EXPLORE

A COLLECTION OF MAPS AND DIAGRAMS THAT EXPLAIN THE WORLD

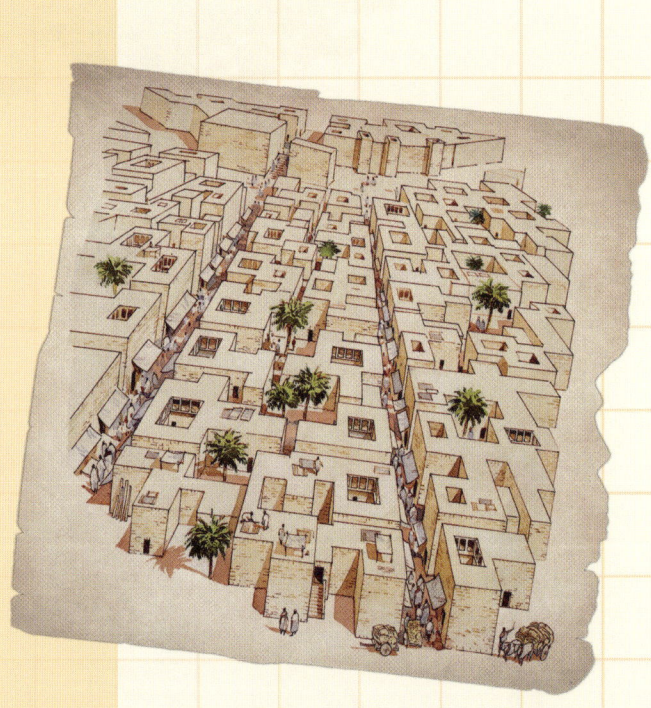

Project Editor Kat Teece
Senior Art Editor Charlotte Milner
US Editor Jane Perlmutter
US Senior Editor Shannon Beatty
Project Art Editor Bettina Myklebust Stovne
Editor Rea Pikula
Designers Sonny Flynn, Brandie Tully-Scott
Managing Editor Gemma Farr
Senior Acquisitions Editor James Mitchem
Managing Art Editor Diane Peyton Jones
Production Editor Dragana Puvacic
Production Controller Inderjit Bhullar
Jacket Designers Charlotte Milner, Brandie Tully-Scott
Subject Consultants Sophie Allan, Lisa Burke,
Jonathan Dale, Stephen Haddelsey, Hannah Pritchard

First American Edition, 2024
Published in the United States by DK Publishing,
a division of Penguin Random House LLC
1745 Broadway, 20th Floor, New York, NY 10019

Copyright © 2024 Dorling Kindersley Limited
A Penguin Random House Company
25 26 27 28 10 9 8 7 6 5 4 3 2
007–338554–Oct/2024

A catalog record for this book
is available from the Library of Congress.
ISBN: 978-0-7440-9848-8

DK books are available at special discounts when purchased
in bulk for sales promotions, premiums, fund-raising,
or educational use.
For details, contact: DK Publishing Special Markets,
1745 Broadway, 20th Floor, New York, NY 10019
SpecialSales@dk.com

Printed and bound in China

www.dk.com

MIX
Paper | Supporting
responsible forestry
FSC™ C018179

This book was made with Forest
Stewardship Council™ certified
paper – one small step in DK's
commitment to a sustainable future.
Learn more at **www.dk.com/uk/**
information/sustainability

EXPLORE

A COLLECTION OF MAPS AND DIAGRAMS THAT EXPLAIN THE WORLD

Written by Lizzie Munsey

Illustrated by Studio Muti and Kaley McKean

DK

CONTENTS

WHAT IS A MAP?

Maps are a way of capturing the world around us for us to explore. They can represent things huge or minute, from the entire universe all the way down to the position of particles inside an atom. Many maps help us find directions and travel from place to place. Ideas can be mapped, too—some maps take complex processes or systems and plot them out visually, making them easier for us to understand. Maps are a great way of showing how the different parts of things are arranged.

History of maps

In the past, maps were used to sketch local areas or trade routes. Mapmakers used drawings to show where key sites were located, such as castles. Over time, the pictures were replaced with simple symbols, and maps gradually became more accurate.

A navigation divider is used to measure distances on a map.

TYPES OF MAPS

Maps come in various forms. Topographic maps show a mixture of natural and human-made features, including streets, mountains, forests, and water. Thematic maps focus on a specific topic, such as weather patterns, population, and even where different languages are spoken.

⑦

①

COMPASS

A compass is a tool that always points to north (N), and shows the direction of south (S), east (E), and west (W). Maps often include a north-pointing arrow, so that people can use a compass to find their way around.

②

N

W — E

S

⑧

KEY

A key is a list of the symbols that appear on a map, with notes to show what they mean. It can also use numbers or letters to identify what is shown where.

1. North America
2. South America
3. Europe
4. Africa
5. Asia
6. Australasia
7. Arctic Ocean
8. Southern Ocean
9. Atlantic Ocean
10. Indian Ocean
11. Pacific Ocean

CHAPTER 1
SPACE

People once believed that our planet was at the center of everything in space, and that the sun and other planets moved around us. Now, we know that the Earth moves around the sun, and that we are only one small, insignificant rocky planet among many billions in space. The sun, too, is one star among billions. The universe stretches out almost endlessly beyond us, filled with objects much larger and stranger than our home. Huge swathes of it are filled with nothing at all. Though, as big as the universe is, Earth is the only planet that we know has liquid water, and is home to life.

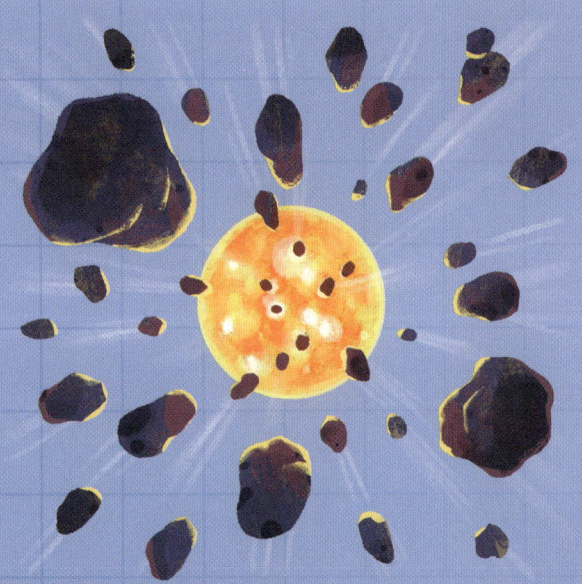

OUR PLANET

Earth may seem like an everyday kind of place, but it is completely unique in the universe. So far, it is the only place we know about that contains life of any kind. One thing that has allowed life forms to survive here is Earth's atmosphere—a layer of gases that wraps around the planet, protecting it from the sun's harmful rays. Without this gas blanket, the surface of the planet would be searingly hot, and impossible to survive on.

How Earth formed

Once, Earth was nothing but an area of gas, rocks, and lumps of space ice. A force called gravity pulled these things together into a baby planet. Over time, Earth grew as more rocks crashed into it. Then the planet cooled down, eventually becoming the Earth we know today.

INSIDE EARTH

Earth is not the same all the way through—it has layers. The layers inside Earth are made of rock, metal, or a mixture of both. Some layers are solid and others liquid.

˅

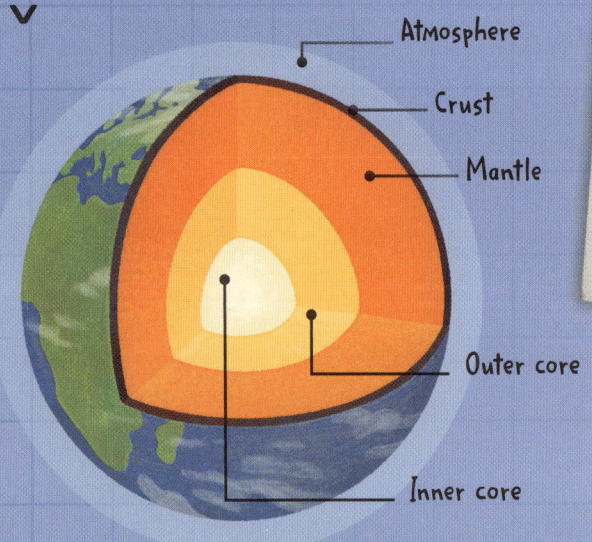

Atmosphere

Crust

Mantle

Outer core

Inner core

˄
WATERY PLANET

So far, Earth is the only planet in the solar system that has been proven to have liquid water. There is frozen water elsewhere, and evidence suggests that water once flowed on Mars, though it is dry today.

EARTH'S ATMOSPHERE

EXOSPHERE

This is the very outermost layer of the atmosphere, which blends into space.

THERMOSPHERE

This is the last complete layer of the atmosphere, before it fades out. Temperatures here are very high.

MESOSPHERE

Here, temperatures are extremely cold. They can drop to an incredible −148°F (~100°C).

STRATOSPHERE

This section includes the ozone layer. It absorbs some harmful rays from the sun, protecting Earth.

TROPOSPHERE

All of Earth's weather happens in this layer. It holds the air we breathe, and a huge 80 percent of the atmosphere's gases.

KARMAN LINE

This line marks where space begins, at 62 miles (100 km) above sea level.

SATELLITES

These machines monitor Earth from high above, and can send information down to us.

INTERNATIONAL SPACE STATION

This space lab is in permanent orbit around Earth, with a number of astronauts onboard.

AURORAS

Beautiful swirling auroras occur when particles from the sun meet Earth's magnetic field.

METEORITES

Most meteors burn up in the mesosphere, creating streaks of light called meteorites.

AIRPLANE

Large planes fly in the stratosphere, where there is no weather to slow them down.

WEATHER BALLOON

These balloons can collect information about what's happening in the atmosphere.

6,215 (10,000)

430 (690)

53 (85)

31 (50)

12 (20)

0 MILES (0 KM)

A map of Earth's atmosphere

SATURN

NEPTUNE

MERCURY

VENUS

JUPITER

THE SUN

EARTH

URANUS

MARS

SIZES AND DISTANCES

The map above does not accurately
show the sizes of the planets or their
varying distances from the sun.
Actually, Jupiter is so big that all the
other planets could fit inside it, and
the outer four planets are much more
spaced out than the inner four.

THE
SUN

MERCURY

VENUS

EARTH

MARS

JUPITER

SATURN

A map of the solar system

SOLAR SYSTEM KEY

MOONS
Some of the planets have moons—objects that orbit around them.

PLUTO
This is a dwarf planet, because it shares its orbit with other material.

KUIPER BELT
This region at the edge of the solar system contains millions of icy and rocky objects.

ASTEROID BELT
Between Mars and Jupiter is a band containing many space rocks, known as asteroids.

SPACE JUNK
Human space exploration has littered the solar system with pieces of old spacecraft and other human-made items.

COMET
These lumps of ice and dust leave bright streaks across the night sky.

PROBE
These robotic spacecraft have been launched into space by us humans.

 URANUS   NEPTUNE

THE SOLAR SYSTEM

Earth travels around the sun, but it is not alone in its journey. In fact, the sun is circled by a whole family of planets, which move in constant orbit around it. Some of the planets even have their own families of moons. Together, the sun, the eight planets, their moons, and various other space objects are known as our solar system.

THE BIRTH OF THE SOLAR SYSTEM

Around 4.6 billion years ago, our solar system was born from a cloud of gas and dust. The cloud collapsed inward, clumping into lumps that became the sun and a spinning disk of gas around it. The disk later formed into the planets.

THE MOON

Study the moon closely and you will see that its surface is pockmarked with craters, left behind by collisions with space rocks. Alongside the craters are "mares,"or "seas"—darker areas of rock that formed when lava from ancient volcanic eruptions cooled. There are also signs of human presence here— equipment left behind by the robotic and crewed missions that we have sent to explore our planet's closest companion in space.

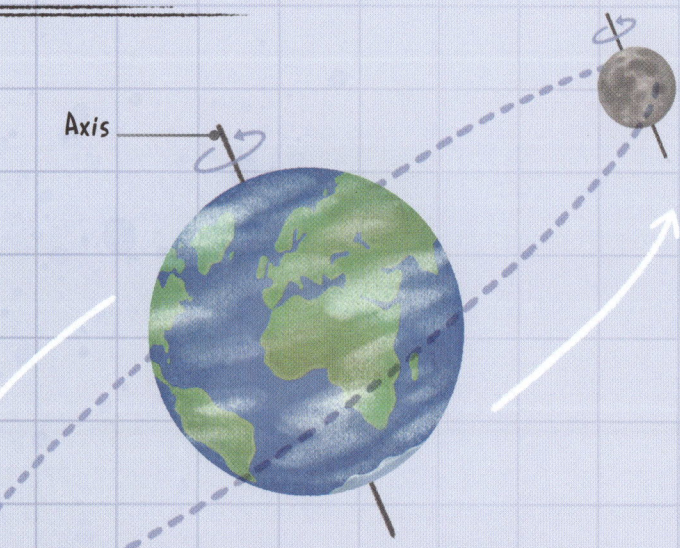

Axis

The moon's journey

The moon moves in constant looping orbits around Earth. It spins on its axis as it goes, so that we on Earth always see the same side of it.

THE APOLLO MISSIONS

So far, the only space missions that have taken humans to the moon's surface were those of the Apollo program, between 1969 and 1972. A total of 12 men walked on the moon itself, including Buzz Aldrin (pictured here), who was the second man to set foot on the moon, after Neil Armstrong.

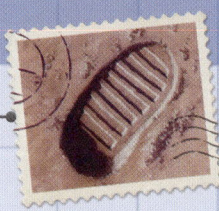

Footprints from old missions remain on the moon.

❮ CHANGING MOON

Over each month, the moon's shape appears to shift—but it doesn't actually change. As it travels around its orbit, different parts of the moon's surface are lit up by the sun. The moon is said to wax, or grow, in the first part of the month, and wane, or shrink, toward the end.

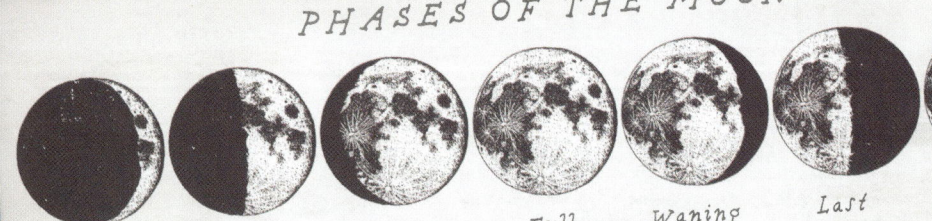

PHASES OF THE MOON

Waxing crescent · First quarter · Waxing gibbous · Full moon · Waning gibbous · Last quarter · Waning crescent

MOON LANDINGS AND OTHER SITES OF INTEREST

PLATO CRATER

MARE IMBRIUM
(SEA OF RAINS)

MARE
SERENITATIS
(SEA OF
SERENITY)

MARE
CRISIUM
(SEA OF
CRISES)

OCEANUS
PROCELLARUM
(OCEAN OF
STORMS)

MARE
TRANQUILLITATIS
(SEA OF TRANQUILITY)

COPERNICUS CRATER

MARE
FECUNDITATIS
(SEA OF
FERTILITY)

MARE
NECTARIS
(SEA OF
NECTAR)

MARE
HUMORUM
(SEA OF
MOISTURE)

MARE
NUBLUM
(SEA OF
CLOUDS)

TYCHO CRATER

1 APOLLO 11—First crewed mission to the moon, 1969

2 APOLLO 16—Fifth crewed mission to the moon, 1972

3 LUNA 2—First spacecraft to land on the moon, 1959

4 APOLLO 17—Final Apollo moon mission, 1972

5 LUNA 16—First robotic spacecraft to return rock samples back to Earth, 1970

6 KAGUYA—Japanese mission to map the moon's surface, which ended in 2007

7 LCROSS—One of a series of spacecraft searching for frozen water, sent in 2009

8 SURVEYOR 1—First US spacecraft to make a controlled landing, 1966

9 LUNA 9—First spacecraft to make a controlled landing, 1965

10 LUNA 17—First spacecraft to deploy a lunar rover, 1970

11 CHANG'E 3—Chinese mission to land a probe and rover, 2013

A map of the moon

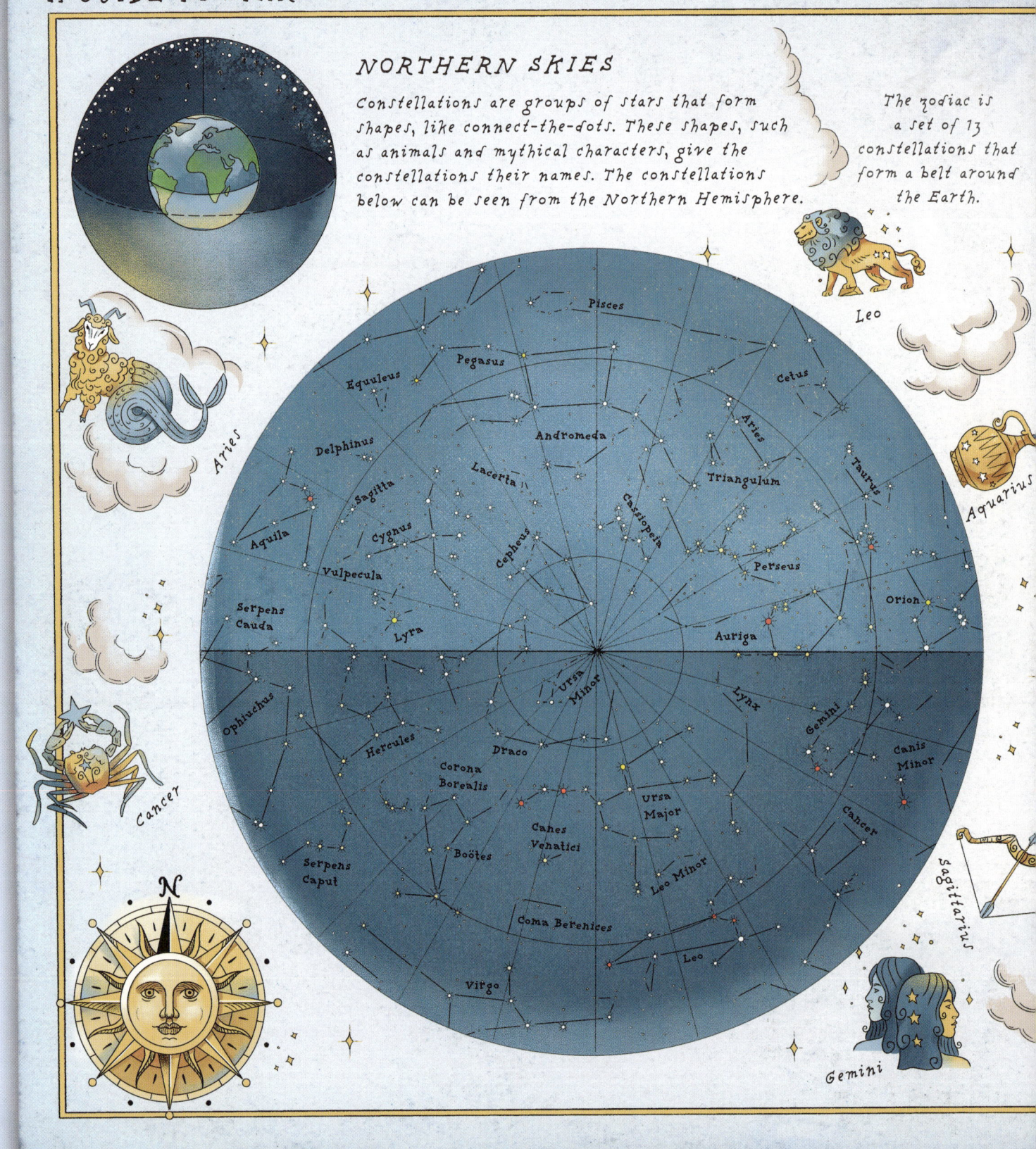

NORTHERN SKIES

Constellations are groups of stars that form shapes, like connect-the-dots. These shapes, such as animals and mythical characters, give the constellations their names. The constellations below can be seen from the Northern Hemisphere.

The zodiac is a set of 13 constellations that form a belt around the Earth.

A map of the northern and southern skies

The nearest star, Proxima Centauri, is 24,984,00,000,000 miles (40,208,000,000,000 km) away.

Red dwarf

SOUTHERN SKIES

The constellations below can be seen from the southern hemisphere. As the Earth orbits the sun and our view changes, the constellations in both hemispheres appear to move across the sky.

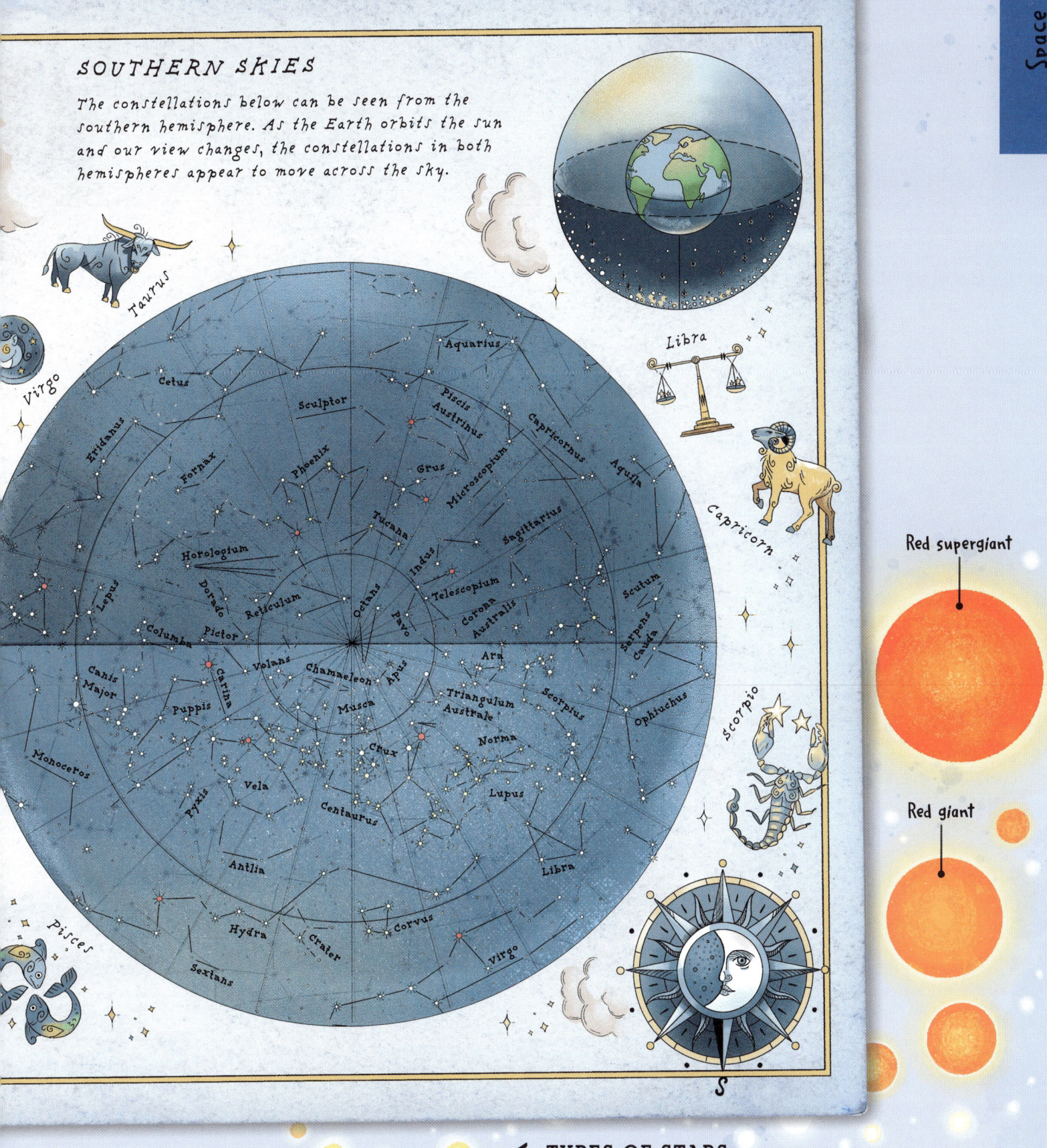

Taurus

Virgo

Cetus

Aquarius

Sculptor

Piscis Austrinus

Capricornus

Eridanus

Fornax

Phoenix

Grus

Microscopium

Aquila

Horologium

Tucana

Indus

Sagittarius

Lepus

Dorado

Reticulum

Telescopium

Scutum

Columba

Pictor

Octans

Pavo

Corona Australis

Serpens Cauda

Canis Major

Carina

Volans

Chamaeleon

Apus

Ara

Ophiuchus

Puppis

Musca

Triangulum Australe

Scorpius

Monoceros

Crux

Norma

Pyxis

Vela

Centaurus

Lupus

Antlia

Libra

Pisces

Hydra

Crater

Corvus

Virgo

Sextans

Libra

Capricorn

Scorpio

S

Red supergiant

Red giant

Sunlike stars

◀ TYPES OF STARS

Stars are grouped based on how big, bright, and hot they are, which affects their color. They do not stay the same for their whole existence—they change color and size depending on where they are in their life cycle.

17

Galaxies

Most stars do not exist alone in space—they cluster together with clouds of gas, dust, and other stars, forming galaxies. The galaxy that we call home is the Milky Way. We can only see a tiny part of the Milky Way from Earth, but astronomers have used their findings to map out its likely form. It contains about 100 billion stars, and is just over 100,000 light years wide.

TYPES OF GALAXIES

Spiral galaxy

These galaxies have curved arms that spiral outward from a central bulge. They spin slowly in place.

Barred spiral galaxy

A barred spiral is similar to a spiral, but with a bar across its center. Our own galaxy, the Milky way, is a barred spiral.

Elliptical galaxy

Round or oval, these galaxies contain older stars, and little gas. Most of them are thought to contain enormous black holes.

Irregular galaxies

We call galaxies without clear shapes "irregular." These galaxies often contain large numbers of young stars.

Lenticular galaxy

These galaxies are shaped like the lens of a magnifying glass—circular, with narrow edges and a thick central bulge.

The Milky Way >

Two main arms spiral out from the barred center of our galaxy: the Scutum-Centaurus and Perseus arms. A number of smaller arms then branch off from these two main arms.

Star movement

The galaxy does not rotate like a disk—its stars follow individual orbits around the center. The farther a star is from the center, the longer it takes to complete an orbit.

Our solar system

We are about one-third of the way out of the Milky Way's center, in the Orion arm.

Sagittarius A*
This supermassive black hole sits in the center of the Milky Way.

Galactic center
This area contains older stars.

The Local Group
The Milky Way is part of a band of galaxies known as the Local Group. So far, more than 50 galaxies have been found in the group, but there may be more that we cannot see.

THE LOCAL GROUP

THE UNIVERSE

Beyond our own planet are others, all circling around the Sun as part of the Solar System. Beyond the Solar System are other stars and planets. All together, the vast expanse of space and space objects are known as the Universe. So far, humans have not travelled further than the far side of the Moon, but our uncrewed craft have gone to the very edge of the Solar System, and on into outer space.

^

STUDYING THE UNIVERSE

Telescopes allow us to see further into the Universe than we can with just our eyes. Over hundreds of years, our telescopes have become more and more advanced. Some telescopes are launched into space itself, giving us views we could never dream of from Earth.

OUR PLACE IN SPACE

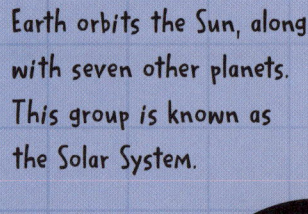

Earth orbits the Sun, along with seven other planets. This group is known as the Solar System.

MILKY WAY

Our Sun is one of billions that form a galaxy called the Milky Way. It is spiral shaped, and our Solar System is in one of the spiral arms.

THE LOCAL GROUP

The Milky Way is one of a cluster of more than 50 galaxies. Together, they are known as the Local Group.

THE LANIAKEA SUPERCLUSTER

The Local Group is part of a colossal supercluster of groups of galaxies, which is called the Laniakea Supercluster.

THE COSMIC WEB

The Universe contains a web of superclusters, with huge empty voids between them. From Earth, we can only see a fraction of it.

EXOPLANETS

You will know that there are eight planets in our Solar System. But did you know that there are planets elsewhere in the Universe, too? We call any planet outside the Solar System an exoplanet. A few of them seem to be similar to Earth.

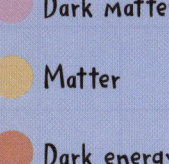

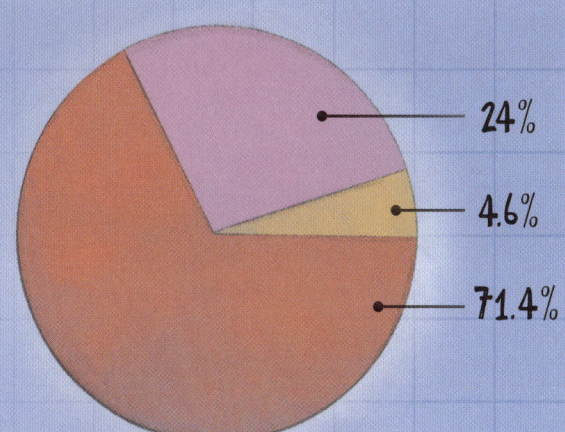

- Dark matter
- Matter
- Dark energy

24%
4.6%
71.4%

The dark Universe

Scientists believe that we can only see a tiny fraction of what is out there in the Universe. The unseen Universe is thought to be made up of two things – masses that we can't see, called dark matter, and an unknown source of energy, called dark energy.

SPACE BODIES

ASTEROID

This is a rocky or metallic space object that orbits the Sun.

Our Universe is home to a range of different things, which we call "bodies". Most of them are made up of gas, rock, ice, and metal.

COMET

This ball of ice and dust forms two tails when it travels near the Sun.

PLANET

This is a large round body, which orbits the Sun with nothing else in its path.

DWARF PLANET

This is a large round body that orbits the Sun, but shares its path with other objects.

MOON

This rocky body orbits a planet. Some planets have lots of moons.

STAR

This is a colossal burning ball of gas and plasma. Some are orbited by planets.

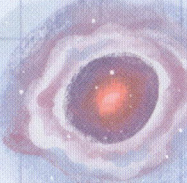

NEBULA

This is a huge cloud of dust and gas. Some are the remains of dying stars.

THE UNIVERSE THROUGH TIME

About 13.8 billion years ago, our universe seems to have suddenly appeared from nothing. This very important event is known as the big bang. At first, everything happened very fast, with matter developing within a fraction of a second. The expansion continued more slowly after that, with stars and galaxies forming over millions of years.

Space between galaxies expands

First galaxies form, after the big bang

Beginning of known Universe

Gravity pulls clusters of galaxies together

An expanding universe

Our universe has been spreading out since the moment of the big bang. Other galaxies are still moving away from us, which suggests the universe is continuing to expand. Scientists think the universe will either expand forever, or, eventually, collapse back into a small point, in a "big crunch."

COSMIC RADIATION

The big bang left behind a blaze of microwave radiation across the universe. In 1964, a special antenna was able to detect the radiation for the first time. This was important evidence of the big bang.

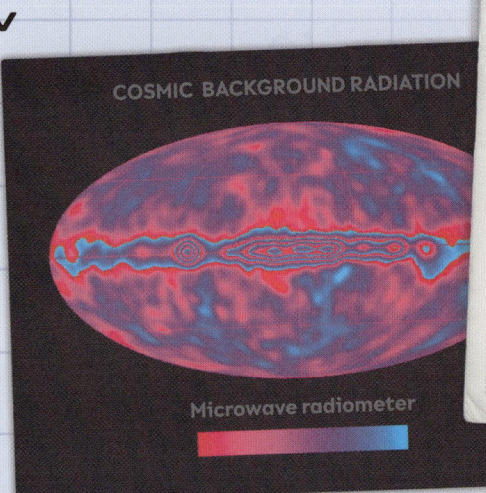

COSMIC BACKGROUND RADIATION

Microwave radiometer

AN IMPORTANT DISCOVERY

Edwin Hubble was an astronomer from the US. By 1929, he proved that galaxies were moving away from each other, which meant that the universe was expanding.

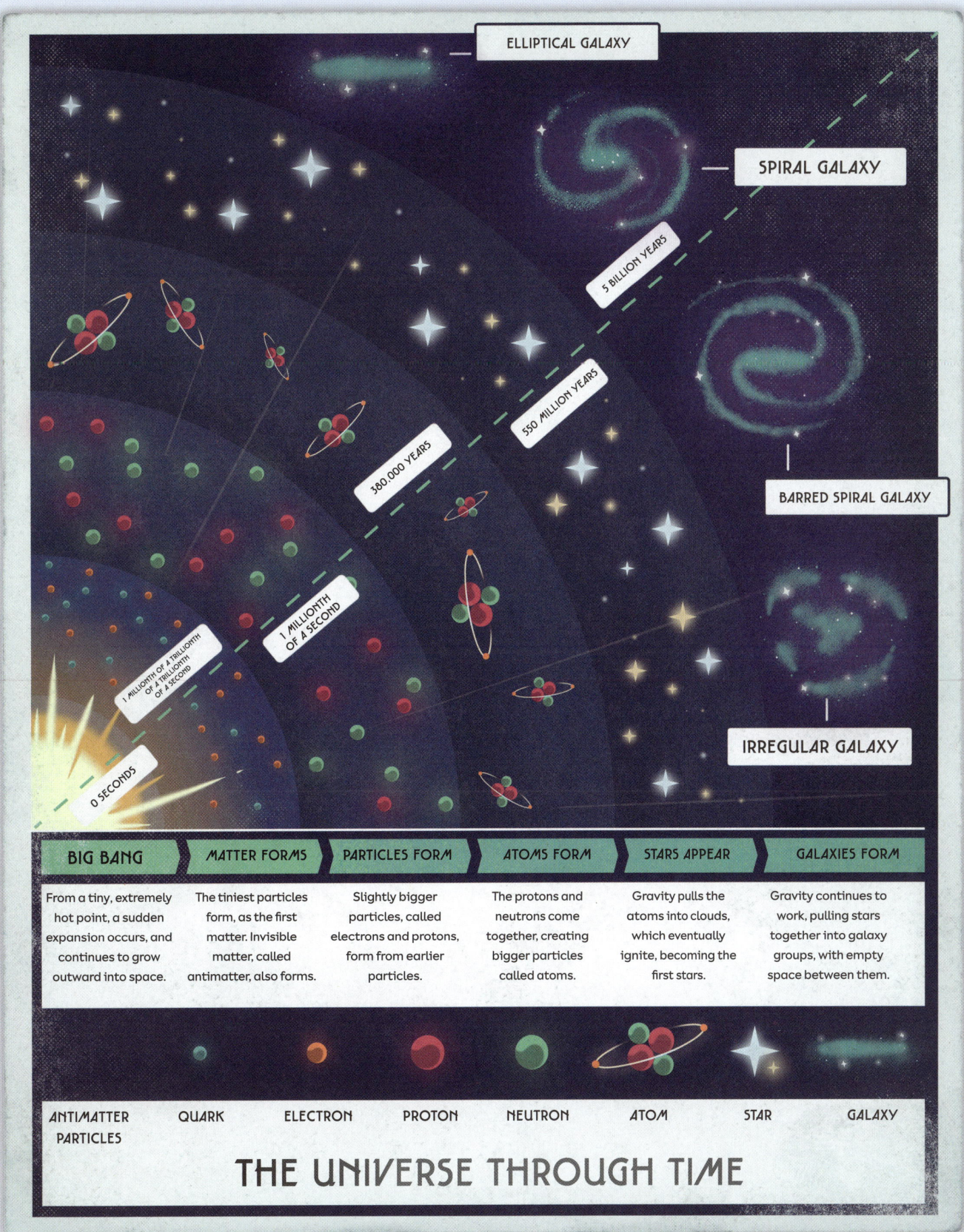

ELLIPTICAL GALAXY

SPIRAL GALAXY

5 BILLION YEARS

550 MILLION YEARS

380,000 YEARS

BARRED SPIRAL GALAXY

1 MILLIONTH OF A SECOND

1 MILLIONTH OF A TRILLIONTH OF A TRILLIONTH OF A SECOND

IRREGULAR GALAXY

0 SECONDS

BIG BANG	MATTER FORMS	PARTICLES FORM	ATOMS FORM	STARS APPEAR	GALAXIES FORM
From a tiny, extremely hot point, a sudden expansion occurs, and continues to grow outward into space.	The tiniest particles form, as the first matter. Invisible matter, called antimatter, also forms.	Slightly bigger particles, called electrons and protons, form from earlier particles.	The protons and neutrons come together, creating bigger particles called atoms.	Gravity pulls the atoms into clouds, which eventually ignite, becoming the first stars.	Gravity continues to work, pulling stars together into galaxy groups, with empty space between them.

ANTIMATTER PARTICLES   QUARK   ELECTRON   PROTON   NEUTRON   ATOM   STAR   GALAXY

THE UNIVERSE THROUGH TIME

A time map of the universe

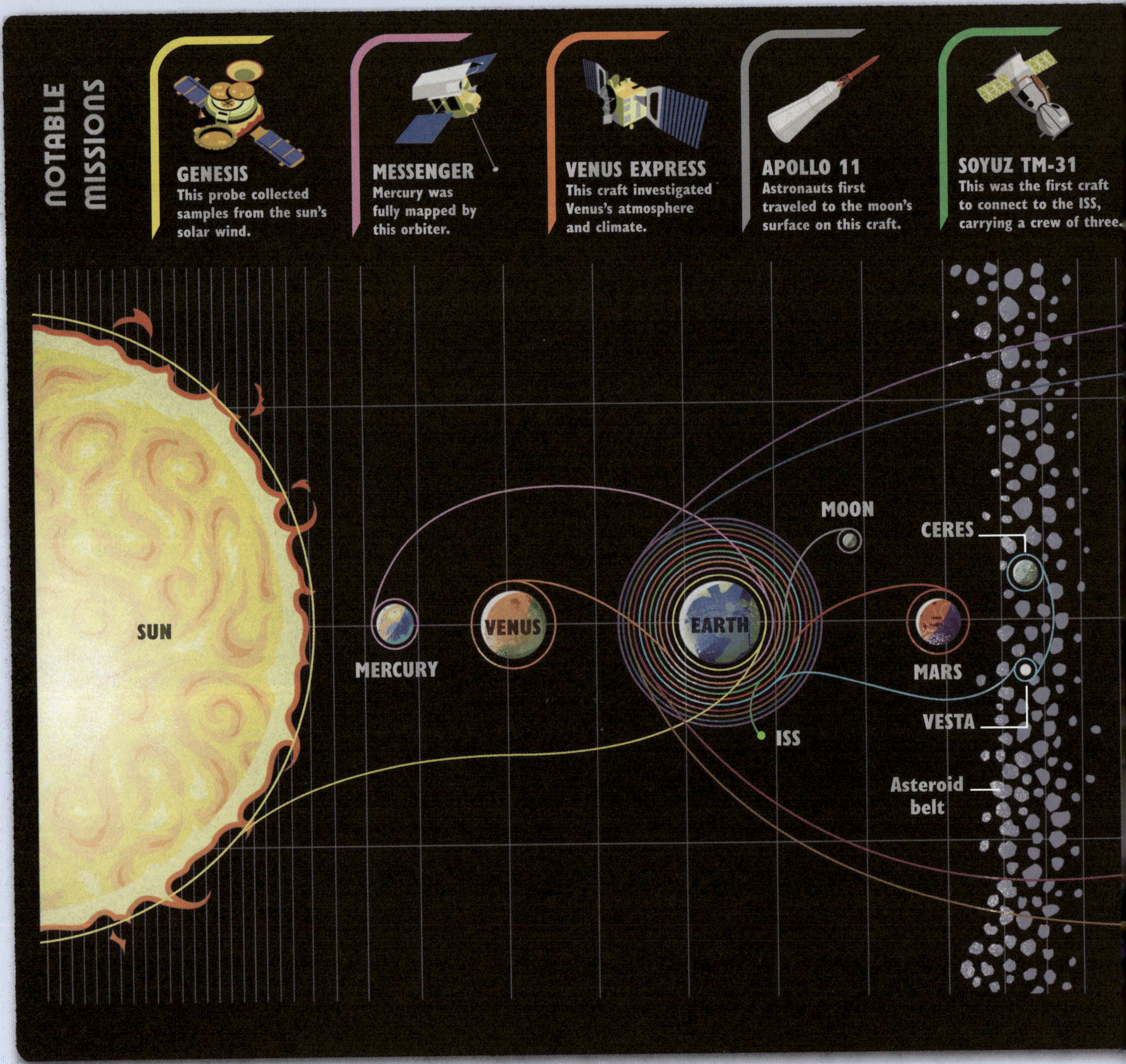
NOTABLE MISSIONS
GENESIS
This probe collected samples from the sun's solar wind.
MESSENGER
Mercury was fully mapped by this orbiter.
VENUS EXPRESS
This craft investigated Venus's atmosphere and climate.
APOLLO 11
Astronauts first traveled to the moon's surface on this craft.
SOYUZ TM-31
This was the first craft to connect to the ISS, carrying a crew of three.
SUN
MERCURY
VENUS
EARTH
MOON
ISS
MARS
CERES
VESTA
Asteroid belt

A map of notable space missions

SPACE MISSIONS

Since the 20th century, we humans have sent thousands of spacecraft into space, along with hundreds of astronauts. These space missions aim to teach us more about our solar system and the universe around it. Sending spacecraft to visit other parts of space allows us to take close-up photographs, and even gather samples of rocks to take back to Earth for scientists to study.

APOLLO 11

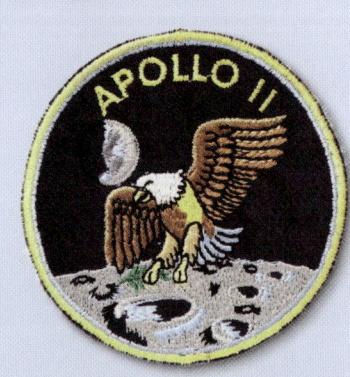

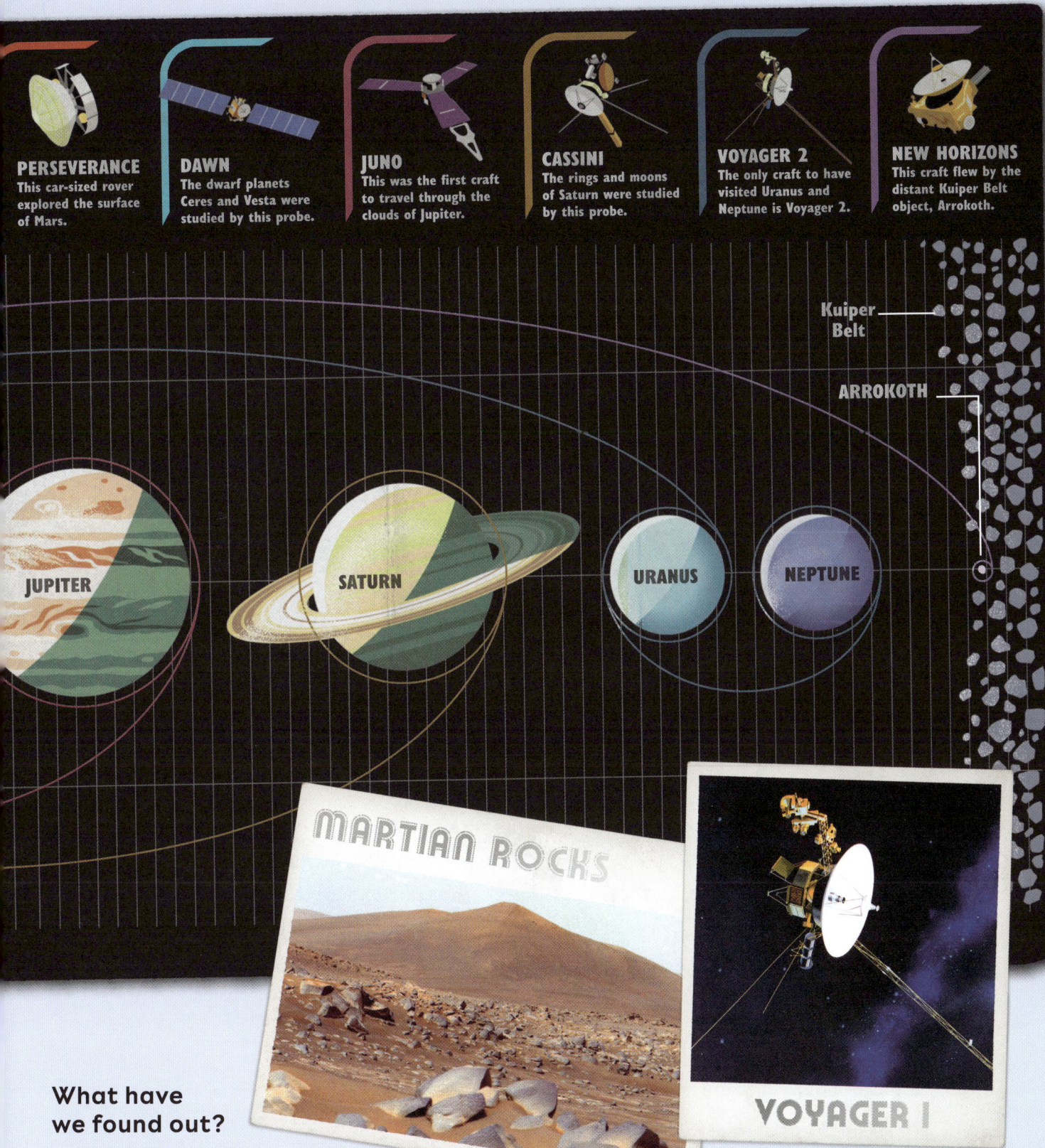

PERSEVERANCE
This car-sized rover explored the surface of Mars.

DAWN
The dwarf planets Ceres and Vesta were studied by this probe.

JUNO
This was the first craft to travel through the clouds of Jupiter.

CASSINI
The rings and moons of Saturn were studied by this probe.

VOYAGER 2
The only craft to have visited Uranus and Neptune is Voyager 2.

NEW HORIZONS
This craft flew by the distant Kuiper Belt object, Arrokoth.

Kuiper Belt

ARROKOTH

JUPITER

SATURN

URANUS

NEPTUNE

MARTIAN ROCKS

VOYAGER I

What have we found out?

So far, humans have only traveled to the moon on missions such as Apollo 11. Most space missions use robotic spacecraft, which send information back to Earth without any risk to human life. Some spacecraft land, others fly past objects and observe them without touching down.

A rover took this photo on Mars's surface.

∧ HOW FAR HAVE WE GONE?

So far, only two spacecraft have traveled beyond our solar system. Voyagers 1 and 2 were launched in 1977 and passed the Kuiper Belt in 2012. They will continue until they run out of power.

25

CHAPTER 2
SCIENCE AND TECHNOLOGY

The word "science" comes from the Latin word for "knowledge." Scientists attempt to find out exactly how things work. They study the world around us, investigating what everything is made of and how it behaves. This includes the natural world—how animals live, where they live, and how they have changed over the years. It includes looking at the substances things are made of, and how they act in different circumstances. Cutting-edge technologies, from the Internet to the plane, can only be made thanks to thousands of years of scientific research.

ATOMS

If you looked very closely at an object, or even a living thing, you would find that it was made of very tiny parts. In fact, everything in the entire universe is made up of miniscule building blocks, called atoms. There are 118 different types of atoms, which link together or join with other types of atoms to form a huge range of different substances. Inside atoms are smaller particles still, which are called protons, neutrons, and electrons.

SUBATOMIC PARTICLES

Protons and neutrons are made up of even smaller particles, such as quarks. Quarks are so tiny that they are nearly impossible to detect.

v

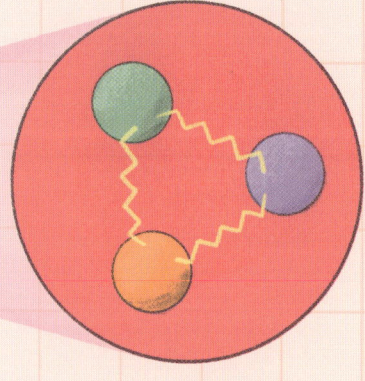

Inside an atom

Each atom is made up of even tinier particles. In the center is a group of particles called the nucleus, which contains protons and neutrons. Electrons travel around the nucleus, positioned in rings known as shells.

Neutrons are found in the nucleus, at the heart of the atom.

Protons are found in the nucleus, along with neutrons.

Electrons orbit around the outside of the nucleus.

MODELS OF THE ATOM

Over the years, the models of atoms used by scientists have evolved, with a series of new discoveries changing the model.

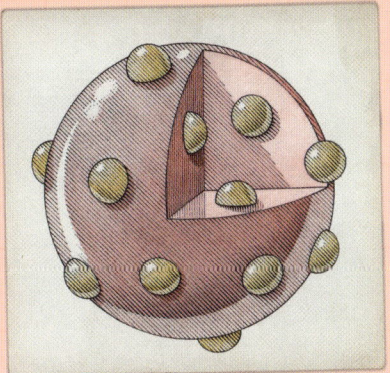

PLUM PUDDING MODEL

Electrons were discovered by British physicist J. J. Thompson, in 1904. He suggested that electrons were studded across a sphere, like raisins in a plum pudding.

PLANETARY MODEL

In 1911, a physicist from New Zealand, Ernest Rutherford, suggested that electrons formed a scattered cloud. He went on to discover protons in the nucleus.

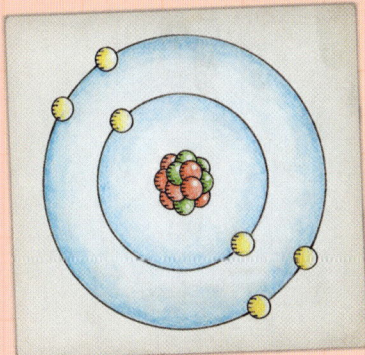

SHELL MODEL

Later, it was found that electrons orbit the nucleus in shells, and that there are also particles called neutrons in the nucleus. This model is still used today.

ATOMIC ENERGY

^
ATOMS INTO MOLECULES

Atoms can join with other atoms to form molecules. The atoms in a molecule share electrons with each other, which bonds them together. Molecules contain anything from two to a million atoms.

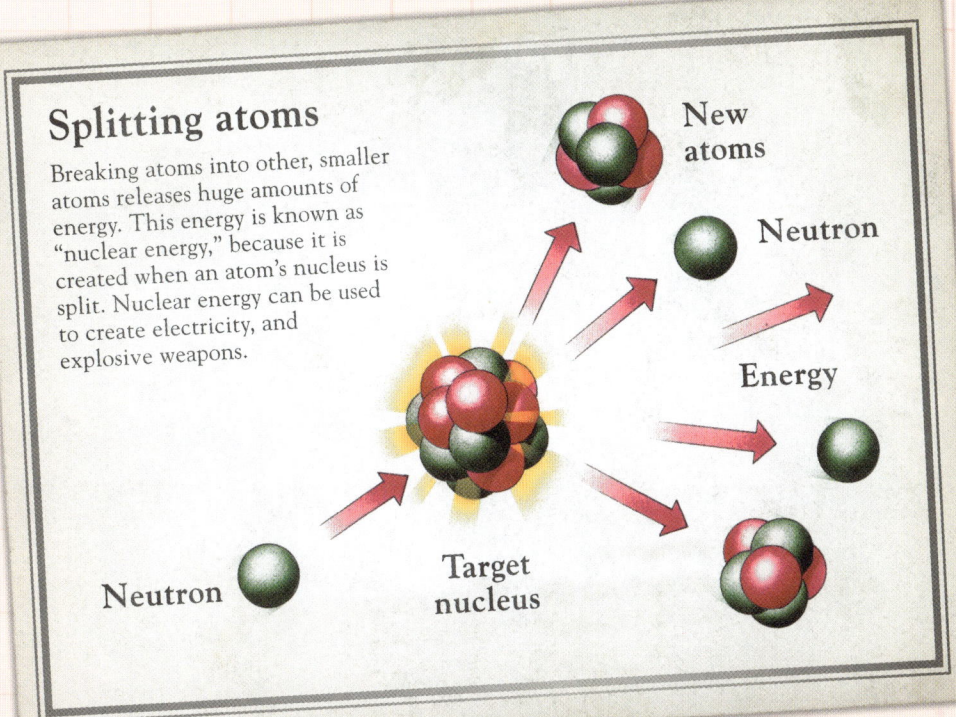

Splitting atoms

Breaking atoms into other, smaller atoms releases huge amounts of energy. This energy is known as "nuclear energy," because it is created when an atom's nucleus is split. Nuclear energy can be used to create electricity, and explosive weapons.

New atoms

Neutron

Energy

Neutron

Target nucleus

THE ELEMENTS

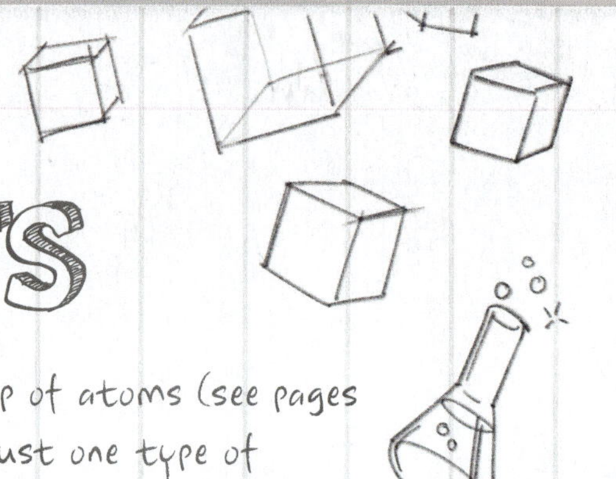

Everything in our world is made up of atoms (see pages 28-29). Substances that contain just one type of atom are called elements. Elements come together in different ways to create all the things we see in the world, such as trees, animals, and even us!

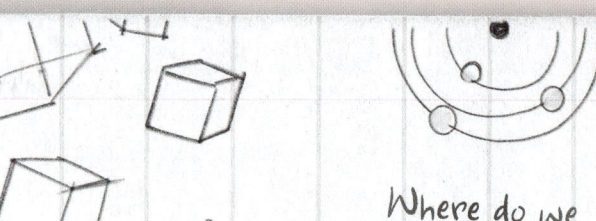

Where do we find elements?

Elements are all around us! Some of them are the basic building blocks of everything in nature. Others are created by scientists, in laboratories.

THE PERIODIC TABLE OF ELEMENTS

This chart of the elements is known as the periodic table. The elements are arranged in rows and columns in order of atomic number, with color codes that group them by type.

An element's symbol is usually the first letter, or first letter and another letter, from its name (or from an old name).

1 H Hydrogen																	2 He Helium
3 Li Lithium	4 Be Beryllium											5 B Boron	6 C Carbon	7 N Nitrogen	8 O Oxygen	9 F Fluorine	10 Ne Neon
11 Na Sodium	12 Mg Magnesium											13 Al Aluminum	14 Si Silicon	15 P Phosphorus	16 S Sulfur	17 Cl Chlorine	18 Ar Argon
19 K Potassium	20 Ca Calcium	21 Sc Scandium	22 Ti Titanium	23 V Vanadium	24 Cr Chromium	25 Mn Manganese	26 Fe Iron	27 Co Cobalt	28 Ni Nickel	29 Cu Copper	30 Zn Zinc	31 Ga Gallium	32 Ge Germanium	33 As Arsenic	34 Se Selenium	35 Br Bromine	36 Kr Krypton
37 Rb Rubidium	38 Sr Strontium	39 Y Yttrium	40 Zr Zirconium	41 Nb Niobium	42 Mo Molybdenum	43 Tc Technetium	44 Ru Ruthenium	45 Rh Rhodium	46 Pd Palladium	47 Ag Silver	48 Cd Cadmium	49 In Indium	50 Sn Tin	51 Sb Antimony	52 Te Tellurium	53 I Iodine	54 Xe Xenon
55 Cs Cesium	56 Ba Barium	57 La Lanthanum	72 Hf Hafnium	73 Ta Tantalum	74 W Tungsten	75 Re Rhenium	76 Os Osmium	77 Ir Iridium	78 Pt Platinum	79 Au Gold	80 Hg Mercury	81 Th Thallium	82 Pb Lead	83 Bi Bismuth	84 Po Polonium	85 At Astatine	86 Rn Radon
87 Fr Francium	88 Ra Radium	89 Ac Actinium	104 Rf Rutherfordium	105 Db Dubnium	106 Sg Seaborgium	107 Bh Bohrium	108 Hs Hassium	109 Mt Meitnerium	110 Ds Darmstadtium	111 Rg Roentgenium	112 Cn Copernicium	113 Nh Nihonium	114 Fl Flerovium	115 Mc Moscovium	116 Lv Livermorium	117 Ts Tennessine	118 Og Oganesson

		58 Ce Cerium	59 Pr Praseodymium	60 Nd Neodymium	61 Pm Promethium	62 Sm Samarium	63 Eu Europium	64 Gd Gadolinium	65 Tb Terbium	66 Dy Dysprosium	67 Ho Holmium	68 Er Erbium	69 Tm Thulium	70 Yb Ytterbium	71 Lu Lutetium
		90 Th Thorium	91 Pa Protactinium	92 U Uranium	93 Np Neptunium	94 Pu Plutonium	95 Am Americium	96 Cm Curium	97 Bk Berkelium	98 Cf Californium	99 Es Einsteinium	100 Fm Fermium	101 Md Mendelevium	102 No Nobelium	103 Lr Lawrencium

GUIDE

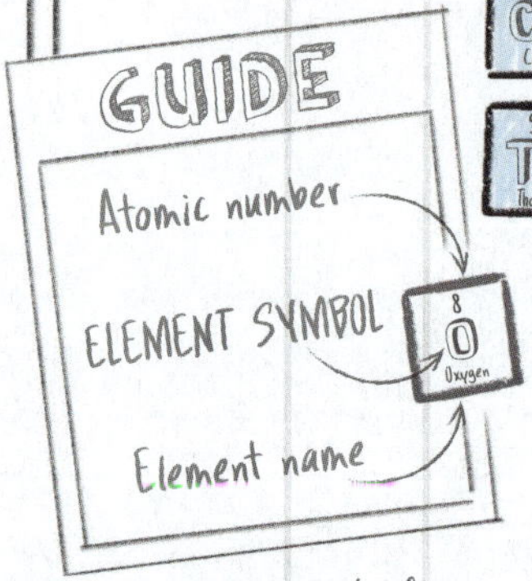

Atomic number

ELEMENT SYMBOL — 8 O Oxygen

Element name

Each element has a unique atomic number, which is the number of protons in its atoms (see pages 28-29).

KEY

METALS
These are usually shiny, solid, and hard.

NONMETALS
Most nonmetals are gas or liquid at room temperature.

METALLOIDS
These elements are partway between metals and nonmetals.

UNKNOWN
These elements have not been created yet!

Diamond crystal

THE JOURNEY OF CARBON

Carbon is one element, but it appears in different forms, depending on how its atoms are arranged. There are millions of different forms of carbon, including all life on Earth!

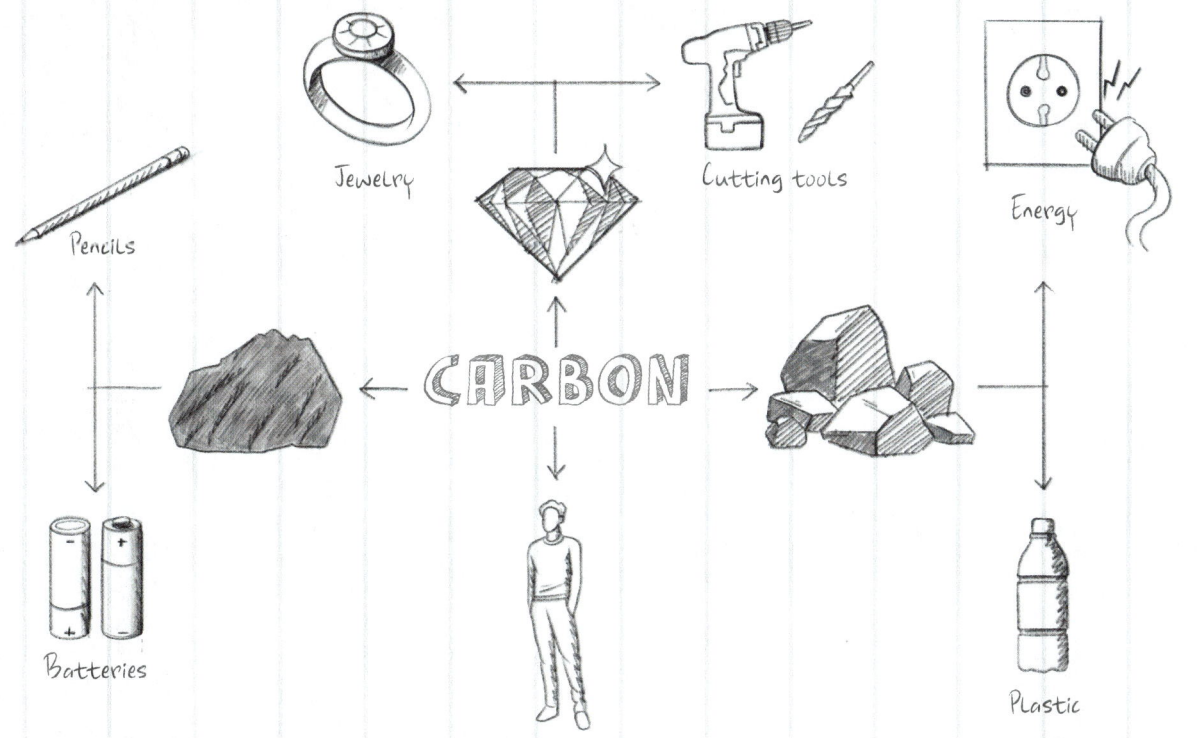

Pencils

Jewelry

Cutting tools

Energy

CARBON

Batteries

Plastic

KEY

Diamond

The carbon atoms in diamond are connected in a superstrong pyramid pattern, making it the hardest natural substance on Earth.

Graphite
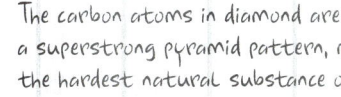
The atoms in graphite are linked in sheets, which slide past each other. This makes it soft and crumbly.

Coal
The atoms inside coal are arranged in a big jumble—it doesn't have a regular structure.

The human body
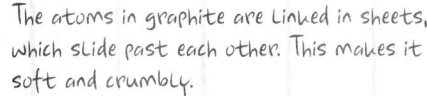
Almost one-fifth of the human body is made-up of carbon!

Compounds

When two or more elements join together, they form something known as a compound. Water (H_2O) is a compound of hydrogen and oxygen.

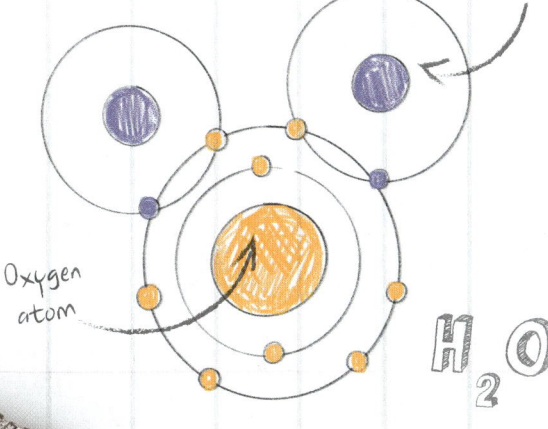

Hydrogen atom

Oxygen atom

H_2O

Graphite

ELECTRICITY

Flowing through wires hidden inside objects, or tucked behind walls, electricity powers all kinds of everyday things—from light bulbs above our heads to handheld devices.

What is electricity?

Electricity is a type of energy, which can be used to make light and heat—such as in light bulbs. A flow of electricity is created when tiny particles with an electrical charge, called electrons, move from one place to another. Electricity can be created inside tiny batteries or in massive power stations.

① Power source

Electricity is made inside a power source, such as a battery. It flows through wires connected to this source.

You can learn more about electrons on pages 28-29.

② On/off switch

A break in a wire stops electricity from flowing. Pressing the on/off switch connects the wires to allow electricity to flow and turn the device on, or disconnects the wire to stop the flow and turn the device off.

③ Conductor

The wires that connect power sources to other devices are made of materials that electricity can pass through, such as the metal copper. The metal wires are encased in materials that electricity can't pass through, such as rubber. This keeps the electricity safely inside.

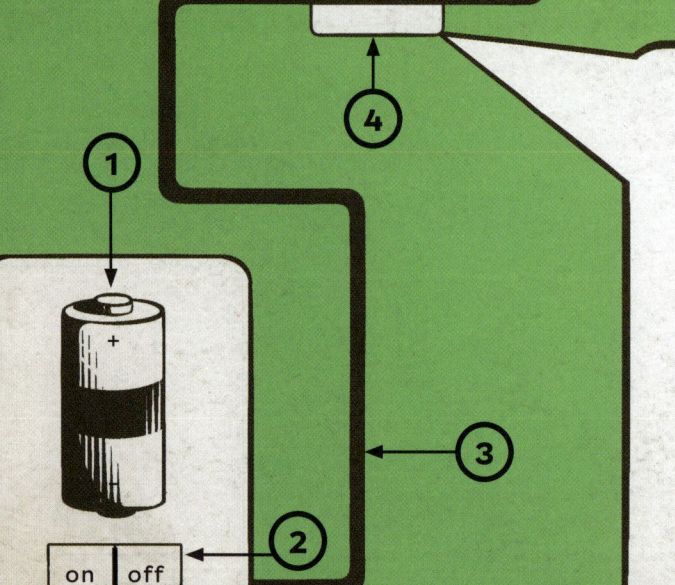

④ Electrons

When an electron jumps from one atom to the next, it pushes an electron out of that next atom. This continues down the wire, creating a flow of electricity to the device.

Atom

Electron

Wire

THE FLOW OF ELECTRICITY

⑤ Light bulb

The light bulb lights up when the electricity reaches it.

A map of electrical flow

MAKING ELECTRICITY

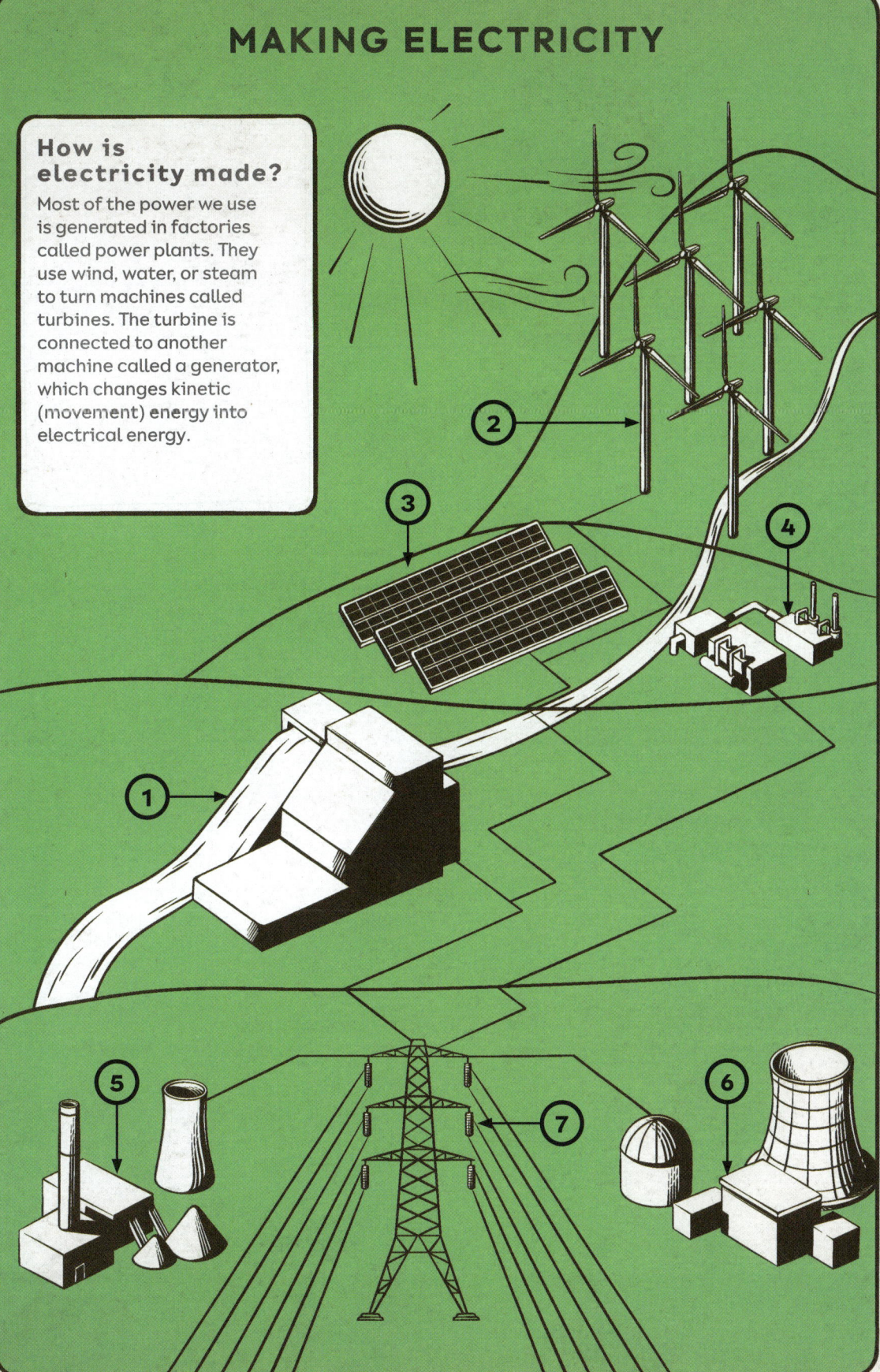

How is electricity made?

Most of the power we use is generated in factories called power plants. They use wind, water, or steam to turn machines called turbines. The turbine is connected to another machine called a generator, which changes kinetic (movement) energy into electrical energy.

1 Water
In nature, water is constantly on the move. The flow of both rivers and of tides can be used to make electricity.

2 Wind
Strong winds can turn turbines. This works best in areas with high levels of wind, such as on hills.

3 Sun
The sun produces huge amounts of energy. We can use solar panels to turn that energy into electricity.

4 Geothermal
In some places on Earth, it is very hot underground. This heat can be used to produce steam, which can turn turbines.

5 Fossil fuels
Coal, gas, and oil are all fossil fuels. They can be burned to heat up water and produce steam to turn turbines.

6 Nuclear
Breaking apart some atoms creates huge amounts of energy. This energy can be used to heat water into steam, which can turn turbines.

7 Pylons
Huge networks of wires link power plants with places that use electricity. Tall structures, called pylons, hold up the wires.

CELLS

If you were to look incredibly closely at your finger—or any other body part—under a microscope, you would see that your whole body is made up of tiny parts, called cells.

These cells are like miniscule building blocks, and they are found inside all living things. Some life forms have just one cell, while others have millions or trillions. Humans have around 100 trillion! There are a few key differences in the makeup of a plant cell compared to an animal one.

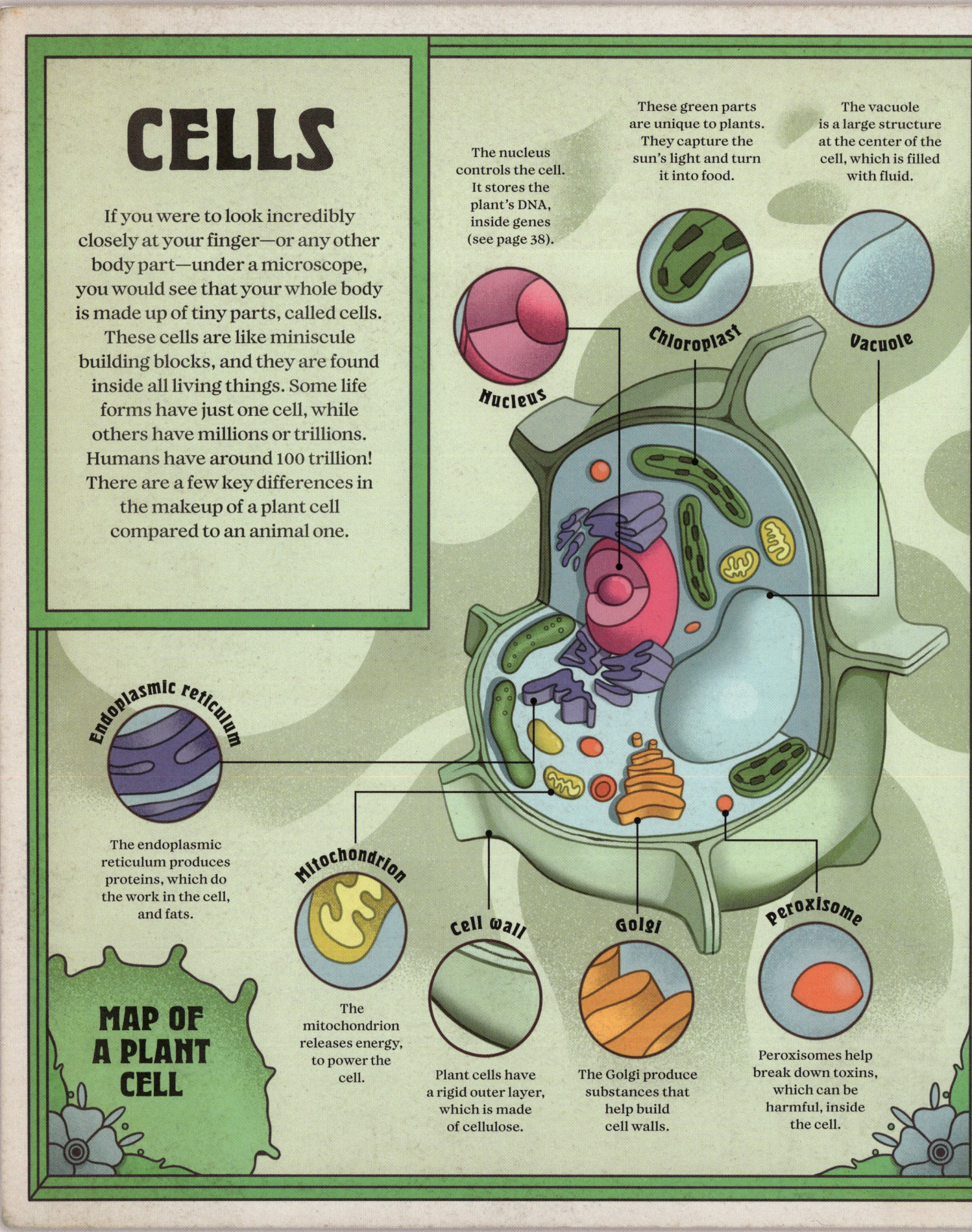

The nucleus controls the cell. It stores the plant's DNA, inside genes (see page 38).

These green parts are unique to plants. They capture the sun's light and turn it into food.

The vacuole is a large structure at the center of the cell, which is filled with fluid.

Nucleus

Chloroplast

Vacuole

Endoplasmic reticulum

The endoplasmic reticulum produces proteins, which do the work in the cell, and fats.

Mitochondrion

The mitochondrion releases energy, to power the cell.

Cell wall

Plant cells have a rigid outer layer, which is made of cellulose.

Golgi

The Golgi produce substances that help build cell walls.

Peroxisome

Peroxisomes help break down toxins, which can be harmful, inside the cell.

MAP OF A PLANT CELL

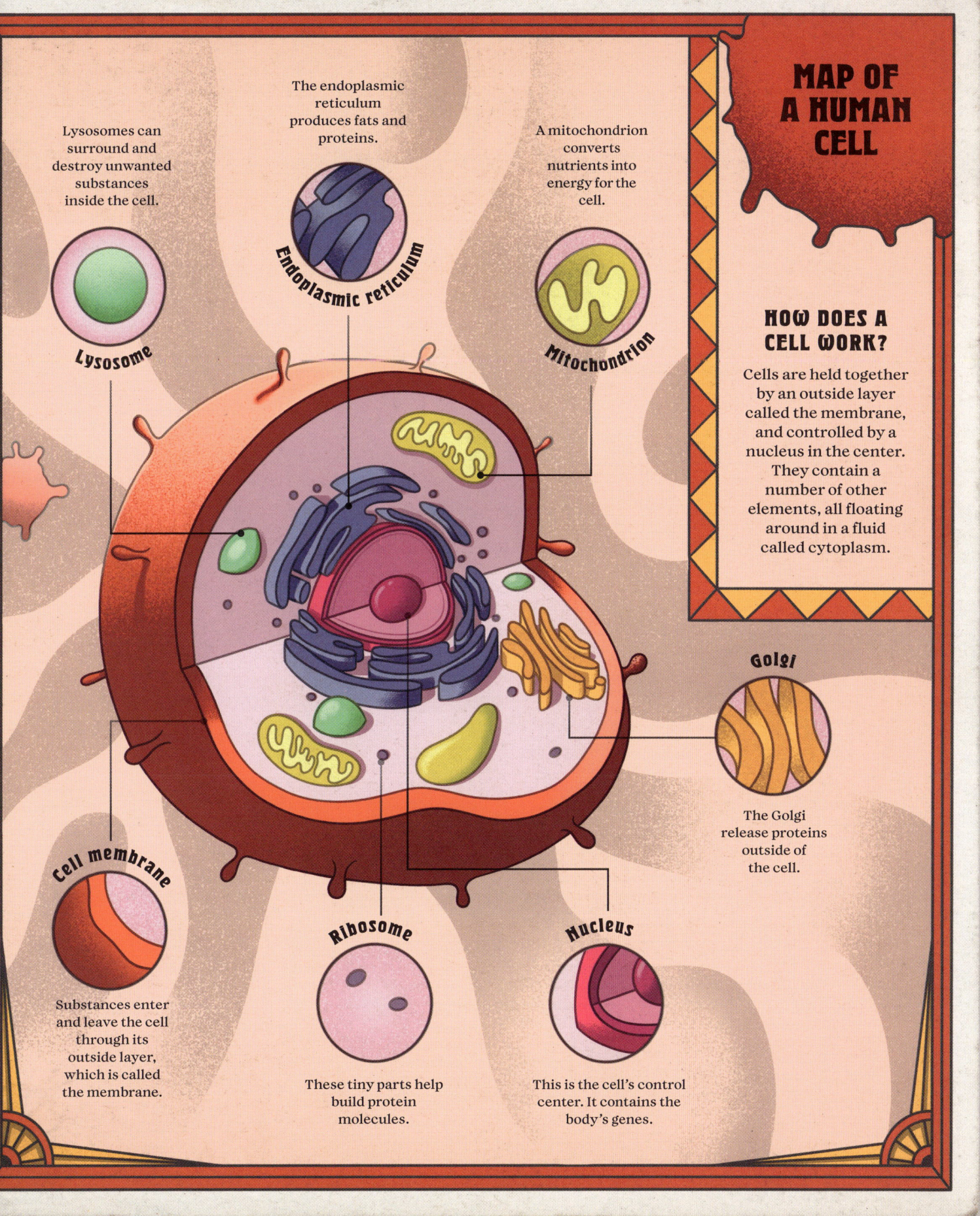

Lysosomes can surround and destroy unwanted substances inside the cell.

The endoplasmic reticulum produces fats and proteins.

A mitochondrion converts nutrients into energy for the cell.

Lysosome

Endoplasmic reticulum

Mitochondrion

HOW DOES A CELL WORK?

Cells are held together by an outside layer called the membrane, and controlled by a nucleus in the center. They contain a number of other elements, all floating around in a fluid called cytoplasm.

Golgi

The Golgi release proteins outside of the cell.

Cell membrane

Substances enter and leave the cell through its outside layer, which is called the membrane.

Ribosome

These tiny parts help build protein molecules.

Nucleus

This is the cell's control center. It contains the body's genes.

AN OCEAN ECOSYSTEM

4

ENERGY
The sun provides energy for the entire ecosystem. Plants use sunlight to grow. They then provide food for other ecosystem members.

WATER
All life forms need water to stay alive. Sea animals often get the water they need from their food, not by drinking it.

OXYGEN
Animals need oxygen to stay alive, while plants produce it as a waste gas. Some animals absorb oxygen from the air, others from water.

CONSUMER
All consumers get their energy by eating other living things. That could mean plants, such as seaweed, or other animals.

2C

DECOMPOSER
The decomposers eat other life forms that have already died, and are rotting away. No energy is wasted!

2B

2A

5

PRODUCER
The seaweed uses light from the sun to make its own energy. It provides food for plant-eating animals, as a producer.

SHELTER
Seagrass offers a lifesaving hiding place for small young animals as they grow.

3

1

KEY **1.** Seaweed **2A.** Killer Whale **2B.** Seal **2C.** Lobster **3.** Seagrass **4.** The sun **5.** Shrimp

WHAT IS AN ECOSYSTEM?

An ecosystem is the combination of plants and animals that live in one particular place on Earth. We divide ecosystems into different groups, such as those on land, in fresh water, and in salt water.

ECOSYSTEMS

Our world is home to a huge variety of life. These life forms all live and die alongside one another, in webs known as ecosystems. Each part of an ecosystem has a role to play. Most ecosystems contain similar roles, though they can be played by different living things.

KEY

1. PRODUCER
Phytoplankton are miniscule plants, so tiny that they can only be seen with a microscope.

2. PRIMARY CONSUMER
Tiny animals called zooplankton eat the phytoplankton. "Primary" means "first."

3. SECONDARY CONSUMER
Coral polyps are unable to leave their position. They use fronds to capture zooplankton for food.

4. TERTIARY CONSUMER
The butterfly fish grazes on small animals, including coral. "Tertiary" means "third."

5. APEX PREDATOR
A shark is an apex predator—it eats other animals and has no predators itself.

A CORAL REEF FOOD WEB

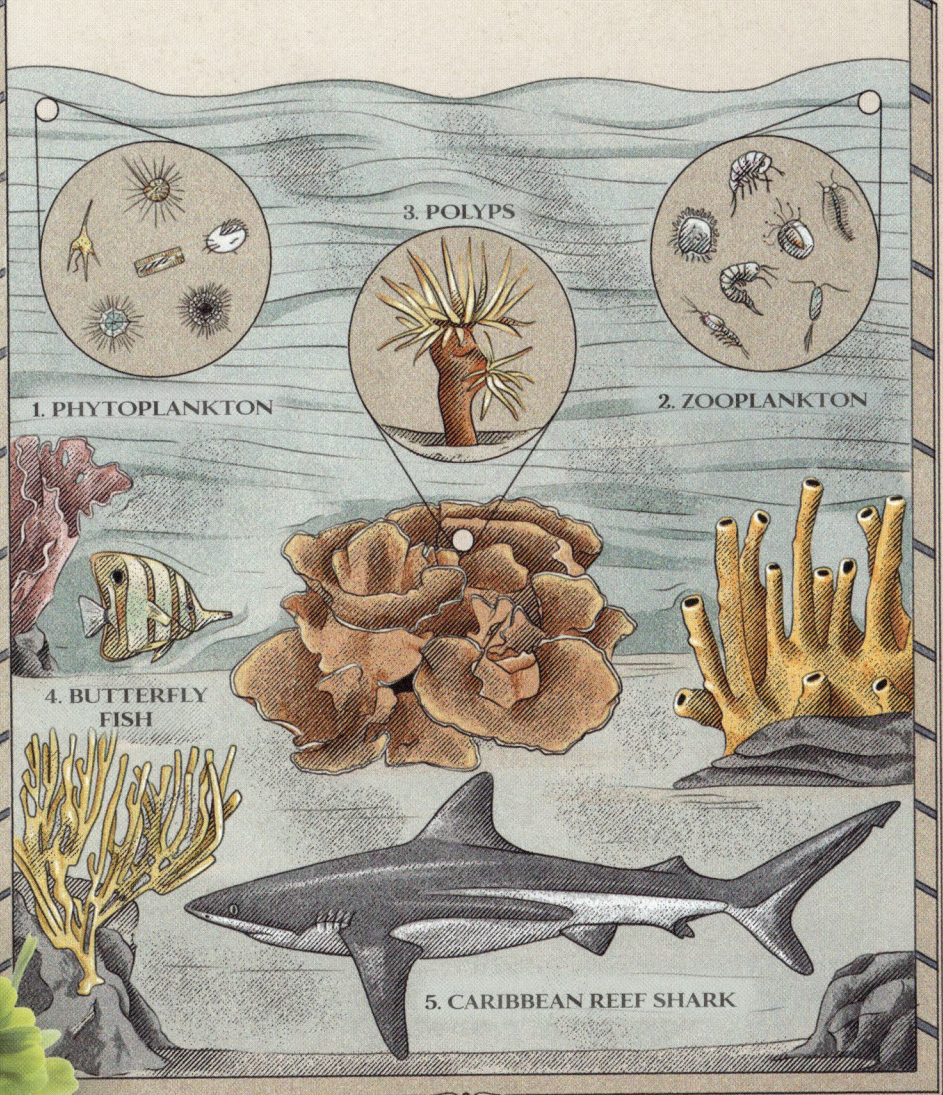

3. POLYPS

1. PHYTOPLANKTON

2. ZOOPLANKTON

4. BUTTERFLY FISH

5. CARIBBEAN REEF SHARK

EVOLUTION

The plants and animals we see around us today have not always existed. Over millions of years they have changed, a tiny bit at a time. Some of these changes are beneficial—they might help the animal adapt to its environment and survive more easily. Others are less helpful, and have led to some types of plants and animals dying out entirely. Eventually, enough tiny changes can change one species of plant or animal into another entirely. This process of change is called evolution.

Fossil of a starfish

^
FOSSIL EVIDENCE

Fossils preserve traces of the life that once lived on Earth. We can study ancient fossils to see which life forms have changed over time, as well as which have stayed the same.

Genes

Animal bodies contain sets of instructions that determine their features, such as hair color. These sets of instructions are called genes, and they occur in pairs—one gene comes from the mother, and one from the father.

Each of these parents has one brown gene and one white gene.

A different gene can be passed on to different offspring.

One gene from each parent is passed on to the offspring.

The brown genes are dominant—any animal with the gene will be brown.

The white genes are recessive—an animal must inherit two of them to be white.

< NATURAL SELECTION

Some features help animals survive . For example, a white hare will be better camouflaged in snow than a brown hare. This means the white hare is more likely to be able to survive in snowy places and pass on its genes, so the next generation is more likely to be white.

FOX EVOLUTION

ANCIENT FOX

All modern foxes are the distant descendants of one species, called their common ancestor. This may have been *Prohesperocyon*—an animal with similar features that lived c.36.6 million years ago—or a close relative.

COMMON ANCESTOR

FOXES EVOLVE

Over time, natural selection has created a range of different fox species. Each species is adapted to survive in the particular environment in which it lives.

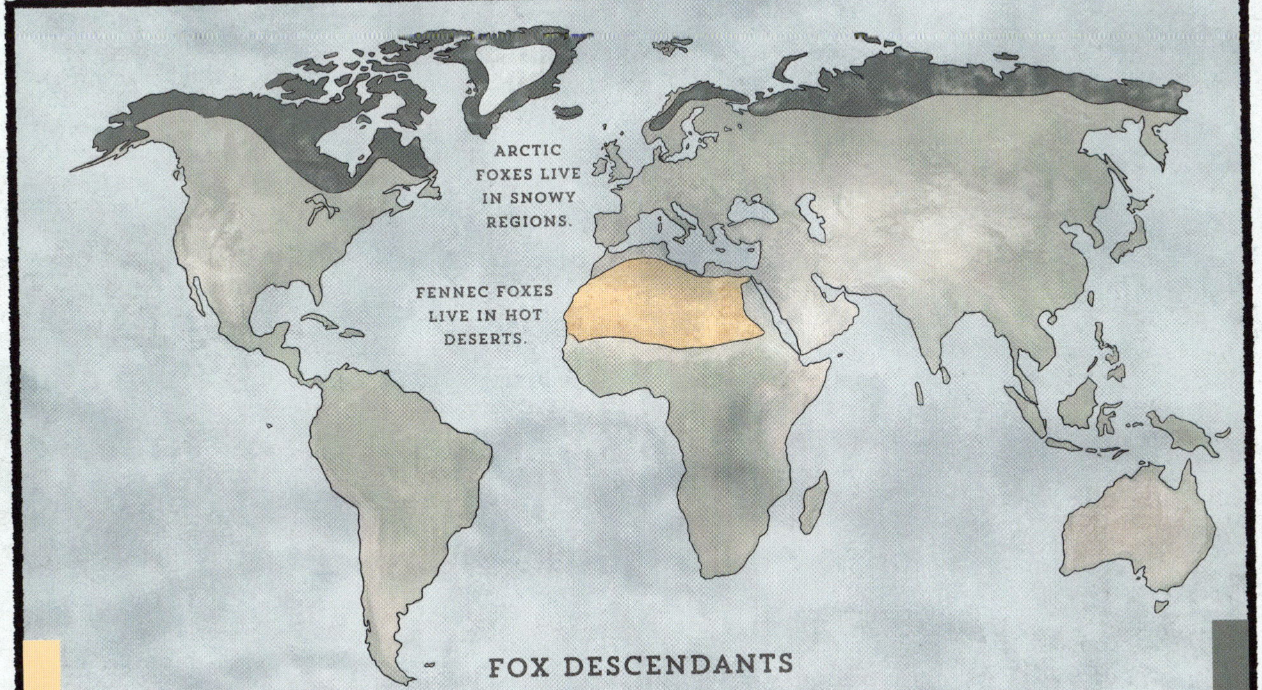

ARCTIC FOXES LIVE IN SNOWY REGIONS.

FENNEC FOXES LIVE IN HOT DESERTS.

FOX DESCENDANTS

FENNEC FOX

This species of fox lives in the hot deserts of North Africa. It has particularly large ears to help it lose excess body heat and stay cool.

A SAND-COLORED COAT HELPS THE FOX HIDE FROM PREDATORS.

HEAT LEAVES THE BODY VIA LARGE EARS.

FURRY SOLES PROTECT THE FEET AGAINST HOT SAND.

ARCTIC FOX

The thick, warm coat of this fox turns white during winters in the Arctic. Camouflaged against the snow, it sneaks up on prey and hides from predators.

THE MUZZLE IS SHORT—SO LESS EXPOSED TO COLD.

A WHITE WINTER COAT BLENDS IN WITH THE SNOW.

THICK FUR KEEPS THE FOX WARM.

A map showing how foxes have evolved to suit their environments

THE HUMAN BODY

Your body is made up of organs, bones, tissue, and muscles, all held together in a sack of waterproof skin. That sounds simple, but every single part of your body has a job to do. Without bones, you couldn't stand. Without muscles, you couldn't move! Most of your body parts are essential for your very survival. All the different parts of the body work together to keep you alive, day after day.

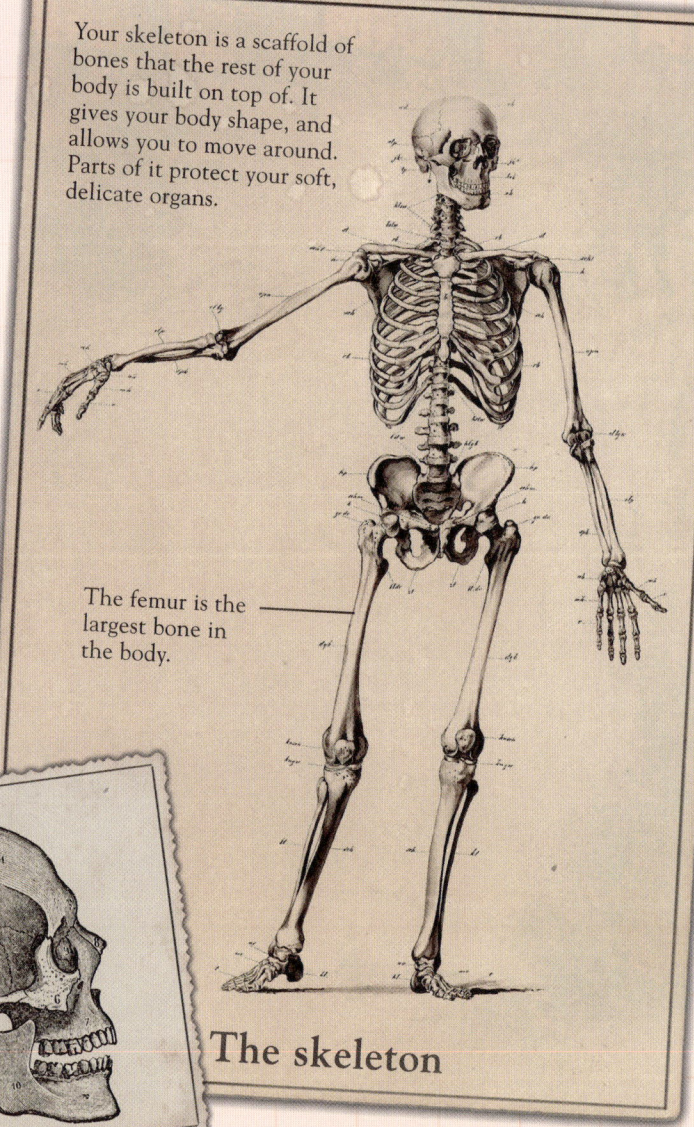

Your skeleton is a scaffold of bones that the rest of your body is built on top of. It gives your body shape, and allows you to move around. Parts of it protect your soft, delicate organs.

The femur is the largest bone in the body.

The skeleton

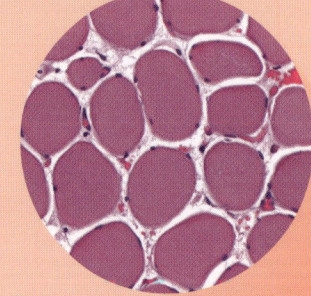

The skull protects the brain—your body's control center.

Human skull

WHAT ARE WE MADE OF?

Your body contains a number of systems, which each do a particular job. Those systems are made up of structures called organs, which are made from tissues, which are made from cells.

CELLS

The smallest building blocks of your body are cells. There are many different types of cells, each specialized to do a particular job.

TISSUES

Cells group together to form tissues. Again, there are different types of tissues. For example, muscle tissue is made up of layers of muscle cells.

BODY SYSTEMS

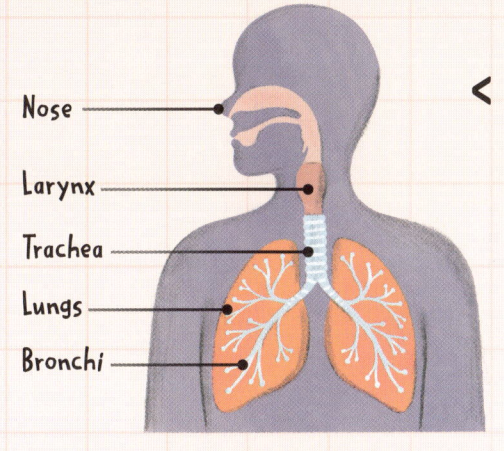

Nose
Larynx
Trachea
Lungs
Bronchi

< RESPIRATORY

Your respiratory system allows you to breathe. The lungs take in oxygen from the air and transfer it to the blood. The waste gas carbon dioxide is then breathed out.

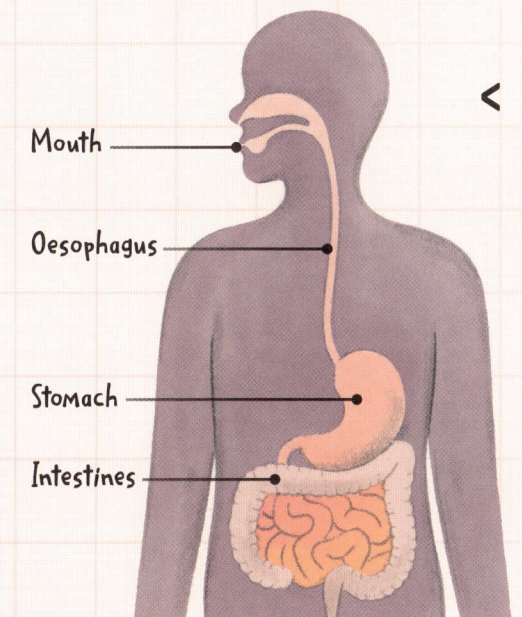

Mouth
Oesophagus
Stomach
Intestines

< DIGESTIVE

We get our energy and nutrients to stay healthy from food. The digestive system takes in food, mashes it up, and extracts all the nutrients. Once all the nutrients are removed, the waste food is pushed out of the body as poop.

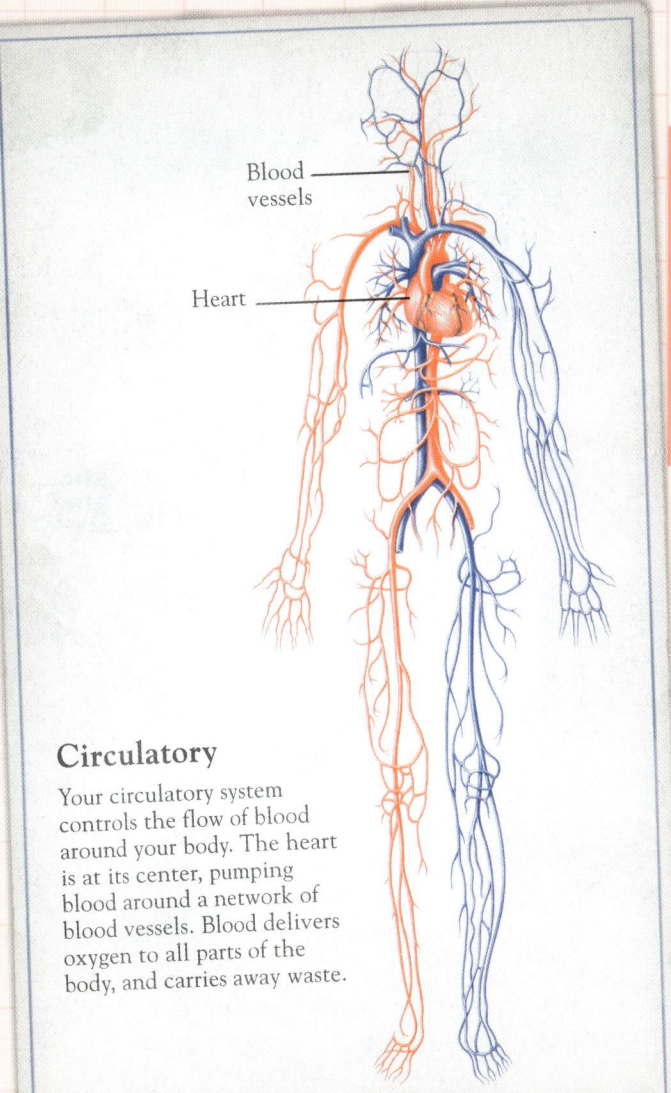

Blood vessels
Heart

Circulatory

Your circulatory system controls the flow of blood around your body. The heart is at its center, pumping blood around a network of blood vessels. Blood delivers oxygen to all parts of the body, and carries away waste.

ORGANS

Your organs are made of a combination of different types of tissues. Each organ performs a certain role. Muscles, for example, help you to move.

ORGAN SYSTEMS

Each body system is made of a group of organs, which work together to perform a function. Different muscles form the muscular system.

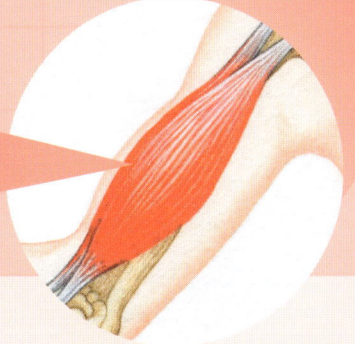

BODY

Your body contains 11 different systems. Together, they fulfill all our needs, including movement, breathing, eating, thinking, and removal of waste.

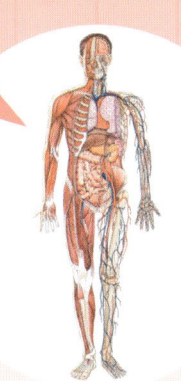

THE BRAIN

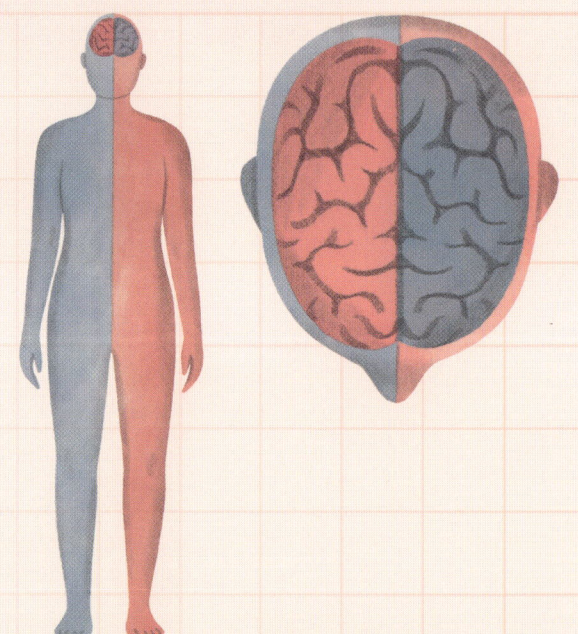

If you were to open your skull and look inside, you would find yourself looking at the control center of your entire body—your brain. All your thoughts happen here. Your ideas begin here. Your brain controls your movements and your heartbeat. It contains your memories, and processes all the information you receive from the outside world. Your brain works constantly, even when you are fast asleep.

The hemispheres

The brain is divided into two hemispheres: left and right. The left-hand side of the brain controls the right-hand side of the body, and the right-hand side of the brain controls the left-hand side of the body.

How do messages travel through the brain?

Brains contain billions of specialized cells, called neurons. These cells carry messages around the brain as electrical signals. The dendrites at one end of the neuron send the signal along the cell—across a structure called the axon—to the synapses, at the opposite end. The synapses send the signal onto the next neuron.

Neuron

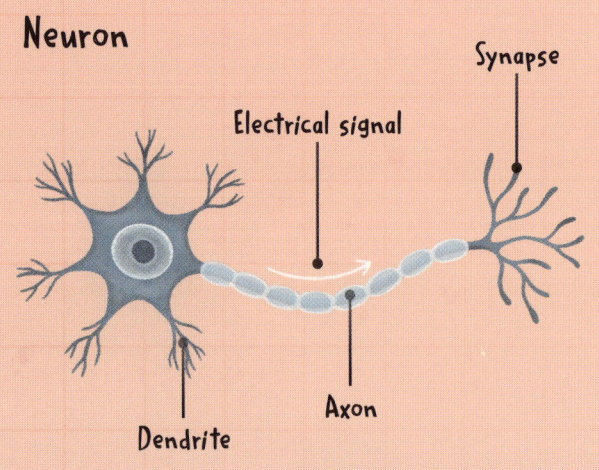

Synapse

Electrical signal

Dendrite

Axon

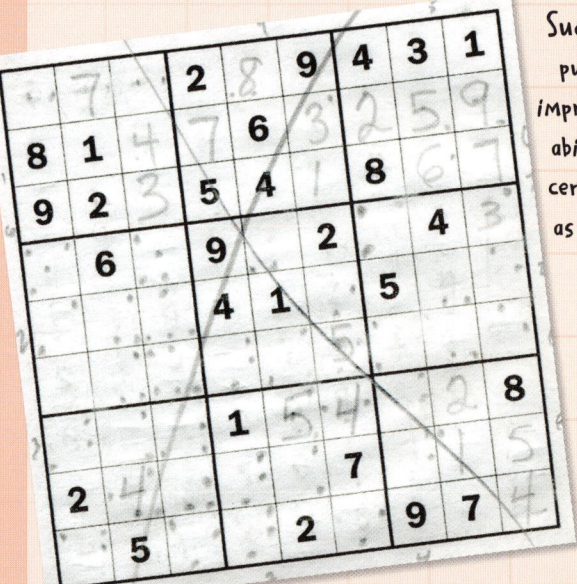

Sudoku and other puzzles can help improve your brain's ability to perform certain tasks, such as remembering.

NEURODIVERSITY

Not all people's brains work the same way—we are all different. The word "neurodiversity" describes the huge variety of ways our individual brains can work.

This badge, shaped like the infinity symbol, represents neurodiversity.

PARTS OF THE BRAIN

The top layer of the brain is called the cerebrum. It is divided into areas called lobes, and each lobe performs different functions for your body. The cerebrum isn't much to look at—it looks a bit like a large, fleshy walnut—but it controls almost everything you do, and uses about a fifth of the energy your body produces.

KEY

- Frontal lobe
- Parietal lobe
- Occipital lobe
- Temporal lobe
- Cerebellum

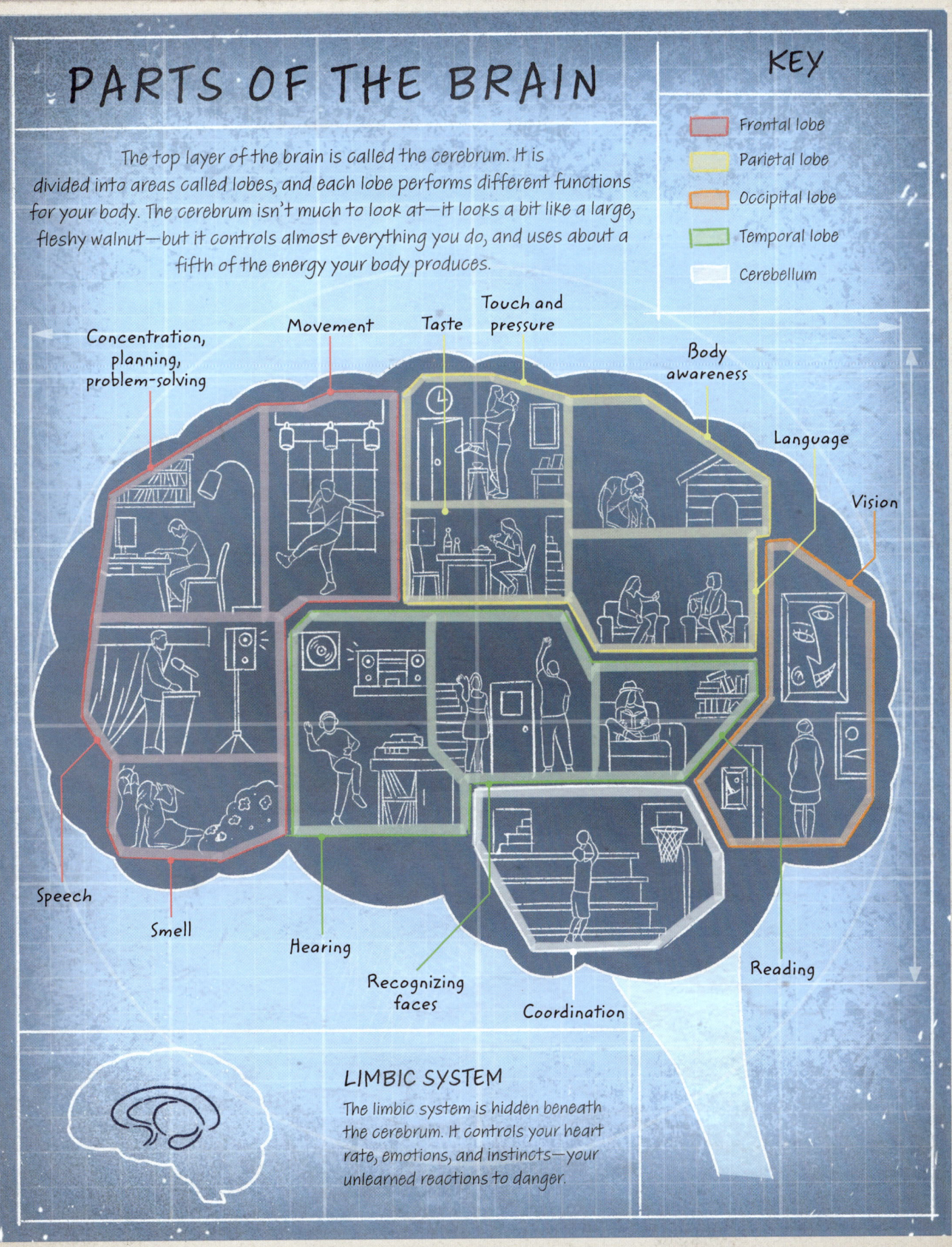

Concentration, planning, problem-solving

Movement

Taste

Touch and pressure

Body awareness

Language

Vision

Speech

Smell

Hearing

Recognizing faces

Coordination

Reading

LIMBIC SYSTEM

The limbic system is hidden beneath the cerebrum. It controls your heart rate, emotions, and instincts—your unlearned reactions to danger.

43

HISTORY'S DEADLIEST PANDEMICS

Smallpox was carried to the Americas by colonizing Europeans.

The Spanish flu was spread by soldiers, who were traveling between continents due to World War I.

ROUTES

Plague of Justinian c.541–42 CE
Bubonic plague spread from Asia or Ethiopia across the eastern Roman Empire, killing 25 million.

Black death 1346–55 CE
An outbreak of bubonic plague spread from Asia into Europe, causing around 50 million deaths.

Smallpox 1500s
Smallpox was common in Europe. It traveled worldwide, killing those who had not been exposed to it.

Spanish flu 1918–20
This outbreak of influenza spread from the US to Europe, killing between 20 and 50 million people.

Influenza is spread by droplets in the air, when people cough or sneeze.

Smallpox is spread by coughing and sneezing.

Pandemics follow frequently traveled paths, such as trade routes.

BOARDING PASS

COVID 19

Passenger	COVID 19		
		Carrier	Human
To	Worldwide		
		Year	2019
Month	December		

A global outbreak of a disease is called a pandemic. Air travel allows us to cross the world quickly, but we take our germs with us. The Covid-19 outbreak began in China in December 2019. It was declared a pandemic just months later, in March 2020.

EPIDEMIOLOGY

Many diseases are spread around by tiny microorganisms, which we know as germs. Germs can travel from person to person and place to place, infecting new people with their diseases. Studying the spread of these diseases is called "epidemiology."

Bubonic plague was spread by fleas, which lived on rats.

The Spanish flu outbreak killed more people than World War I.

Spanish flu reached New Zealand in 1918.

HOW DISEASES SPREAD

KEY ━━━━ **INFECTED** ━━━━ **HEALTHY**

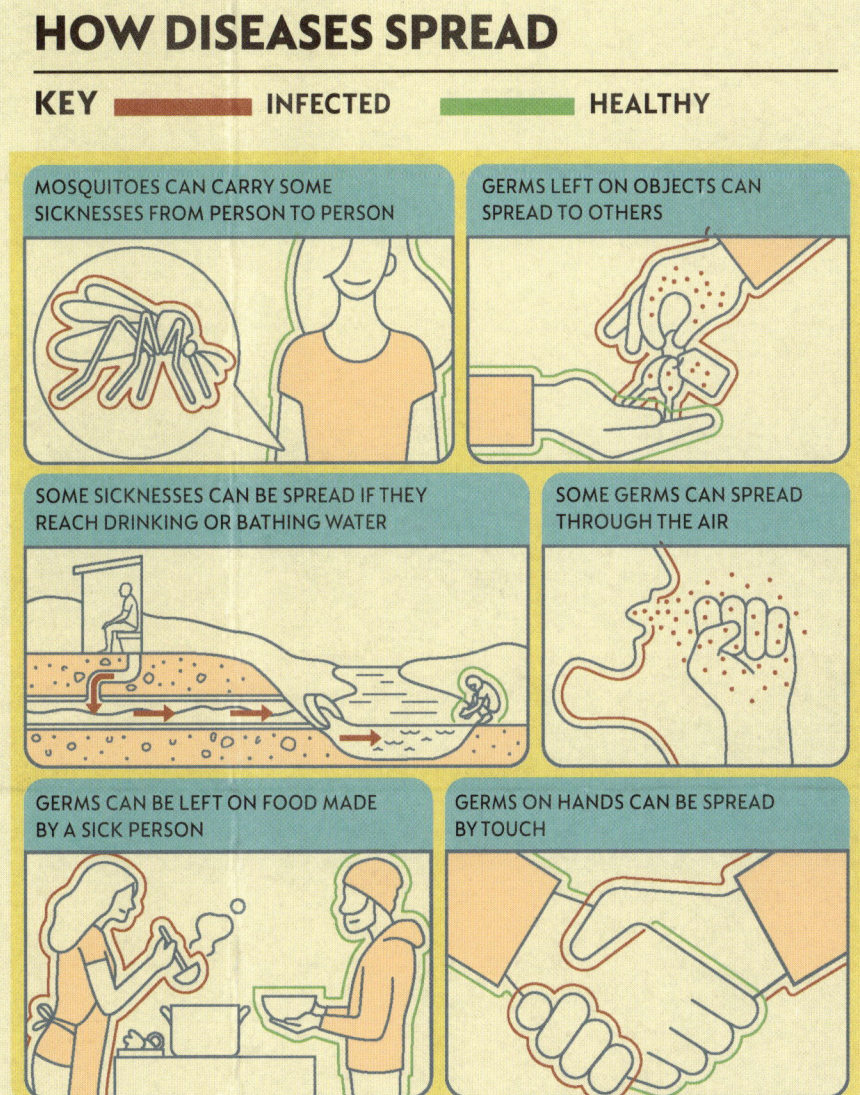

MOSQUITOES CAN CARRY SOME SICKNESSES FROM PERSON TO PERSON

GERMS LEFT ON OBJECTS CAN SPREAD TO OTHERS

SOME SICKNESSES CAN BE SPREAD IF THEY REACH DRINKING OR BATHING WATER

SOME GERMS CAN SPREAD THROUGH THE AIR

GERMS CAN BE LEFT ON FOOD MADE BY A SICK PERSON

GERMS ON HANDS CAN BE SPREAD BY TOUCH

Stopping the spread

To fight a pandemic, we attempt to stop diseases from traveling. Certain actions make it harder for the germs to travel from one person to the next.

Washing hands

Keeping away from each other

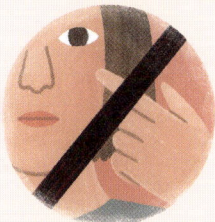

Avoiding touching the eyes, nose, and mouth

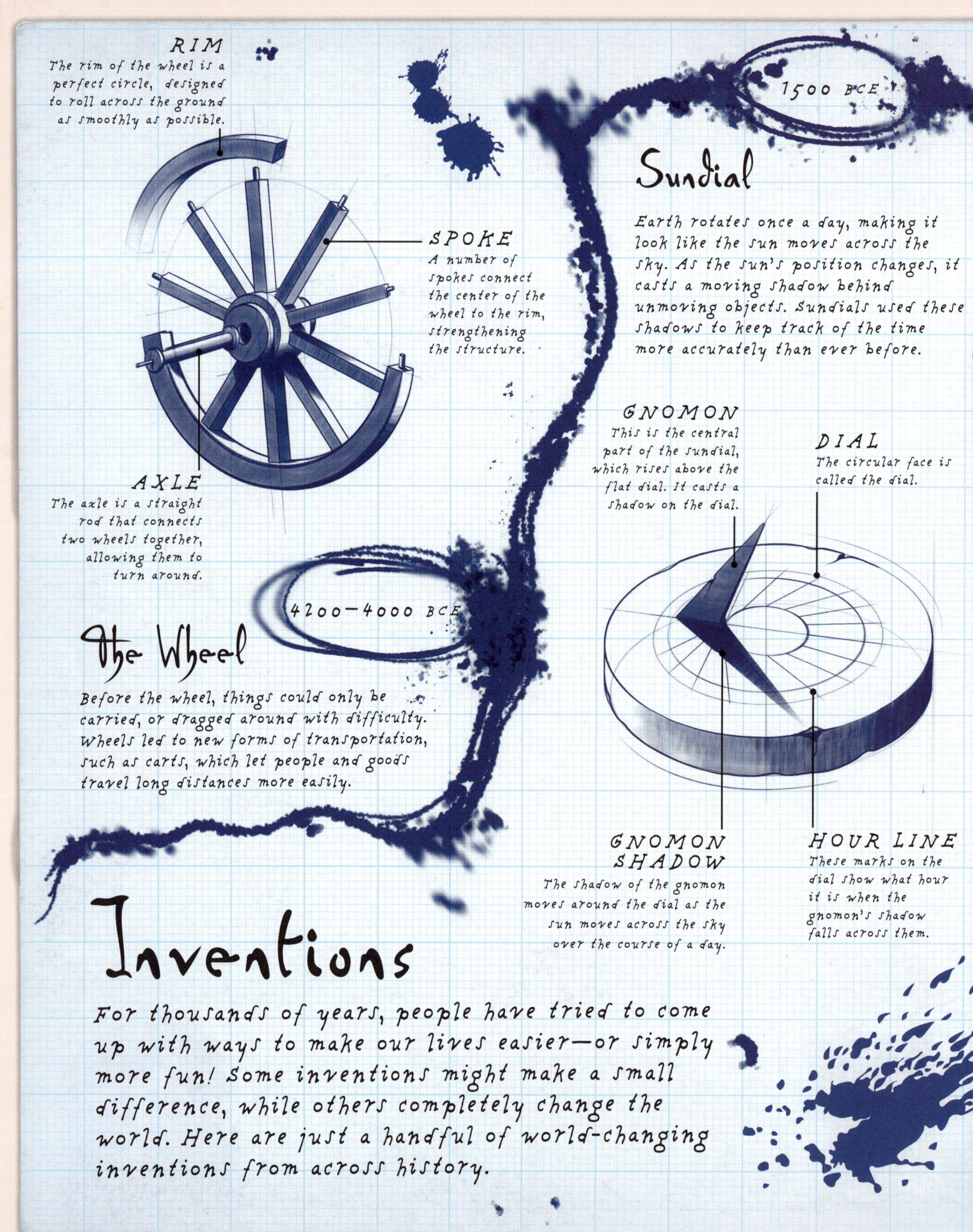

RIM

The rim of the wheel is a perfect circle, designed to roll across the ground as smoothly as possible.

SPOKE

A number of spokes connect the center of the wheel to the rim, strengthening the structure.

AXLE

The axle is a straight rod that connects two wheels together, allowing them to turn around.

Sundial

1500 BCE

Earth rotates once a day, making it look like the sun moves across the sky. As the sun's position changes, it casts a moving shadow behind unmoving objects. Sundials used these shadows to keep track of the time more accurately than ever before.

GNOMON

This is the central part of the sundial, which rises above the flat dial. It casts a shadow on the dial.

DIAL

The circular face is called the dial.

The Wheel

4200–4000 BCE

Before the wheel, things could only be carried, or dragged around with difficulty. Wheels led to new forms of transportation, such as carts, which let people and goods travel long distances more easily.

GNOMON SHADOW

The shadow of the gnomon moves around the dial as the sun moves across the sky over the course of a day.

HOUR LINE

These marks on the dial show what hour it is when the gnomon's shadow falls across them.

Inventions

For thousands of years, people have tried to come up with ways to make our lives easier—or simply more fun! Some inventions might make a small difference, while others completely change the world. Here are just a handful of world-changing inventions from across history.

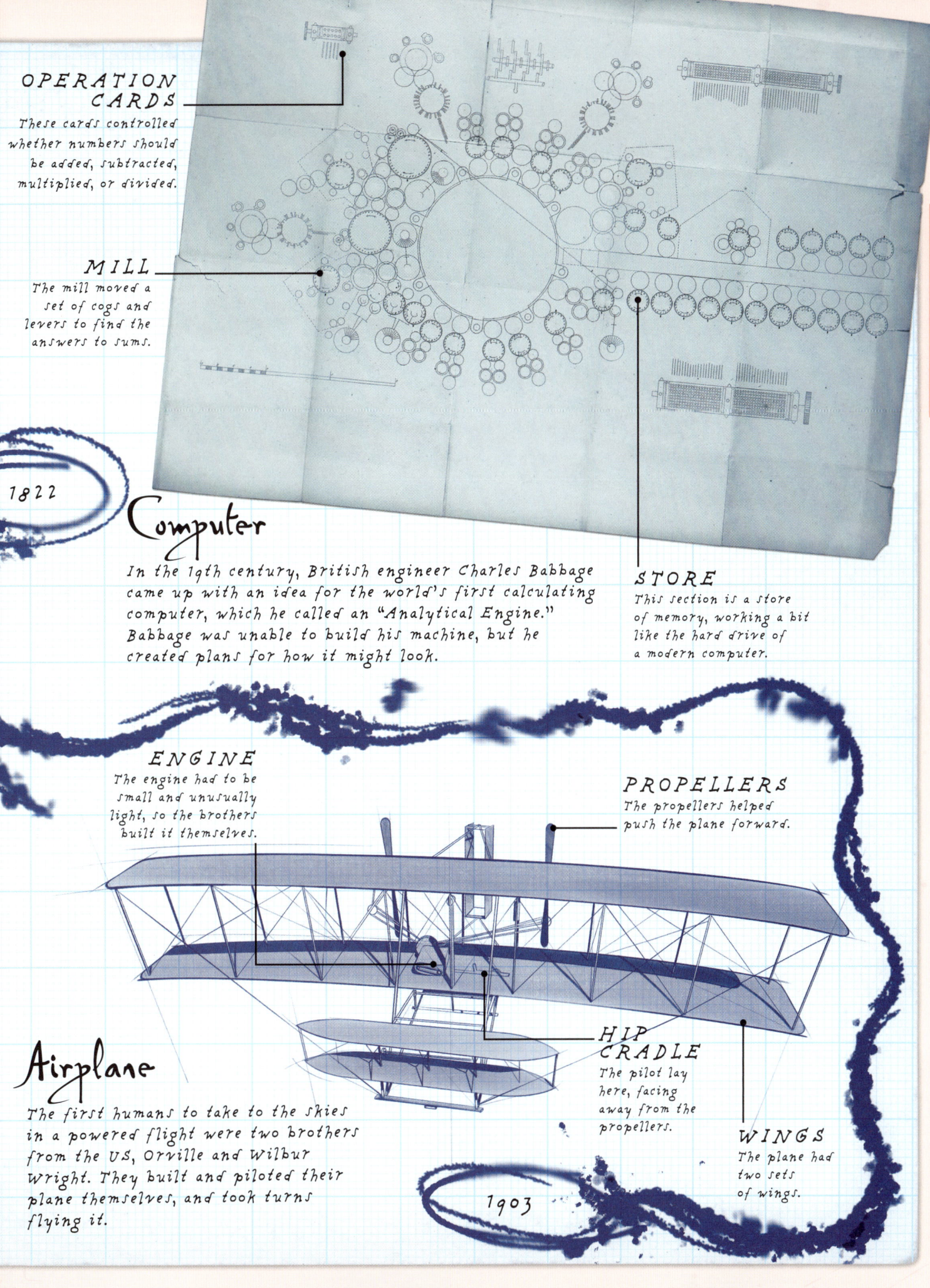

OPERATION CARDS
These cards controlled whether numbers should be added, subtracted, multiplied, or divided.

MILL
The mill moved a set of cogs and levers to find the answers to sums.

1822

Computer

In the 19th century, British engineer Charles Babbage came up with an idea for the world's first calculating computer, which he called an "Analytical Engine." Babbage was unable to build his machine, but he created plans for how it might look.

STORE
This section is a store of memory, working a bit like the hard drive of a modern computer.

ENGINE
The engine had to be small and unusually light, so the brothers built it themselves.

PROPELLERS
The propellers helped push the plane forward.

HIP CRADLE
The pilot lay here, facing away from the propellers.

Airplane

The first humans to take to the skies in a powered flight were two brothers from the US, Orville and Wilbur Wright. They built and piloted their plane themselves, and took turns flying it.

1903

WINGS
The plane had two sets of wings.

47

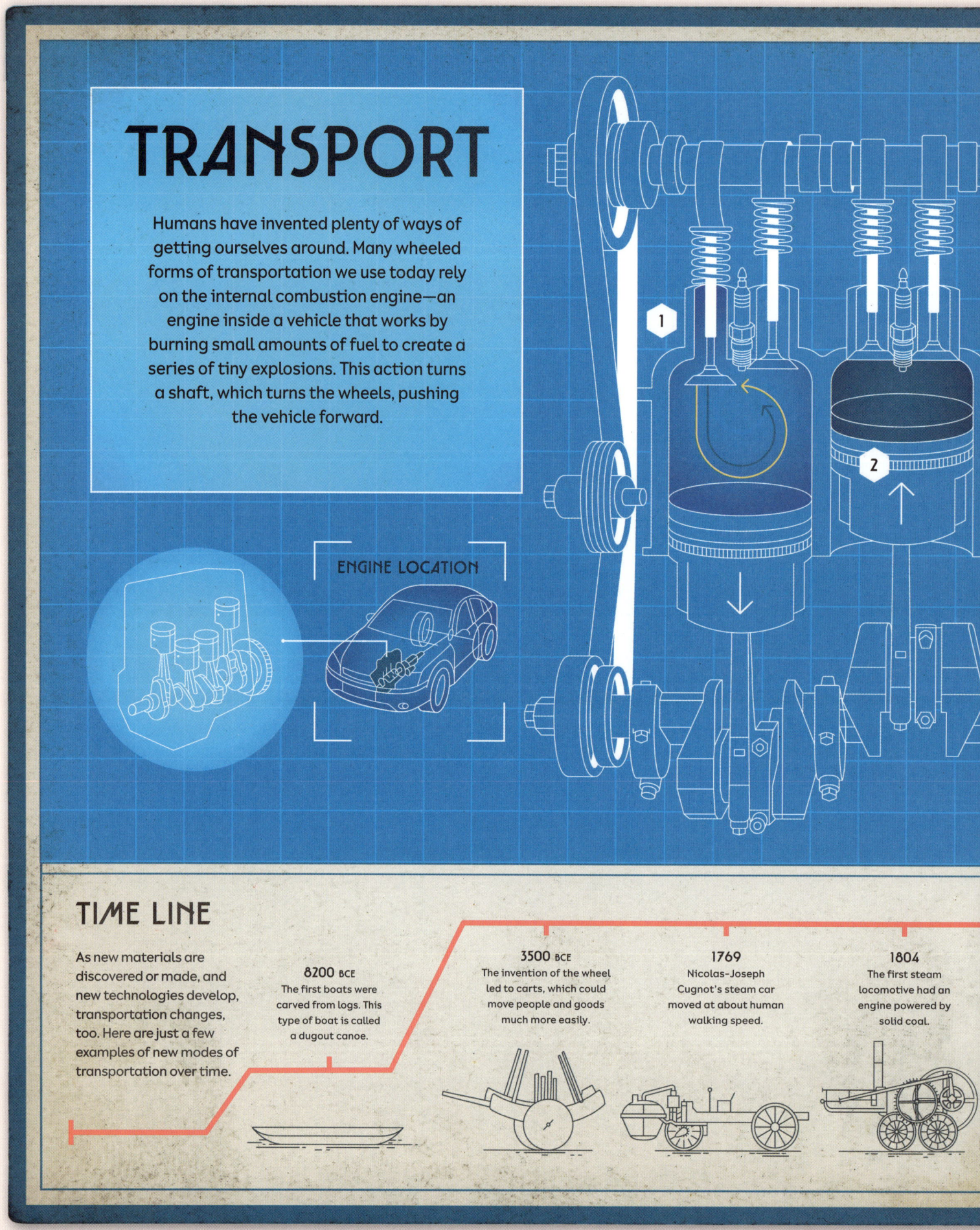

TRANSPORT

Humans have invented plenty of ways of getting ourselves around. Many wheeled forms of transportation we use today rely on the internal combustion engine—an engine inside a vehicle that works by burning small amounts of fuel to create a series of tiny explosions. This action turns a shaft, which turns the wheels, pushing the vehicle forward.

ENGINE LOCATION

TIME LINE

As new materials are discovered or made, and new technologies develop, transportation changes, too. Here are just a few examples of new modes of transportation over time.

8200 BCE
The first boats were carved from logs. This type of boat is called a dugout canoe.

3500 BCE
The invention of the wheel led to carts, which could move people and goods much more easily.

1769
Nicolas-Joseph Cugnot's steam car moved at about human walking speed.

1804
The first steam locomotive had an engine powered by solid coal.

Map of a combustion engine

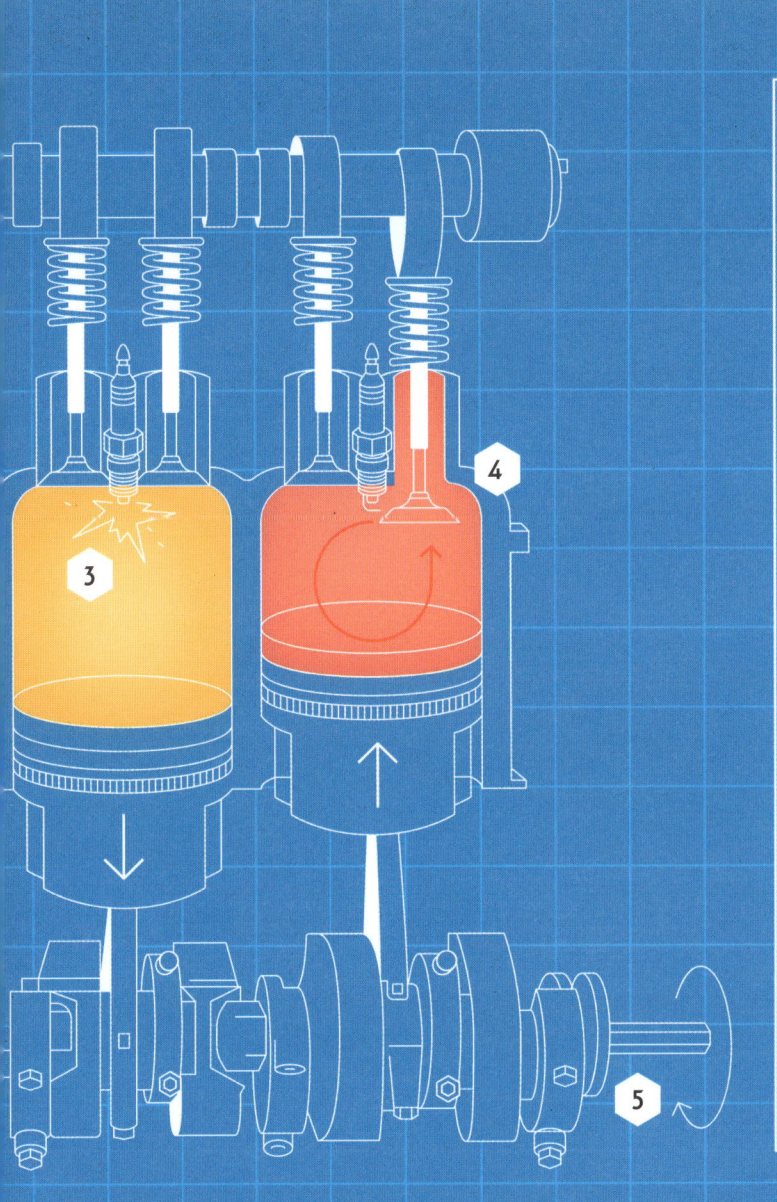

COMBUSTION ENGINE

1 INTAKE VALVE

As the piston moves downward, a mixture of fuel and air are sucked into it through a valve.

2 PISTON

Most engines have four, six, or eight pistons. The same reaction occurs in all of the pistons, in turn.

3 SPARK PLUG

Once the piston reaches the top, a spark ignites the fuel. The bang pushes the piston down again.

4 EXHAUST VALVE

Waste products from the burning fuel are pushed out of the piston through the exhaust valve.

5 CRANKSHAFT

The up-and-down movement of the pistons turns the crankshaft, which turns the wheels.

↑ FUEL

Fuel, such as diesel or gasoline, provides the energy that is needed for the reaction to happen.

↑ AIR

To burn, a reaction needs oxygen. Here, oxygen is provided by the air inside the engine.

↑ WASTE

The waste products from the reaction are gases such as steam and carbon dioxide.

1808

François Isaac de Rivaz invented the first internal combustion engine.

1817

Karl von Drais invented an early bicycle, which had no pedals.

1888

The first electric vehicle ran using an enormous, heavy battery.

1903

The Wright Brothers invented the first working airplane.

1995

The first driverless car was the Navlab5, which drove itself from Pittsburgh to San Diego in the US.

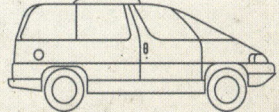

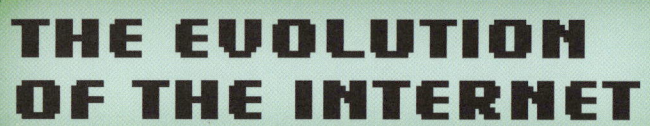

THE EVOLUTION OF THE INTERNET

1969, CALIFORNIA

The first Internet network, the ARPANET, goes online.

1971, MASSACHUSET

The first ever email is sent.

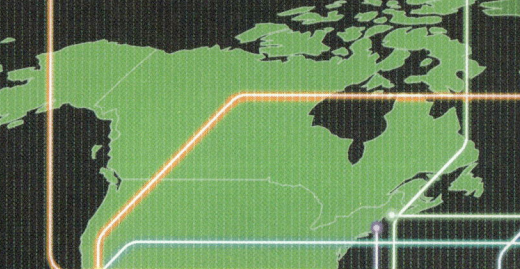

INTERNET EVERYWHERE

Electronic information networks have developed very quickly over the last 50 years or so. The first networks connected devices over short distances. Now, undersea cables connect servers to Internet users on other continents. Devices are also able to connect to the Internet without any wires at all, via satellites. This map shows what percentage of each country's population uses the Internet in modern times.

KEY

No data	0%	10%	20%	30%	40%	50%	60%	70%	80%	90%	100%

WHAT NEXT?

Virtual reality already lets people enter digital environments hosted on the Internet, such as the metaverse. These may become more popular over time.

2007, ESTONIA

The Internet is first used to vote in an election.

2007, CALIFORNIA

The iPhone is invented.

How does the Internet work?

Web page information is stored on machines called servers. Any question we ask on a device is sent to the server, and the answer is sent back to us. Often, this is done via a router in our homes—our computers connect to the router, which connects to the server.

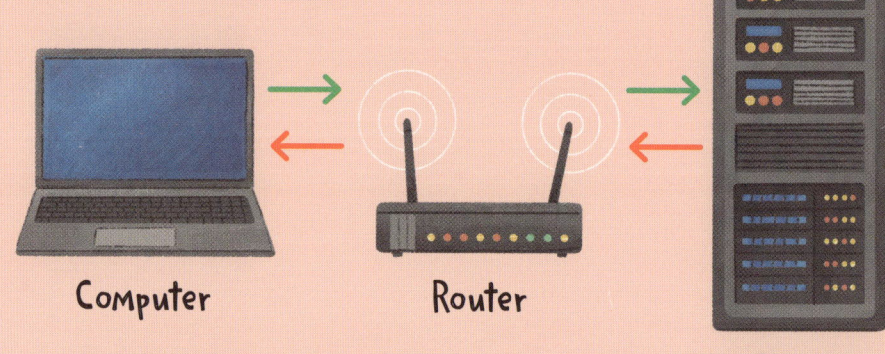

Computer   Router   Server

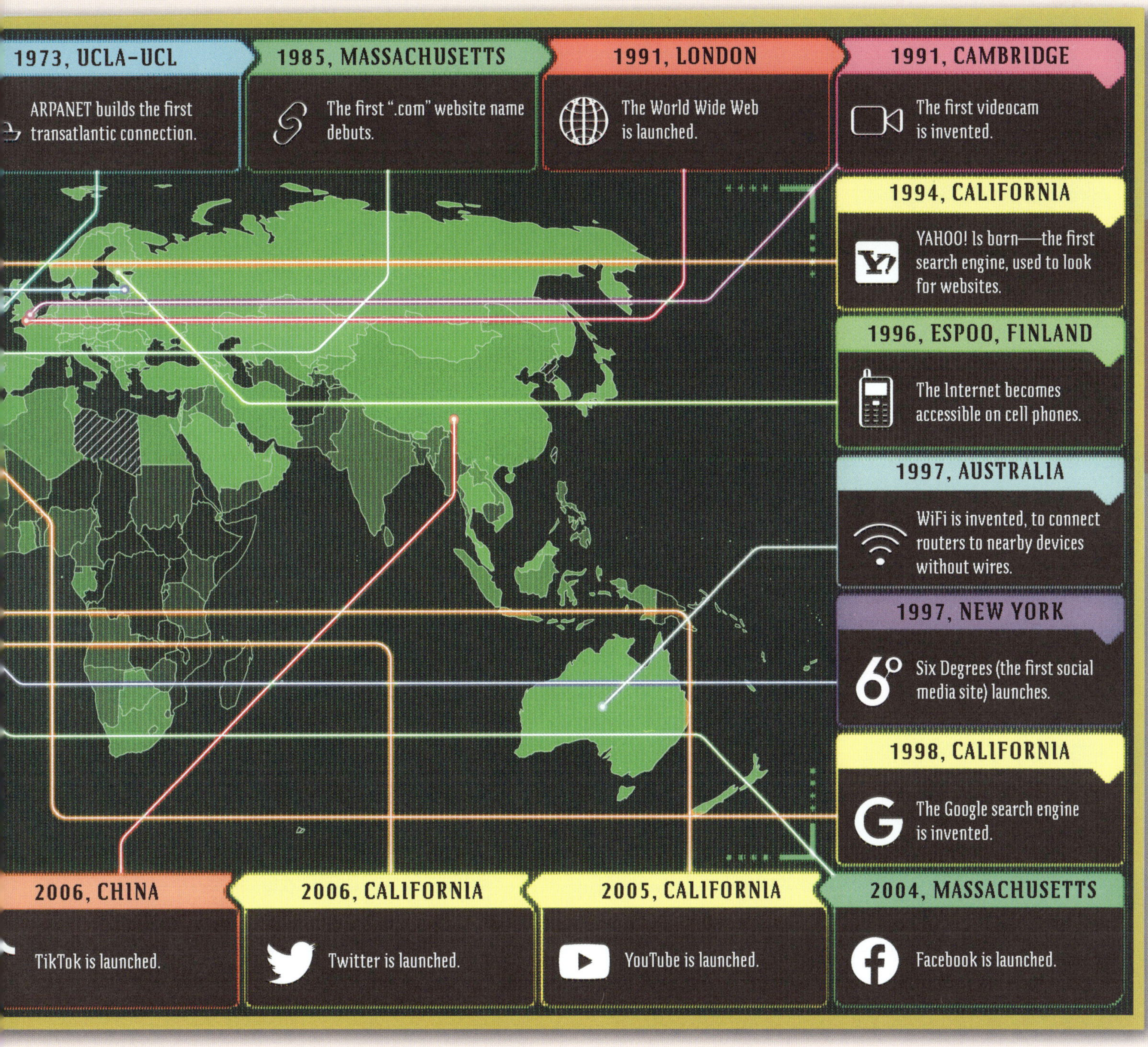

1973, UCLA–UCL

ARPANET builds the first transatlantic connection.

1985, MASSACHUSETTS

The first ".com" website name debuts.

1991, LONDON

The World Wide Web is launched.

1991, CAMBRIDGE

The first videocam is invented.

1994, CALIFORNIA

YAHOO! Is born—the first search engine, used to look for websites.

1996, ESPOO, FINLAND

The Internet becomes accessible on cell phones.

1997, AUSTRALIA

WiFi is invented, to connect routers to nearby devices without wires.

1997, NEW YORK

Six Degrees (the first social media site) launches.

1998, CALIFORNIA

The Google search engine is invented.

2006, CHINA

TikTok is launched.

2006, CALIFORNIA

Twitter is launched.

2005, CALIFORNIA

YouTube is launched.

2004, MASSACHUSETTS

Facebook is launched.

CYBER PROBLEMS

Bad things can be shared on the Internet as well as good things. Our computers can be "infected" by Internet-borne viruses, and hackers can use the Internet to take control of our devices.

∨

THE INTERNET

Our smartphones, tablets, laptops, and desktop computers are all linked together in a vast network—the Internet. The Internet allows us to share and receive information at lightning speed. It is used by households, businesses, and institutions such as schools. All of us would come to a standstill without it! Today, almost everything we do on a computer works via the Internet. We can message friends, shop, watch videos, play games, and even submit homework.

CHAPTER 3
EARTH

Our planet has existed for 4.5 billion years. It has altered and developed over its lifespan, changing from a blob of hot rock and metal into a stable planet with water, land, and a protective blanket of gases called the atmosphere. Today, Earth's surface is a patchwork of different habitats. It has mountains, oceans, forests, and, of course, plenty of humans. Human activity has permanently changed our planet—we have occupied most of it, building cities and farming the land. Humans are not the most plentiful species on the planet, but we are the one with the most influence over what happens where.

ROCKS AND MINERALS

If you took a look beneath the grass and soil under your feet, you would find that the ground is made up of solid rock. This rock is not all the same—it comes in a huge range of shapes, colors, and textures. Rocks can form deep underground or from volcanic eruptions, and over time they can transform into other types of rocks.

What is a rock?

Rocks are solid substances found in nature. They are made up of a mix of other natural substances, called minerals. Rocks can be organized into three different groups, based on how they formed, called "sedimentary," "igneous," and "metamorphic."

Marble is a metamorphic rock.

IGNEOUS ROCK SPECIMENS

 OBSIDIAN

 BASALT

PUMICE

 SCORIA

 GRANITE

 GABBRO

THE ROCK CYCLE

Like animals that go through metamorphosis, rocks are part of a cycle of change. They form, get worn away, and reform. This constant process of change is known as the rock cycle. It can take millions of years for rock to change from one form to another.

ROCK TYPES

IGNEOUS ROCK

Hot, liquid rock—called lava above ground and magma below—cools and hardens into igneous rock.

PROCESSES

WEATHERING

Water and wind slowly wear away rocks, breaking bits off.

GEMSTONES

These minerals can be cut and polished to create jewels. They sometimes form in cracks around magma chambers, when hot liquids and gases cool and harden.

GEMSTONE SPECIMENS

 EMERALD

 RUBY

 SAPPHIRE

TOPAZ

 AQUAMARINE

What is a mineral?

A mineral is a natural substance that is made up only of itself, with nothing else mixed in. Minerals have a crystal structure, though for many minerals this can only be seen under a microscope.

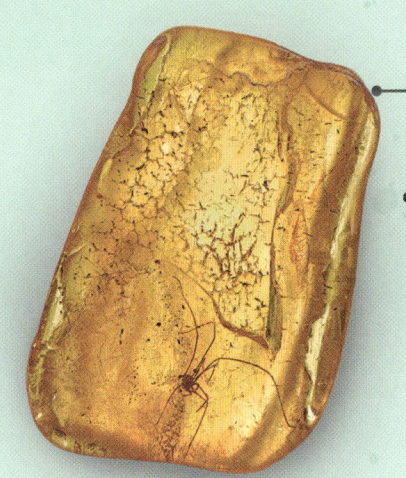

This amber contains a preserved spider.

Turquoise can be blue or green.

< LIVING ROCK

Amber is fossilized tree resin. It was once liquid and sticky, but became solid over millions of years. Small creatures can sometimes be seen trapped inside the stone.

SEDIMENTARY ROCK SPECIMENS

BRECCIA

CHALK

LIMESTONE

CHERT

CALICHE

COAL

SEDIMENTARY ROCK

This rock forms when tiny pieces of mud, sand, or sea-animal skeletons get squashed tightly together.

SQUASHING

As mud or sand builds up, it becomes heavy, squashing the layers below.

METAMORPHIC ROCK

Deep underground, huge heat and pressure can change igneous and sedimentary rock into metamorphic rock.

HEATING

If rock is heated enough it will melt, becoming liquid.

METAMORPHIC ROCK SPECIMENS

MARBLE

ANTHRACITE

GNEISS

HORNFELS

MARIPOSITE

SERPENTINE

A map of the rock cycle

FOSSILS

Most of the species of plants and animals that have ever lived on Earth are now extinct. How do we know that? Well, we've found their remains and traces of their lives, such as footprints, as fossils. These rocks allow us a glimpse of what lived on our planet long before we did. All kinds of different life forms have become fossils, from shellfish to impressive dinosaurs. Some familiar-looking fossils are the ancestors of modern animals, and can tell us how they changed over time.

What are fossils?

Fossils are stone formed from the remains and traces of living things. They help us figure out what ancient animals looked like—but they don't always tell the whole picture. It is often only the bones that are preserved, because they tend not to rot away or be eaten by scavengers.

Megalosaurus

FINDING FOSSILS

Fossils have been found all over the world, including in bleak deserts such as Antarctica. Here are just a few examples.

BODY FOSSILS

These are the remains of actual parts of a plant, or of an animal's body. They include bones, shells, feathers, wood, and leaves.

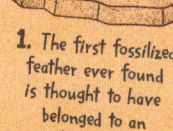

1. The first fossilized feather ever found is thought to have belonged to an archaeopteryx.

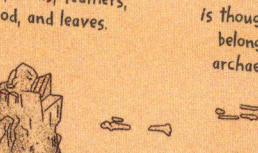

4. These glossopteris leaves show us that Antarctica once had a warm, tropical climate.

5. Named Lucy, this was the most complete skeleton of a human ancestor ever found.

AMBER FOSSILS

Amber is fossilized tree resin. It can have tiny animals trapped inside, such as insects.

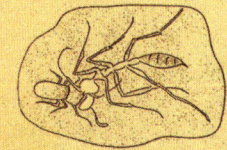

11. This 99-million-year-old ant has been frozen forever inside a piece of amber.

TRACE FOSSILS

These are fossils of animal activities—including tracks, nests, and even poop. They show us how animals behaved.

2. This 2.3 million-year-old skull is the oldest human fossil discovered so far.

3. Dug up in a family yard in England, this ammonite was found to be 65 million years old.

6. A battle between a velociraptor and a protoceratops was preserved in this fossil.

7. Seven-year-old Diego Suárez discovered this strange, beaked dinosaur in 2004.

8. This huge coprolite (fossilized poop) belonged to a Tyrannosaurus rex, and tells us what it ate.

9. This nest of baby Maiasauras shows that some dinosaurs took care of their young.

10. These fossil footprints show many little dinosaurs running in the same direction.

Earth

HOW FOSSILS FORM

Only a tiny fraction of life forms become fossils, because fossilization can only happen in very particular circumstances. Here's how it works:

To have a chance of being fossilized, a life form must die close to water, or in it.

Layers of mud and sand cover the body, increasing the weight and pressure on it.

Minerals from water seep into the bones, gradually turning them into stone.

Millions of years later, the land may be worn away, revealing the fossil.

BIOMES

Not everywhere on Earth looks the same, or has the same weather—some places are warm, others cold, some have trees, others don't, and so on. Regions that share the same climate (temperature and wetness), and support similar groups of plants and animals, are called biomes. Earth's land is divided up into a number of different biomes, and there are plenty more hidden out of sight, underwater.

Desert

The main thing about a desert is that it is extremely dry. Deserts can be hot or cold. They all have less than 10 inches (25 cm) of rain in a year.

Sahara Desert

Andes

Vermont

Temperate forest

These forests have seasons—they are different in spring, summer, fall, and winter. Many of the trees are deciduous, which means they drop their leaves in the fall.

Mountain

High above the ground it is cold and windy. There is less oxygen to breathe than at ground level, too. Different groups of plants and animals can be found at different heights.

Tundra

The tundra is an expanse of frozen, treeless land. More animals can be found here than you might expect, including polar bears, foxes, hares, and caribou.

North American tundra

Russian taiga

Boreal forest

A boreal forest contains mostly conifers—trees with needlelike leaves that they don't drop in winter. Winters are long here, while summers are fairly short.

Polar

These icy regions are the coldest biome, with ice and snow all year round. Fewer plants and animals are able to live here, though a few hardy animals have adapted to the difficult conditions.

Antarctica

Eurasian steppe

Grassland

These rolling plains have plenty of grass but few trees. They are home to burrowers and grass-eating animals, as well as the predators that prey on them.

Mediterranean

This biome occurs on coasts. It is hot in the summer, but cool and wet in the winter. The land often appears dry, with shrubs rather than lush, green plants.

Mediterranean shrubland

Tropical forest

These forests are warm and wet all year round, with plenty of rain. They support more types of plants and animals than any other biome on land.

Amazon Rainforest

WHAT GOES WHERE?

Different biomes occur in different places around the world, depending on how hot or cold it is in each area, and how much rain there is. It is freezing cold at Earth's poles (at its top and bottom), and warmer around the middle.

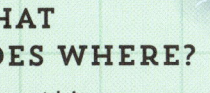

- Temperate forest
- Tropical forest
- Boreal forest
- Mediterranean shrubland
- Desert and dry shrubland
- Arctic tundra
- Polar
- Grassland
- Mountain

FORESTS

Our planet is home to billions of trees, which grow together in vast groups known as forests. Forests produce the oxygen we need to breathe, and help slow climate change by absorbing carbon dioxide—they are magical places! Not all our forests are same. There are three main types, which grow in different areas. Other types of plants grow alongside the trees in forests, and many different types of animals rely on forests for their food and shelter.

Which forest is where?

Forests grow in different places depending on the climate—how hot it is and how much rain there is. Temperate forests occur where temperatures are mild. Boreal forests grow near polar areas, where it is very cold. Tropical forests grow in warm areas near Earth's equator, but only where there is a lot of rain.

● Boreal   ● Temperate   ● Tropical

This map shows where to find Earth's forests.

TEMPERATE FORESTS

Deciduous trees make up this type of forest. These trees have wide, flat leaves that change color in the fall and drop off in winter, before growing again in spring.

BOREAL FORESTS

The trees in boreal forests are conifers, which have thin, needlelike leaves all year round. We sometimes call trees that don't drop their leaves "evergreens."

TROPICAL FORESTS

Also known as rainforests, tropical forests have extremely tall trees, which are mostly evergreens. They are home to millions of different animal species.

LAYERS OF THE RAINFOREST

230 FT (70 M)

98 FT (30 M)

20 FT (6 M)

5 FT (1.5 M)

0 FT 0 M

Emergent layer
The tops of the very tallest trees pop up above the rainforest's canopy, forming the emergent layer.

Canopy
The trees branch out here, forming a thick layer of leaves that very little light can penetrate.

Understory
Beneath the canopy it is dark and wet. Plants that need a lot of light cannot grow here, but there are plenty of vines and mosses.

Forest floor
All the forest's leaves fall here, creating a layer of rotting mulch. Some young trees try to reach upward toward the canopy.

Earth

1 Scarlet macaw	**3** Harpy eagle	**5** Emerald tree boa	**7** Strangler fig	**9** Glasswing butterfly	**11** Leaf-cutter ants
2 Blue morpho butterfly	**4** Two-toed sloth	**6** Howler monkey	**8** Jaguar	**10** Capybara	**12** Black caiman

A map of the rainforest

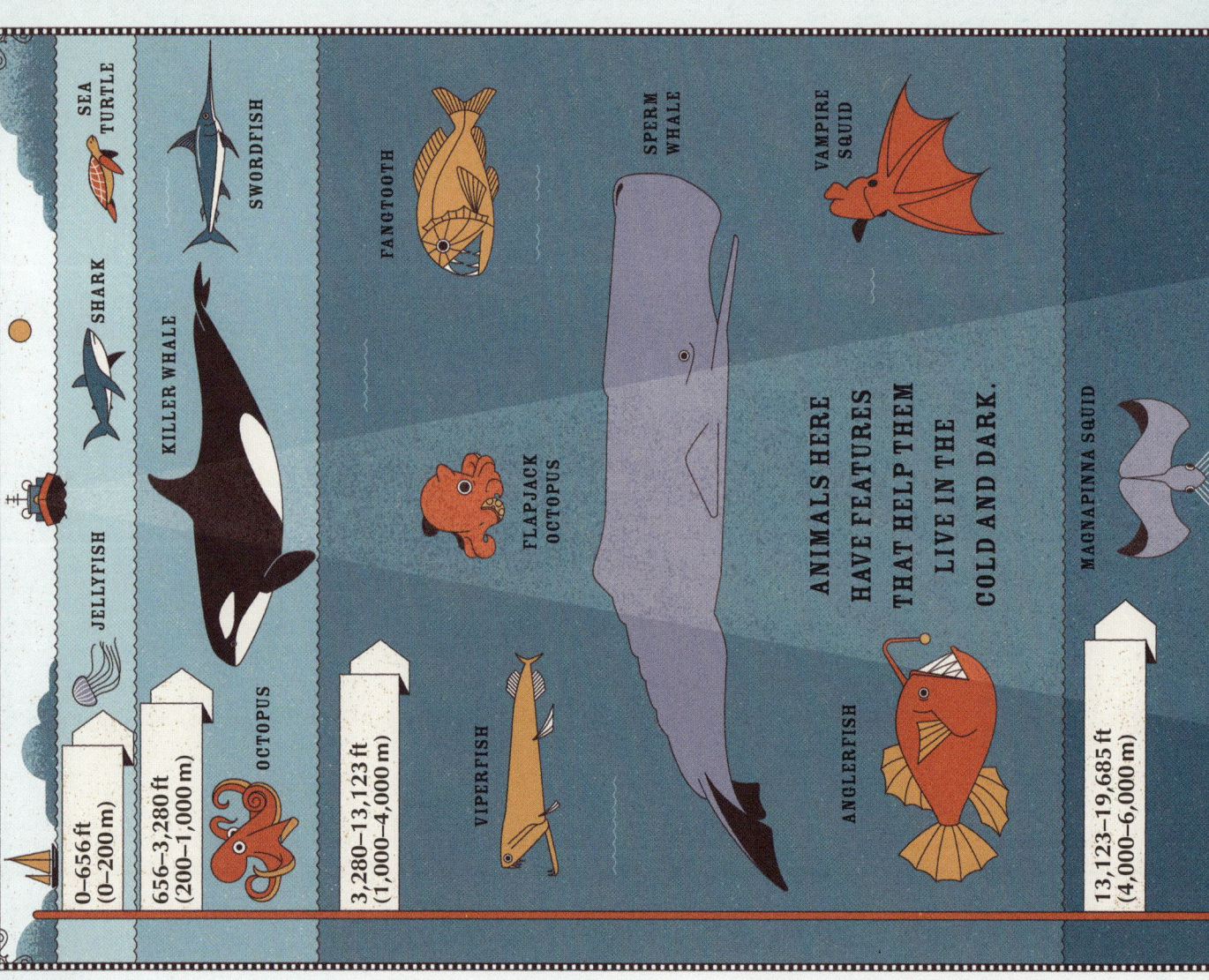

SEA TURTLE

SWORDFISH

SHARK

FANGTOOTH

SPERM WHALE

VAMPIRE SQUID

KILLER WHALE

JELLYFISH

FLAPJACK OCTOPUS

ANIMALS HERE HAVE FEATURES THAT HELP THEM LIVE IN THE COLD AND DARK.

MAGNAPINNA SQUID

OCTOPUS

VIPERFISH

ANGLERFISH

0–656 ft (0–200 m)

656–3,280 ft (200–1,000 m)

3,280–13,123 ft (1,000–4,000 m)

13,123–19,685 ft (4,000–6,000 m)

MAP OF OCEAN DEPTH

SUNLIT ZONE >

As its name suggests, this is the only zone that receives full sunlight. Tiny plankton live here, providing food for huge numbers of larger ocean animals.

TWILIGHT ZONE >

The light here fades to a dim blue light. Far fewer animals live here than in the higher, light-filled sunlit zone. There is less oxygen, and much less available to eat.

MIDNIGHT ZONE >

No light at all penetrates below the twilight zone. It is pitch black, freezing cold, and pressure is high due to the weight of water above. The animals that live here look very different from those higher up.

OCEANS

Water, water, everywhere! Earth's surface features huge expanses of water— our oceans. They are home to a huge range of different types of life forms. But, have you ever thought about what happens beneath the waves?

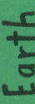

BRITTLE STAR

SOME DEEP-SEA ANIMALS CAN MAKE THEIR OWN LIGHT.

We have accurate maps of just 15% of the ocean floor, though it makes up 70% of Earth's surface.

AMPHIPOD

DEEP-SEA SNAILFISH

CUSK EEL

VERY LITTLE IS KNOWN ABOUT LIFE IN DEEP-SEA TRENCHES.

TRIPOD FISH

Below 19,685 ft (6,000 m)

ABYSSAL ZONE >

Many of the animals in the deepest parts of the ocean live by eating dead animals that drift down to the ocean floor from higher zones. Some of them hunt, but eat very rarely.

What is an ocean?

Oceans are the largest bodies of water on Earth. There are five oceans in total: the Atlantic, Pacific, Indian, Arctic, and Southern Oceans, and they are all connected.

Arctic Ocean

Pacific Ocean

Indian Ocean

Atlantic Ocean

Southern Ocean

Arctic Ocean

Pacific Ocean

HADAL ZONE >

This zone contains the deepest parts of the ocean trenches. Very little life survives here, though there are some bizarre ecosystems with life forms that have developed unusual features and behaviors to survive.

Earth

63

CORAL POLYP

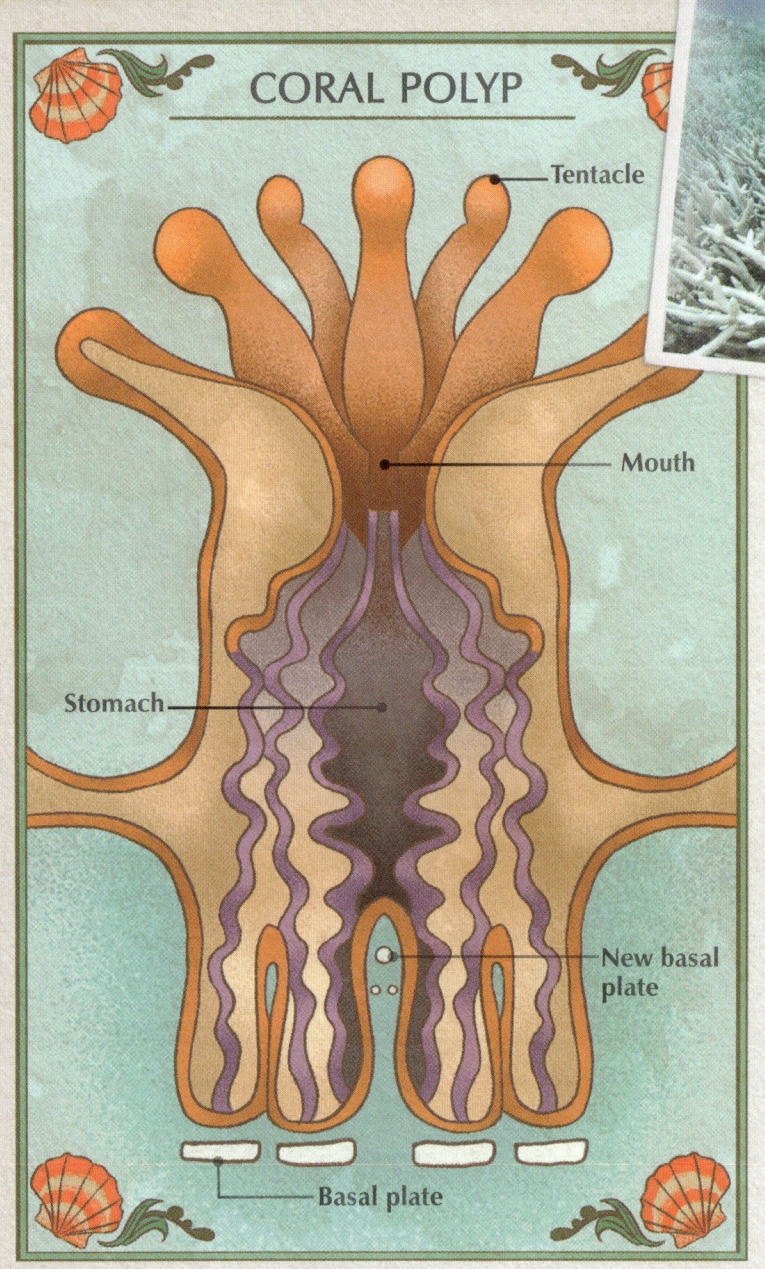

Tentacle

Mouth

Stomach

New basal plate

Basal plate

CORAL BLEACHING

Climate change is heating up oceans all over the world. This has had a devastating effect on coral, damaging the coral and turning it white in a process called "bleaching."

< WHAT IS CORAL?

Corals are formed of groups of tiny individual creatures, called polyps. Each polyp is a separate life form, with its own mouth, gut, and tiny tentacles. The polyps link together to form a larger coral structure. They create basal plates to sit on, and lift off the plates to grow taller.

CORAL REEF

Not far beneath the surface of warm, tropical oceans hide brightly colored coral reefs. Each coral reef is made up of a collection of individual corals. Corals look similar to plants, but they are actually invertebrates—animals with no internal skeleton. Coral reefs and the spaces around them provide shelter for a huge range of different plants and animals, including baby fish.

People often travel to see coral reefs.

A Flowerpot coral

This hard coral has long, feathery, daisylike polyps that can be extended. It comes in a range of colors, and eats plankton.

MAP OF A CORAL REEF

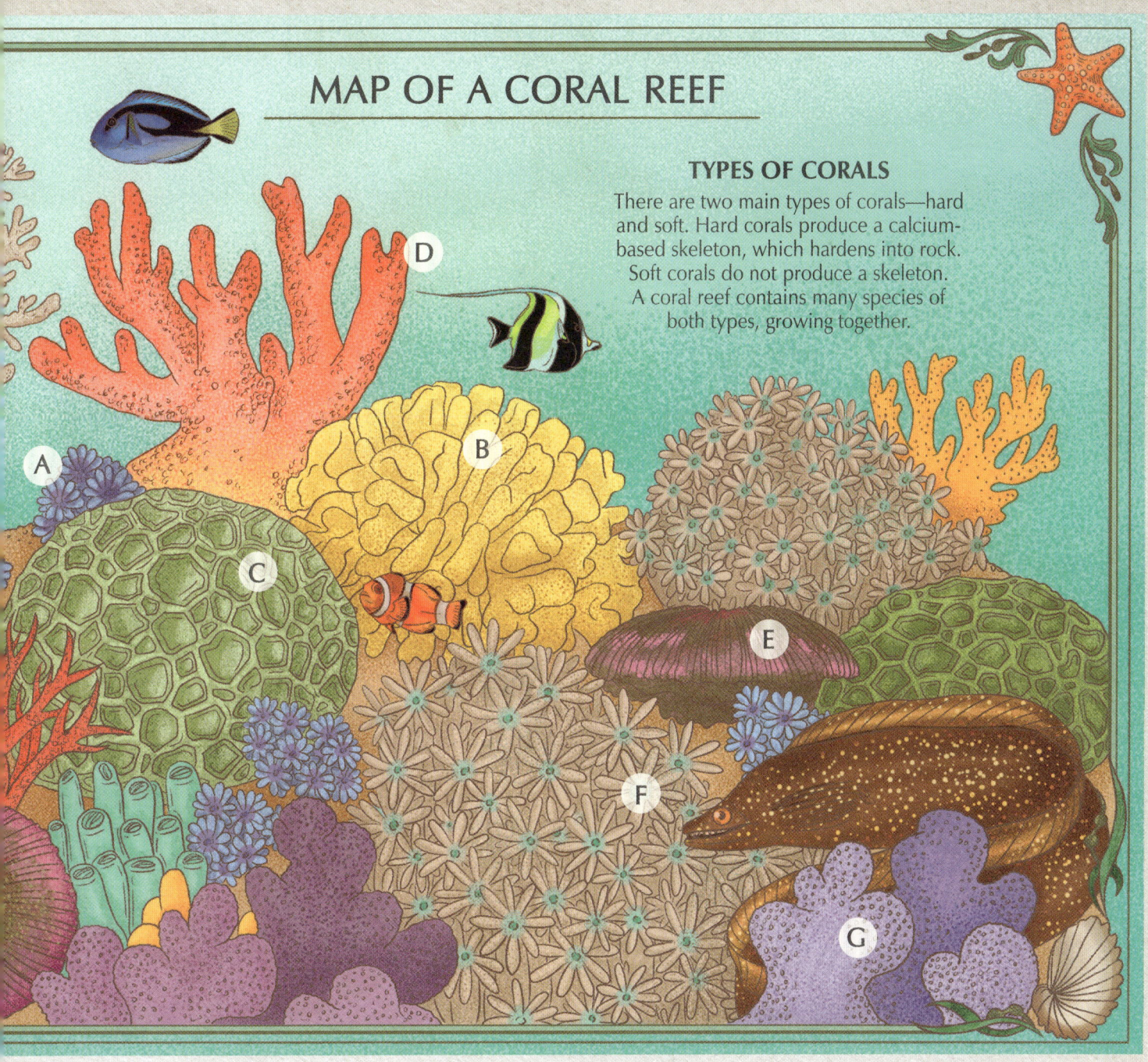

TYPES OF CORALS

There are two main types of corals—hard and soft. Hard corals produce a calcium-based skeleton, which hardens into rock. Soft corals do not produce a skeleton. A coral reef contains many species of both types, growing together.

Earth

B Cauliflower coral

Named after the vegetable it looks a little like, this stony coral comes in many colors, including blue.

C Honeycomb coral

As this hard coral grows, it forms a large dome, which can eventually reach more than 3 ft 3 in (1 m) across.

D Finger coral

This slow-growing coral forms long, thin structures that look a little like fingers. Its polyps only extend their tentacles at nighttime.

E Mushroom coral

This hard coral always has six tentacles, or a number of tentacles that is a multiple of six.

F Organ-pipe coral

This soft coral has long, organ-pipelike tubes. Each tube is made up of polyps with eight feathery, starlike tentacles.

G Hump coral

Another hard coral, hump coral grows into a rounded, "hump" shape. It likes growing in places where there aren't any other corals nearby.

EARTHQUAKES

The ground we walk on is not as solid as it feels. It is part of Earth's outer layer, the crust, which is split up into huge chunks, called tectonic plates. The tectonic plates shift around, rubbing and bumping against each other. These movements send vibrations rippling through the crust beneath us, which can cause earthquakes. Most earthquakes happen at the places where tectonic plates meet, which are called boundaries.

Earthquake-proof buildings

If a structure is too rigid, which means it cannot bend, it can break during an earthquake. So, some buildings are designed to flex (bend) when the ground shakes.

The Tokyo Skytree has a flexible core to protect it during earthquakes.

< MEASURING QUAKES

There are many ways of measuring earthquakes. They are often given a number—a low number means less damage is caused, while higher numbers link to more damage.

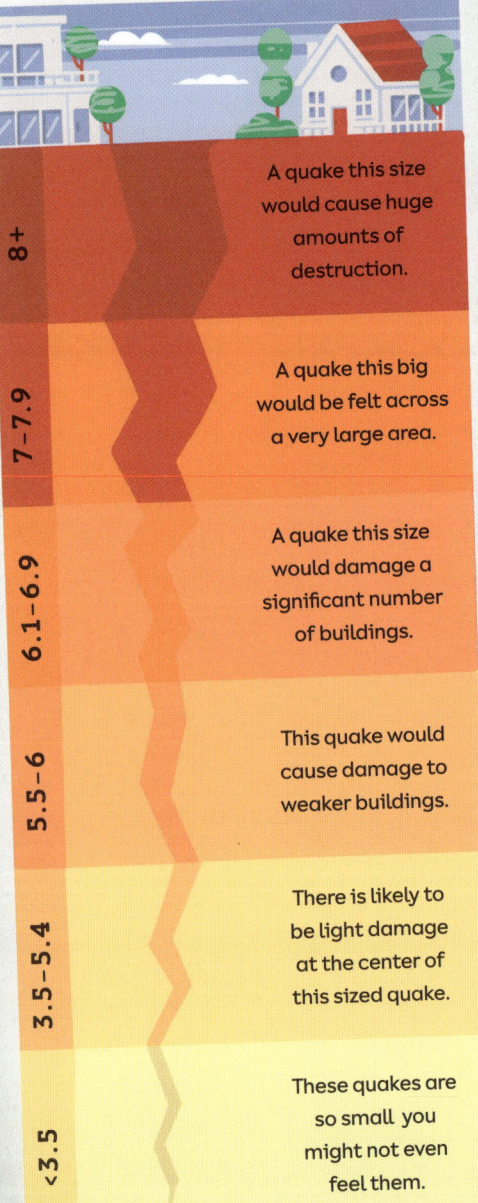

EARTHQUAKE MAGNITUDE CLASSES

Magnitude	Description
8+	A quake this size would cause huge amounts of destruction.
7–7.9	A quake this big would be felt across a very large area.
6.1–6.9	A quake this size would damage a significant number of buildings.
5.5–6	This quake would cause damage to weaker buildings.
3.5–5.4	There is likely to be light damage at the center of this sized quake.
<3.5	These quakes are so small you might not even feel them.

MAP OF TECTONIC PLATES

NORTH AMERICAN PLATE

CARIBBEAN PLATE

AFRICAN PLATE

COCOS PLATE

PACIFIC PLATE

NAZCA PLATE

SOUTH AMERICAN PLATE

SOUTH AMERICAN PLATE

TSUNAMIS >

If an earthquake occurs beneath the ocean, it can trigger a tsunami. These large waves become taller as they get closer to land, reaching heights of up to 100 ft (30.5 m).

Mount Pinatubo volcano—three days before it erupted in June, 1991

< RING OF FIRE

The boundary around the edge of the Pacific plate is home to so many active volcanoes that it is known as the Ring of Fire. This is one of the most active parts of Earth's crust. Many earthquakes occur here, as well as fiery volcanic eruptions.

 PLATE BOUNDARY   RING OF FIRE

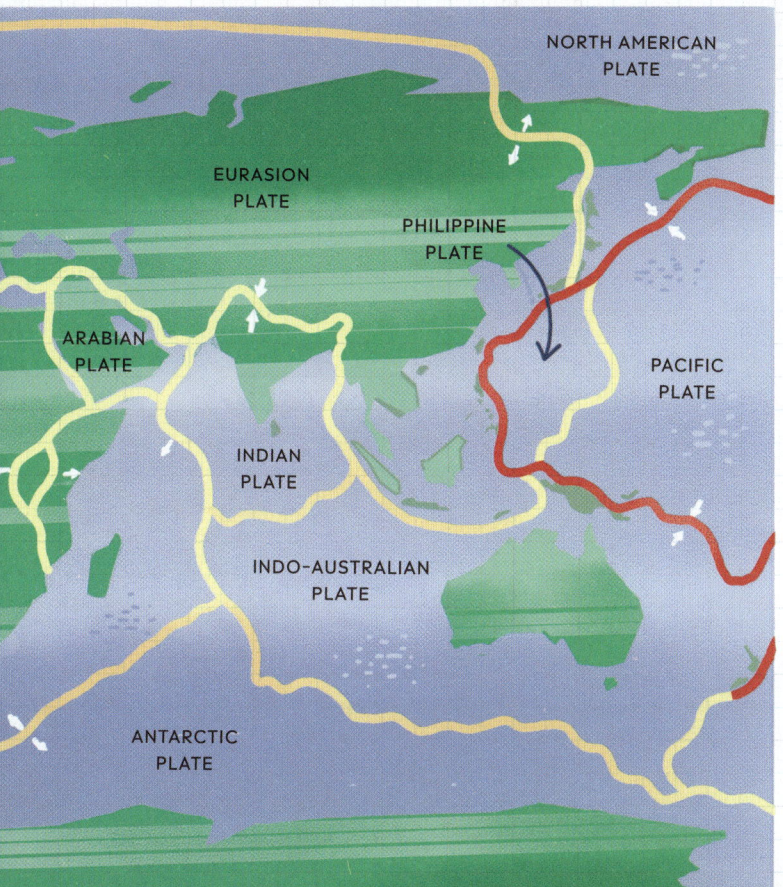

NORTH AMERICAN PLATE

EURASION PLATE

PHILIPPINE PLATE

ARABIAN PLATE

PACIFIC PLATE

INDIAN PLATE

INDO-AUSTRALIAN PLATE

ANTARCTIC PLATE

TYPES OF PLATE BOUNDARIES

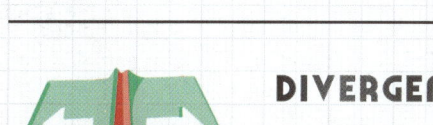

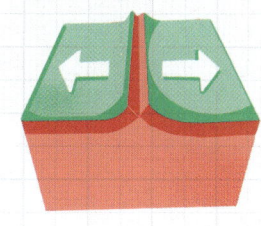

DIVERGENT

At this boundary, two plates move away from each other. New plate material forms in the opening that is created between them.

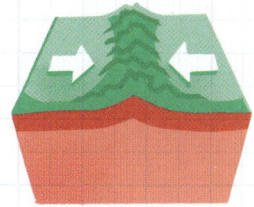

CONVERGENT

Two plates push into each other, creating mountain ranges. If one plate moves beneath the other then volcanoes can form.

TRANSFORM

Here, the two plates scrape along past each other. This movement can shake the ground, creating rippling earthquakes.

MOUNTAINS

Our mountains are the highest places on Earth's surface. Because they are so high up, mountain temperatures are usually cold and the air is thinner, with less oxygen in it. People and animals live in the mountains despite the hard conditions. In fact, people seek out the mountains for fun: to ski, walk, and climb. Mountains are formed by the movements of Earth's tectonic plates, as well as volcanic activity. Many of them are still growing as the plates push together.

MOUNTAIN RANGES

Mountains can grow individually, but they often form in long ridges, known as mountain ranges. Mountain ranges can be hundreds or even thousands of miles long. The longest above-water range is the Andes, at 4,300 miles (7,000 km) long.

MOUNTAIN LIFE

Living on the edge

The plants and animals that live high up in mountains must adapt to survive in these difficult environments. Mountain goats have thick coats for warmth and hooves with two toes that can grab rock and climb.

MOUNTAINS IN SPACE

Mountains don't just occur on Earth—they can develop on other planets. The largest mountain in our solar system is a volcano on the planet Mars, called Olympus Mons. It is about three times taller than Earth's tallest mountain, Everest.

Olympus Mons seen from space

Olympus Mons—73,819 ft (22,500 m)

Everest—29,032 ft (8,849 m)

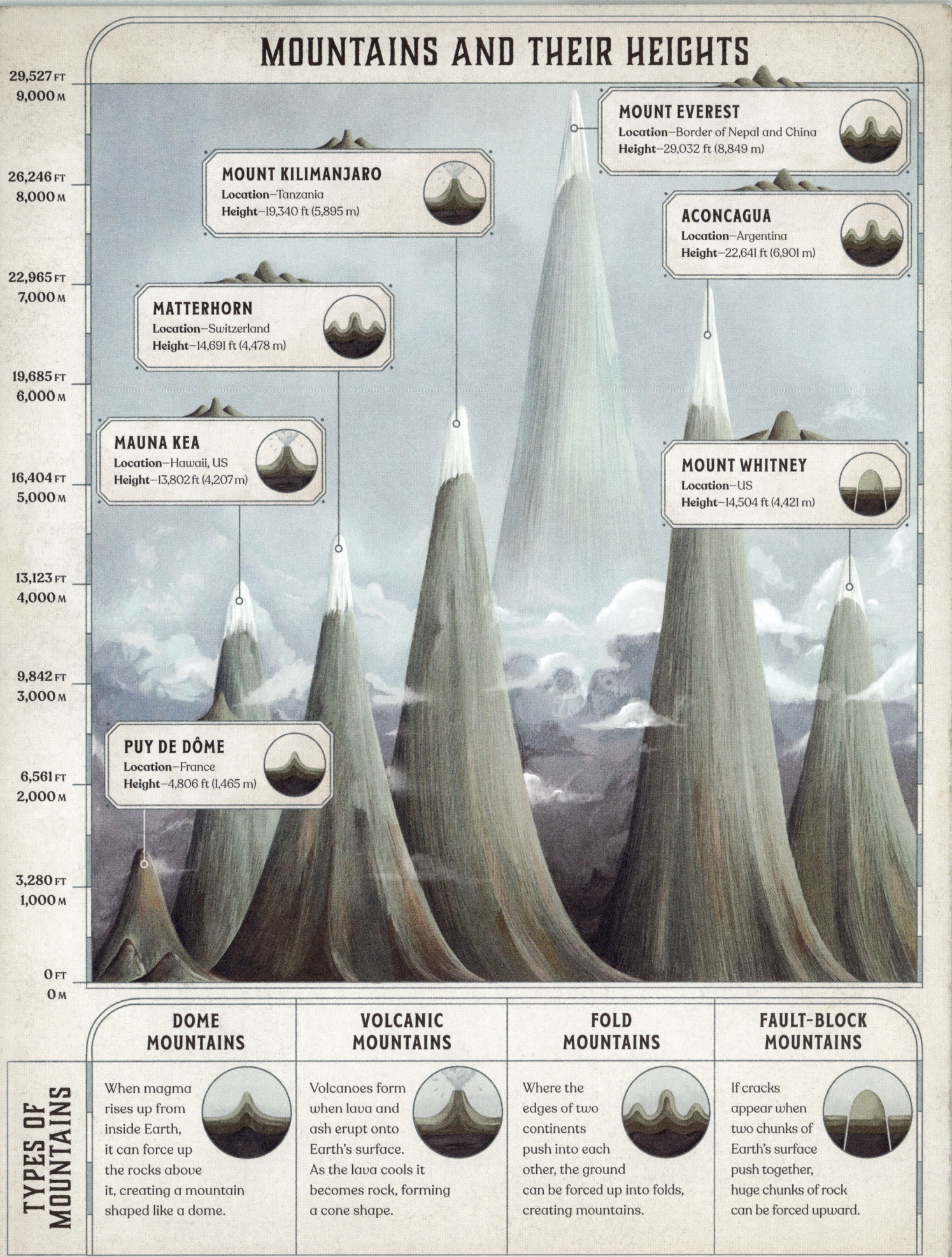

MOUNTAINS AND THEIR HEIGHTS

29,527 FT / 9,000 M	
26,246 FT / 8,000 M	
22,965 FT / 7,000 M	
19,685 FT / 6,000 M	
16,404 FT / 5,000 M	
13,123 FT / 4,000 M	
9,842 FT / 3,000 M	
6,561 FT / 2,000 M	
3,280 FT / 1,000 M	
0 FT / 0 M	

MOUNT EVEREST
Location–Border of Nepal and China
Height–29,032 ft (8,849 m)

MOUNT KILIMANJARO
Location–Tanzania
Height–19,340 ft (5,895 m)

ACONCAGUA
Location–Argentina
Height–22,641 ft (6,901 m)

MATTERHORN
Location–Switzerland
Height–14,691 ft (4,478 m)

MAUNA KEA
Location–Hawaii, US
Height–13,802 ft (4,207 m)

MOUNT WHITNEY
Location–US
Height–14,504 ft (4,421 m)

PUY DE DÔME
Location–France
Height–4,806 ft (1,465 m)

Earth

TYPES OF MOUNTAINS

DOME MOUNTAINS
When magma rises up from inside Earth, it can force up the rocks above it, creating a mountain shaped like a dome.

VOLCANIC MOUNTAINS
Volcanoes form when lava and ash erupt onto Earth's surface. As the lava cools it becomes rock, forming a cone shape.

FOLD MOUNTAINS
Where the edges of two continents push into each other, the ground can be forced up into folds, creating mountains.

FAULT-BLOCK MOUNTAINS
If cracks appear when two chunks of Earth's surface push together, huge chunks of rock can be forced upward.

1. Rainfall
When clouds contain enough water, they release it down to Earth. This is called precipitation.

2. Snow
If it is cold enough, the water droplets in clouds will freeze to snow or hail and fall to the ground.

3. Moving clouds
Clouds drift across the sky, pushed by wind and by heat that rises up from the ground.

LAKE

OCEAN
Most of the world's water is in the oceans. This water is salty because there are minerals dissolved in it.

9. Lakes
Water collects and forms lakes where there are hollows in the ground.

8. Ground water
Some water sinks down into the land, and moves through the soil.

WHY DO RIVERS FLOW? >
All liquid water moves downhill. Moving water forms streams in high areas, which come together as larger rivers. Rivers keep flowing downhill until they eventually reach a larger body of water, such as a lake, sea, or ocean.

KEY

Direction of travel

Evaporation

Transpiration

Snow or hail

Precipitation

The water cycle

Our planet is home to huge quantities of water, which moves constantly. It flows from rivers into the oceans, rises up to make clouds, and rains back down to Earth, in a never-ending looping cycle.

4. Evaporation
As the sun heats the oceans, some of the water turns to vapor (gas) and rises upward into the air.

5. Condensation
As the water vapor rises, it cools and turns into water droplets that clump together, forming clouds.

6. River flow
Rivers carry water downhill, from high ground toward the oceans.

7. Surface flow
Water that falls onto the land runs downhill until it joins a stream or river.

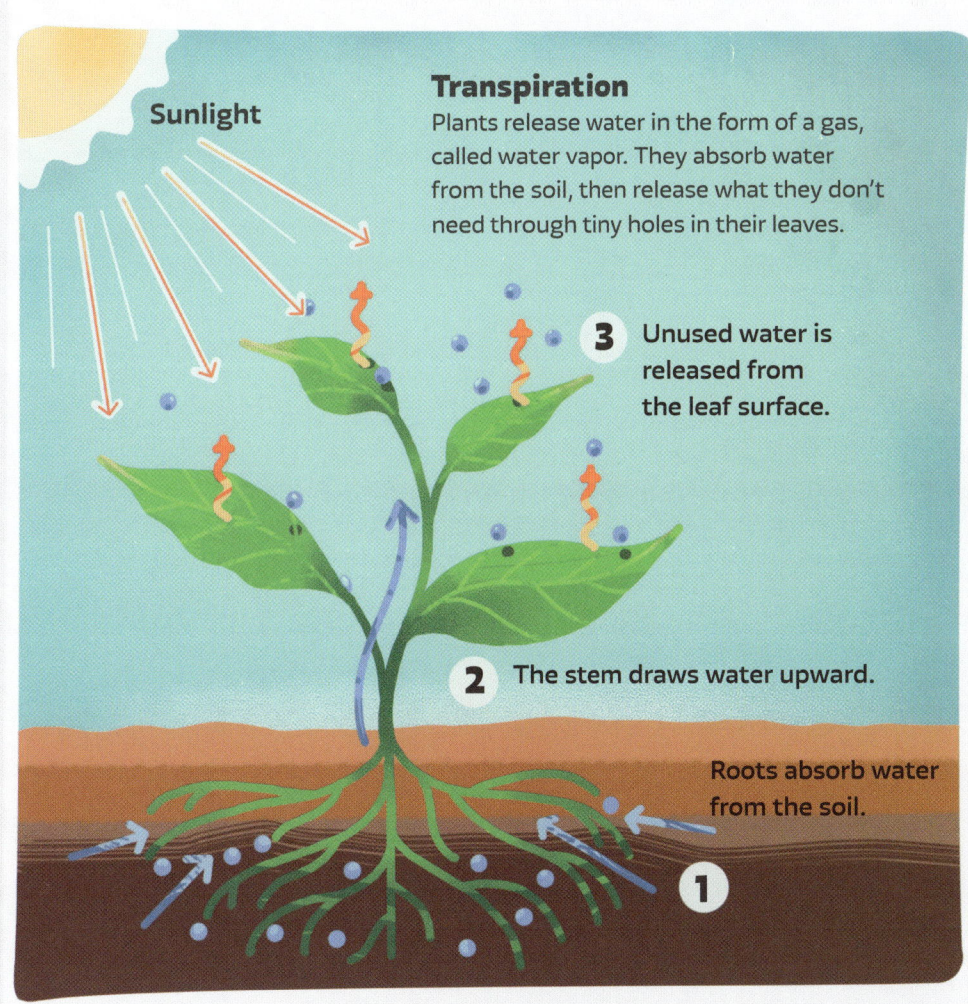

Sunlight

Transpiration
Plants release water in the form of a gas, called water vapor. They absorb water from the soil, then release what they don't need through tiny holes in their leaves.

3 Unused water is released from the leaf surface.

2 The stem draws water upward.

Roots absorb water from the soil.

1

Changing states

The water cycle involves all three forms of water. Solid water, called ice, appears as glaciers or snow. Liquid water flows over the land and forms lakes and oceans. Water vapor (gas) is in the air and clouds.

 Solid

 Liquid

 Gas

SEASONS

WINTER

This is the coldest of the seasons. Many trees are bare of leaves, and there is less food around for animals to eat.

SPRING

In spring, many trees begin to flower and grow leaves again. It gets warmer, the days start to get longer, and the nights get shorter.

SUMMER

This is the hottest of the seasons. The days are long and nights short. Plants grow and begin to form fruit, and the trees have plenty of green leaves.

FALL

In the fall, many trees lose their leaves—they turn gold or red before dropping off. Fruit is ripe and ready to pick, and the nights begin to get longer.

WEATHER

The weather is whatever is happening in the lower atmosphere at a particular moment. It can change from day to day, giving us rain or sunshine, windy weather or calm. Climate is slightly different. This is the average weather in a place—what it is like there generally, rather than in a particular moment. Many parts of the world also have seasons—they have different weather patterns depending on what time of the year it is.

Warm and cold air move in cells.

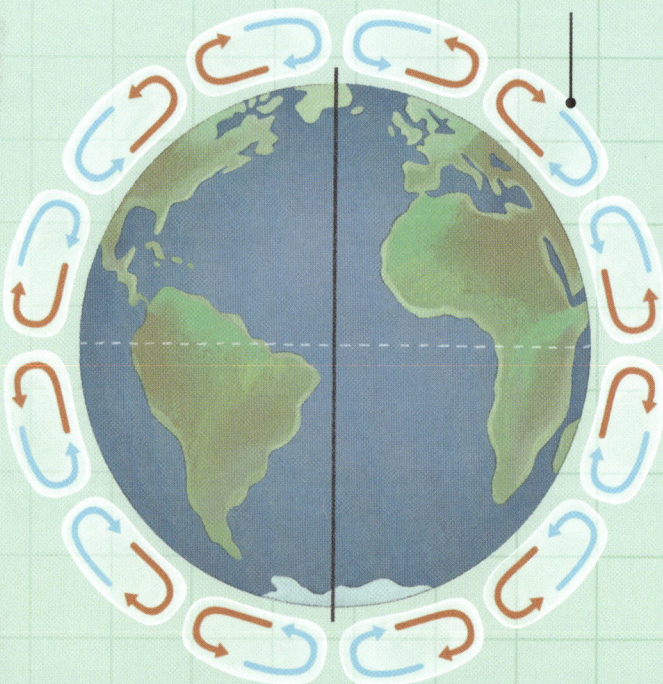

Hot and cold air

The air around Earth moves constantly, rising and falling as it warms and cools. This movement creates bands of air currents around the planet, which are known as cells. There are three cells around Earth's top half and another three around the bottom.

Climate zones

Some parts of our planet are warmer than others. Generally, it is hottest in tropical areas along the equator, which is Earth's widest part, closest to the sun. It is coldest in the polar areas at the top and bottom of the planet. In between are two more zones—fairly cool temperate areas and fairly hot subtropical ones.

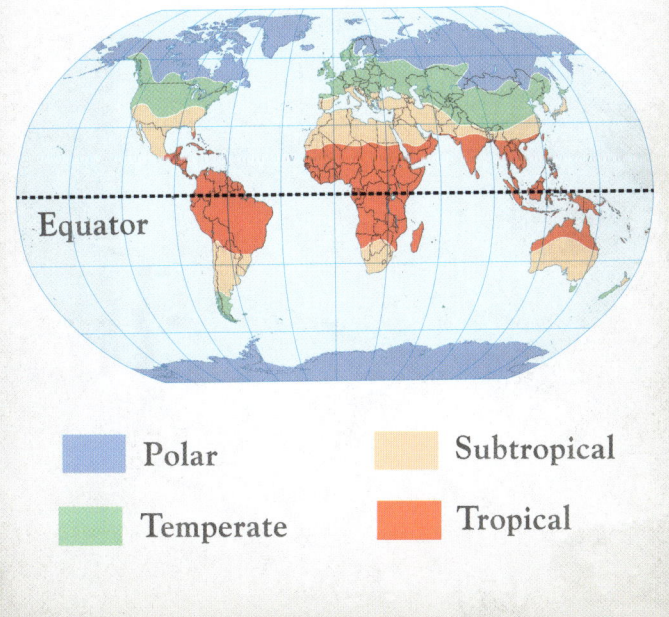

Equator

- Polar
- Temperate
- Subtropical
- Tropical

OCEAN CURRENTS

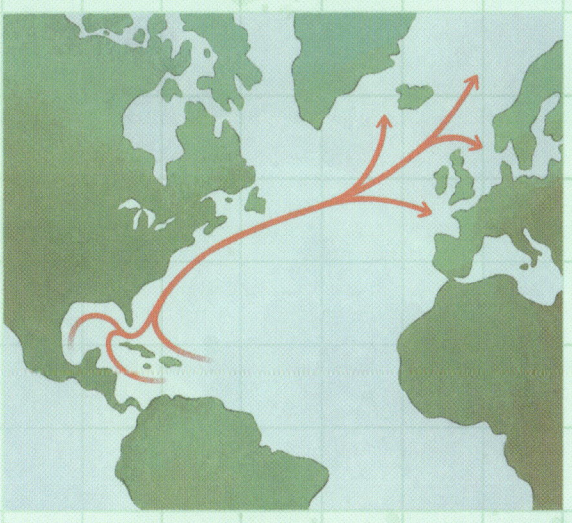

The Gulf Stream

Earth's oceans contain large movements of water, called currents. Some currents are warm and others cool, and they affect the climate on the land nearby. The Gulf Stream takes warm water from the Americas toward Europe.

WILD WEATHER

Most of the time, our weather is fairly tame. There is wind, and probably rain. Given the right conditions, however, weather can be much more extreme...

HURRICANES

Hurricanes are supersized storms that form above warm water in tropical areas. They can move from water to land, bringing torrential rain and extreme winds.

THUNDERSTORMS

A thunderstorm brings heavy rain, snow, or hail. Some storms are accompanied by lightning—bursts of electricity that begin in clouds.

TORNADOES

These columns of wind twist at high speed. They can form under storm clouds, and leave a path of destruction as they spin along the ground.

CLIMATE CHANGE

Climate is the typical weather conditions in an area—so Earth's climate is basically world weather. Climate is not a fixed thing, and Earth has naturally become warmer and cooler over time. We humans, however, have added a new level of complexity to climate change. We release greenhouse gases, at increasingly high levels. This human activity is heating up our planet rapidly, which has negative effects for us and many other forms of life on Earth.

The greenhouse effect

Earth is surrounded by a layer of gases, called its atmosphere. The atmosphere traps heat around our planet, keeping us warm in space. Greenhouse gases trap even more heat around Earth. The "greenhouse effect" is the planet getting hotter and hotter.

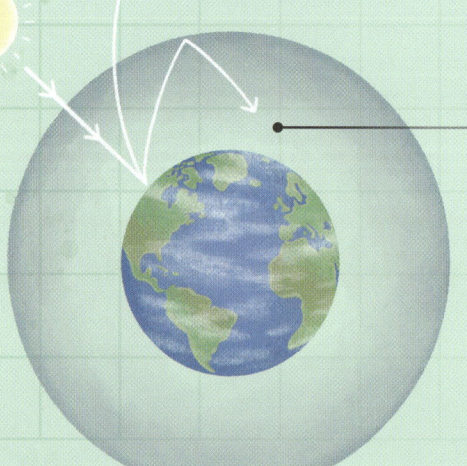

The sun's energy passes through the atmosphere.

Some of the sun's heat is reflected back into space.

Some of the heat is trapped in Earth's atmosphere.

56 MILLION YEARS AGO

The Earth was once warmer than it is today. In fact, it was so warm that there was no ice at the North Pole! This warm period was caused by large amounts of greenhouse gases, which may have been released by volcanic activity.

20,000 YEARS AGO

Then, the Earth began to cool down. We call this time the "Ice Age," because much of the planet was covered in layers of ice and snow. It began to melt around 20,000 years ago.

Fighting climate change

Large amounts of greenhouse gases are released when we burn fossil fuels. Using alternative energy sources, such as wind or water power, will help us reduce the amount of greenhouse gases we create. We can also try to use less energy overall, and travel around less.

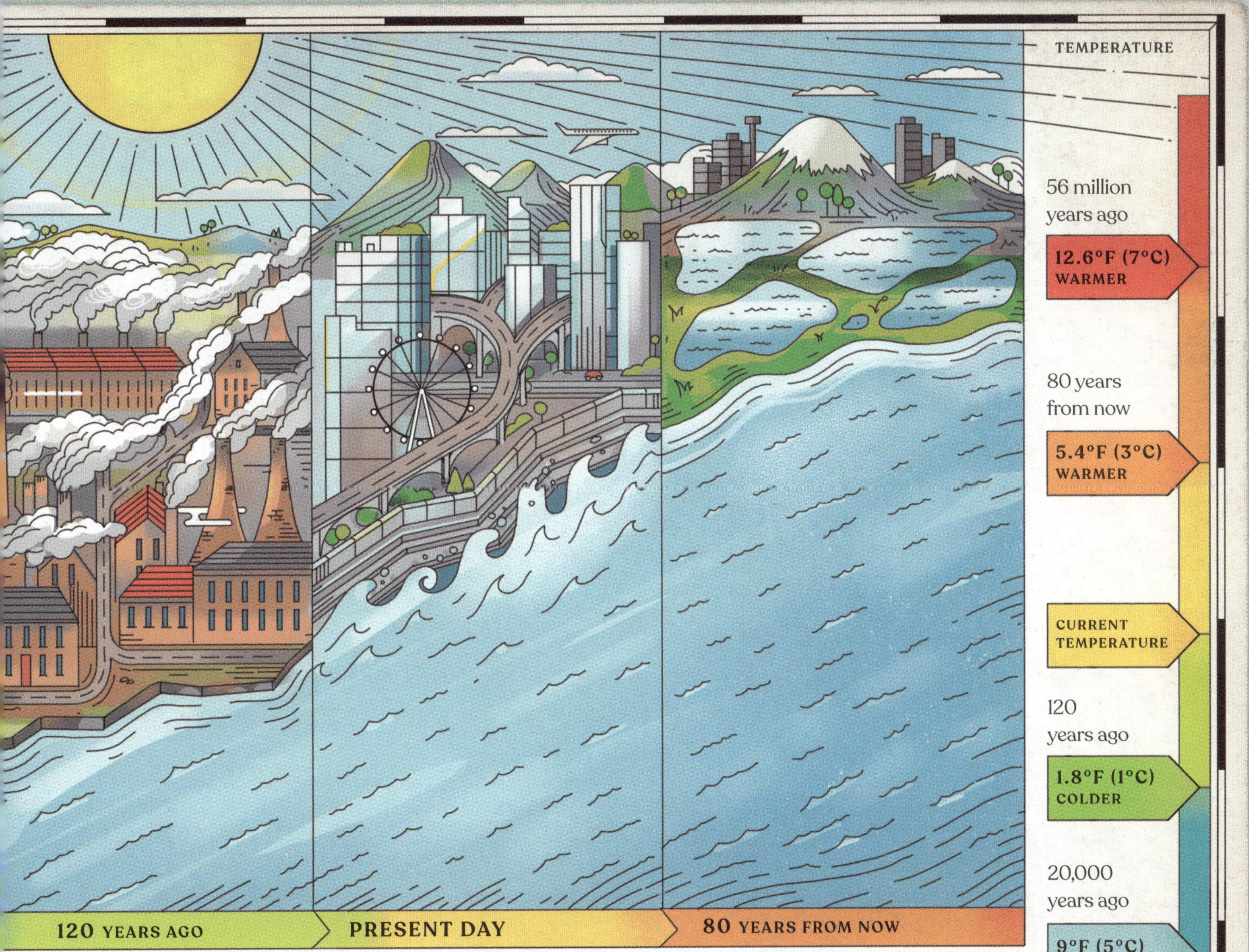

TEMPERATURE

56 million years ago

12.6°F (7°C)
WARMER

80 years from now

5.4°F (3°C)
WARMER

CURRENT
TEMPERATURE

120 years ago

1.8°F (1°C)
COLDER

20,000 years ago

9°F (5°C)
COLDER

120 YEARS AGO

After the Industrial Revolution, humans began building factories, which released greenhouse gases into the air. This made the planet start to warm up faster.

PRESENT DAY

Today, our planet is warming up faster than ever before. Greenhouse gases are produced by our vehicles, factories, and power plants. We are trying to reduce the amount of greenhouse gases we create.

80 YEARS FROM NOW

The Earth is likely to continue getting warmer. As our planet heats up, glaciers and ice sheets are melting, which causes water levels in the oceans to rise. Some coastal areas and low-lying islands are likely to be flooded.

A map of the changing climate

< HABITAT LOSS

Climate change is having an effect on Earth's habitats. For example, our ice caps are melting, which makes life hard for the animals that live on the ice.

WHERE DOES FOOD COME FROM?

Once upon a time, people were only able to eat food that could be produced locally to them. That is no longer the case—today, foods are shipped and flown all over the world. Countries that produce and send the food abroad are called exporters, and this map shows the biggest exporters of some popular foods.

KEY

- Canada
- Chile
- China
- Cote d'Ivoire
- Brazil
- Ecuador
- Spain
- India
- Ireland
- Mexico
- New Zealand
- Morocco
- Italy
- Netherlands

GROW YOUR OWN

Some countries have enough fertile land that, if they wanted to, they would be able to produce enough food for everyone who lives there. But importing allows them to eat a much wider range of different foods.

Something SWEET

MAPLE SYRUP

COCOA BEANS

The US is the world's biggest exporter of food.

The MAIN EVENT

PASTA

RICE

FRUIT and VEGETABLES

TOMATOES

BANANAS

MEAT and SEAFOOD

BEEF

SALAMI

CHICKEN

LAMB

SHRIMP

Extra FLAVOR

BLACK PEPPER

BUTTER

CLIMATE AND FOOD

Many foods can only be grown easily in particular climates. So, countries that want to eat things they can't produce must import them from elsewhere.

Parts of Africa export cocoa, tea, coffee, and spices.

GRAPES

SOY BEANS

GREEN BEANS

POTATOES

LETTUCE

APPLES

ORGANIC

CITIES

Many of our cities are home to hundreds of thousands of people, and some contain millions. When so many people live in one place, we are tightly packed, and the design of the city can make a big difference to our lives. Some cities have layouts that have developed over time, like a jumble, with bits and pieces being added in. Others have been carefully designed to help improve the lives of their citizens.

WHAT IS A CITY?

A city is a human settlement that is larger than a town or village. Cities contain homes, businesses, schools, hospitals, government buildings, open spaces, and all kinds of transportation.

∨

WALKABLE CITY

In some cities, such as Tokyo, in Japan, homes, businesses, parks, and schools are close together. So, people can walk or easily take public transportation to the places they need to get to.

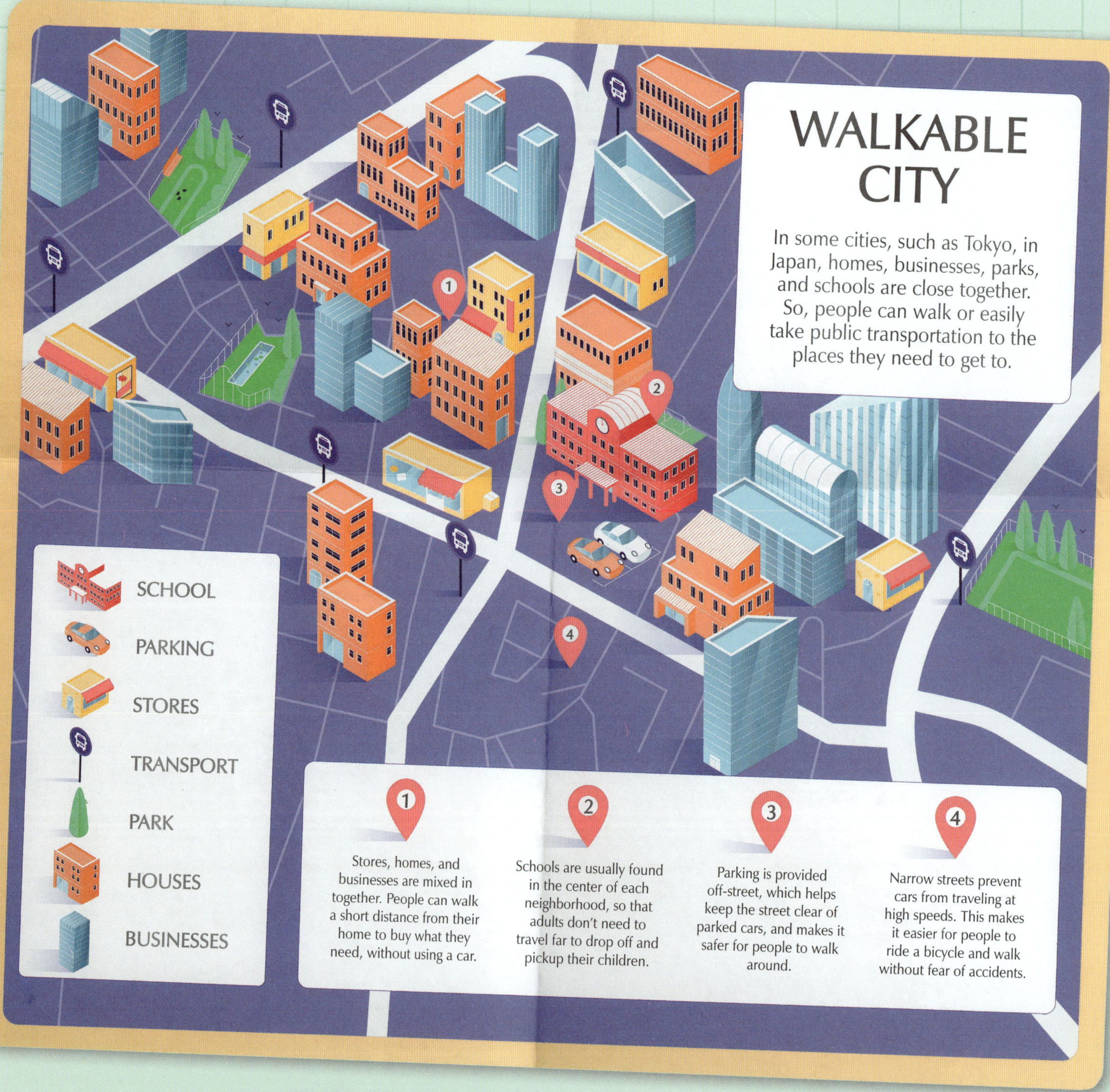

SCHOOL

PARKING

STORES

TRANSPORT

PARK

HOUSES

BUSINESSES

1 Stores, homes, and businesses are mixed in together. People can walk a short distance from their home to buy what they need, without using a car.

2 Schools are usually found in the center of each neighborhood, so that adults don't need to travel far to drop off and pickup their children.

3 Parking is provided off-street, which helps keep the street clear of parked cars, and makes it safer for people to walk around.

4 Narrow streets prevent cars from traveling at high speeds. This makes it easier for people to ride a bicycle and walk without fear of accidents.

FIVE FINGER PLAN

Copenhagen, in Denmark, is designed like a hand—with the city center at its palm and five fingers of built-up areas along railroad lines. The railroads allow easy access to the city center, while also leaving room for green open spaces.

The history of cities

The first cities, built thousands of years ago, had far fewer inhabitants than modern cities, and buildings that were only one or two stories high. Today, huge skyscrapers tower over bustling cities.

The world's tallest skyscraper is the Burj Khalifa in the city of Dubai, United Arab Emirates.

1 The unusual shape of this city was designed to keep people's homes away from the city center, so that it wouldn't get too crowded.

2 The space between the fingers is kept for open green space. Some of it is farmed, other parts are open for people to enjoy.

3 The railroads have been designed to link the fingers where people live to the city center, giving people easy access to what they need.

4 At the very center of the city are commercial (business) buildings, such as the city's financial district. Many people travel to work here.

GREEN SPACES

HOUSES

CITY CENTER

TRANSPORT

BUILDINGS

Buildings give us shelter—they keep us dry and protect us from the wind, cold, and hot sun. But many buildings are far more than simple shelters. They are designed for particular purposes, and come in a huge variety of forms. Some are even works of art! A person who designs new buildings is called an architect. Their designs are turned into reality by engineers, and the actual work is completed by construction workers.

Frame

Walls

Roof

Second floor

First floor

Foundation

Windows

Parts of a building

Buildings can look very different, and be used for different purposes, but they are all composed of the same key parts. The foundation is underground, and keeps the building stable. Each level of the building above that is called a "floor," or "story."

TYPES OF BUILDING

There are many different types of buildings. They can be homes, offices, open to the public, and much more.

SINGLE STORY

A building with just one level and no stairs inside is called a single-story building. Some long single-story homes are called ranches.

Amsterdam, the Netherlands

MULTISTORY

Many buildings have more than one level—building up can give you more rooms while using the same amount of space on the ground.

SKYSCRAPER

Buildings with many levels are called skyscrapers. These are most common in cities, where there is often less land to build on, so people build upward.

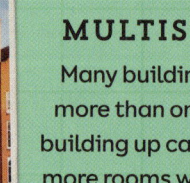

Doha, Qatar

STADIUM

A stadium is a place to watch many kinds of sports. There is a field or track in the center, surrounded by rings of thousands of seats.

National Stadium, China

MUSEUM

A museum is a building that people can visit, to learn about the objects inside, or about a particular subject.

Azerbaijan Carpet Museum

ANCIENT BUILDINGS >

People have been building for thousands of years. The Colosseum was built in 72 CE. It looks circular, but it's actually elliptical (oval). Today much of the building still stands, though some parts have crumbled away.

The Colosseum, Italy

Lotus Temple, India

Museum of Tomorrow, Brazil

< STUNNING SHAPES

Over time, we have learned more and more about building materials and what is possible. Today, architects are able to design swooping, dramatic buildings that would have been impossible for ancient builders to imagine.

IMPORTANT MATERIALS

Most buildings are made from similar materials. Some, such as wood, are found in nature. Others were invented over time. Here are just a few common building materials.

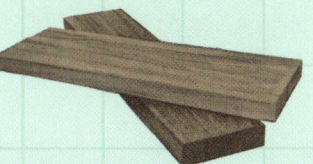

WOOD

Wood is strong and easy to cut to shape. It is often used to make roof structures.

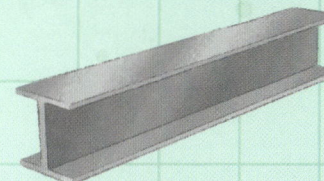

METAL

Steel beams are used to make structures strong. They can support a lot of weight.

BRICK

Bricks are made of hardened clay. They are stacked together to form walls.

GLASS

See-through glass is used to make windows, or even the walls of modern buildings.

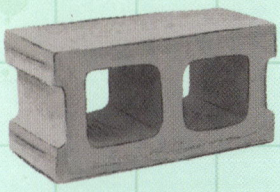

CONCRETE

Concrete blocks can be used like bricks, or liquid concrete can be poured around steel.

LANGUAGE

Our languages are very important because they allow us to communicate with each other. Different languages are spoken in different parts of the world. Today, the three most-spoken languages are Mandarin Chinese, English, and Spanish. People also talk using sign languages, which include hand signs, body movements, and facial expressions. Languages that were once used but are now no longer spoken are known as "dead" languages. Latin is now considered a dead language, but French, Italian, and Spanish all have their roots in it.

How do languages grow?

As people and communities grow and change, their languages evolve with them. People might say words differently, or invent new words. As people move around, they also take words along with them to other places. So, our languages develop over time, and can even pick up useful additions from other languages.

There are more than 7,000 different languages.

Cuneiform tablet

< **WRITTEN LANGUAGE**

Writing facts and stories down allows us to keep a permanent record of them, without having to rely on memory. The first form of writing was called cuneiform. It was invented 5,000 years ago, in an area that is now in Iraq.

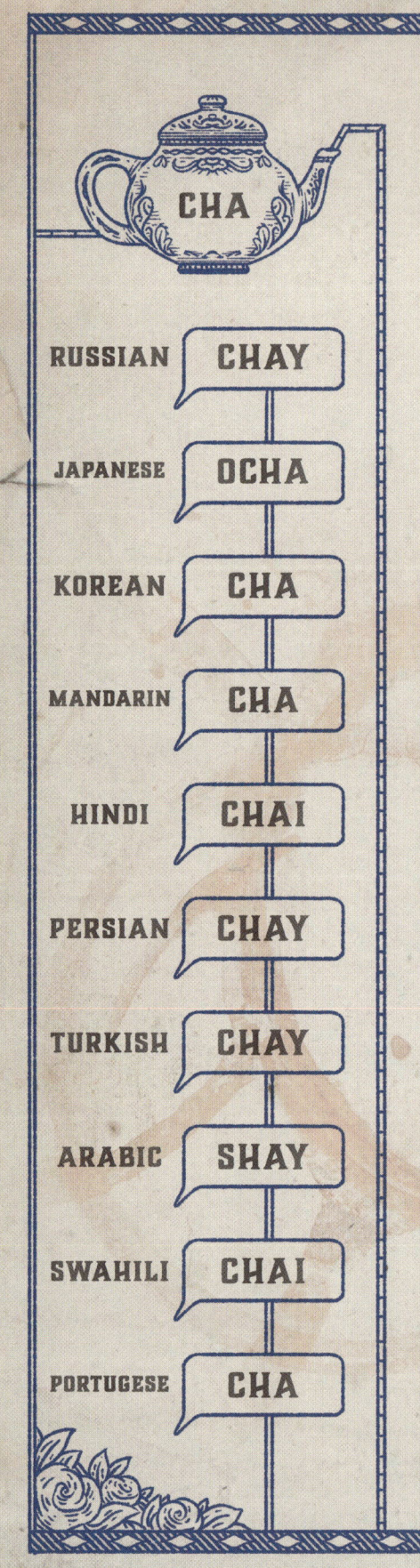

CHA

RUSSIAN	CHAY
JAPANESE	OCHA
KOREAN	CHA
MANDARIN	CHA
HINDI	CHAI
PERSIAN	CHAY
TURKISH	CHAY
ARABIC	SHAY
SWAHILI	CHAI
PORTUGESE	CHA

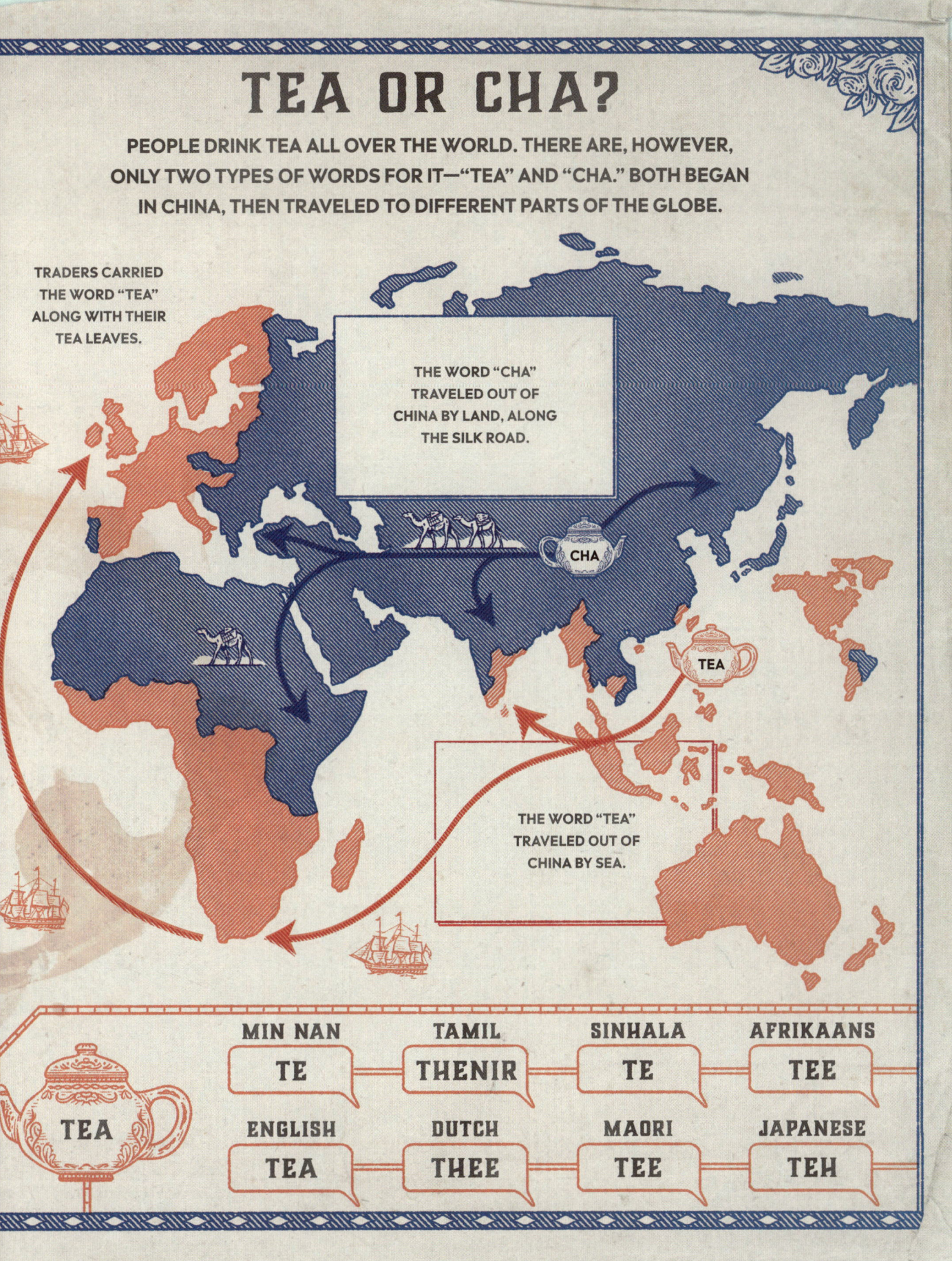

TEA OR CHA?

PEOPLE DRINK TEA ALL OVER THE WORLD. THERE ARE, HOWEVER, ONLY TWO TYPES OF WORDS FOR IT—"TEA" AND "CHA." BOTH BEGAN IN CHINA, THEN TRAVELED TO DIFFERENT PARTS OF THE GLOBE.

TRADERS CARRIED THE WORD "TEA" ALONG WITH THEIR TEA LEAVES.

THE WORD "CHA" TRAVELED OUT OF CHINA BY LAND, ALONG THE SILK ROAD.

CHA

TEA

THE WORD "TEA" TRAVELED OUT OF CHINA BY SEA.

TEA

MIN NAN	TAMIL	SINHALA	AFRIKAANS
TE	THENIR	TE	TEE
ENGLISH	DUTCH	MAORI	JAPANESE
TEA	THEE	TEE	TEH

A map showing how the words "tea" and "cha" spread.

CHAPTER 4
NATURE

"Nature" is the plants, animals, and other life forms that exist on our planet without any human involvement. It comes in a huge range of forms. Microscopic life is so tiny that we cannot see it, while blue whales are so huge that a human could use one of their tongues as a mattress. Animals communicate with each other like we do, though not using speech. They use smells, movements, sounds, or chemical signals. Some types of plants are able to communicate, too! Humans weren't involved in the creation of nature, but our actions are affecting it—we cut down trees and pollute the air, impacting creatures and habitats all over the world.

A GUIDE TO FUNGI

Fungi are not plants or animals—they are a kingdom of their own. There are around 3 million species of fungi, and only some of them have mushrooms. These fruiting bodies are just a small part of a fungus. Beneath the ground, masses of rootlike threads, called hyphae, absorb nutrients and water.

MUSHROOM PARTS

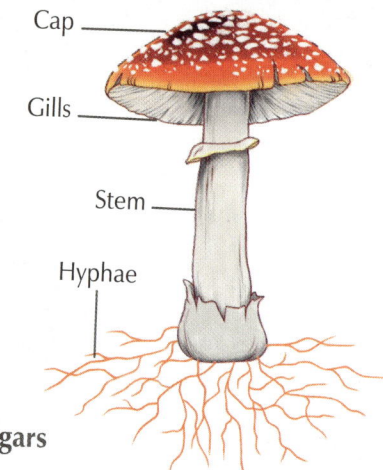

Cap

Gills

Stem

Hyphae

Woods

Underground

 Tree roots

 Fungi hyphae

 Sugars

 Nutrients

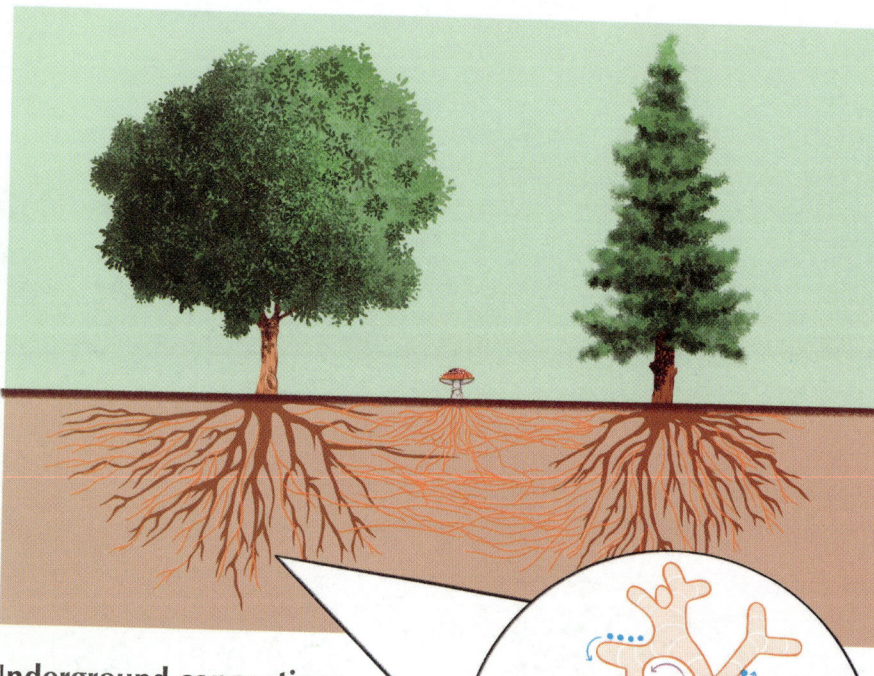

Underground connections

The hyphae of some fungi can form connections with tree roots, growing around them like a sock and pushing inside. The fungi provide the tree with nutrients, and receive sugars in return. Hyphae can connect trees with each other, too.

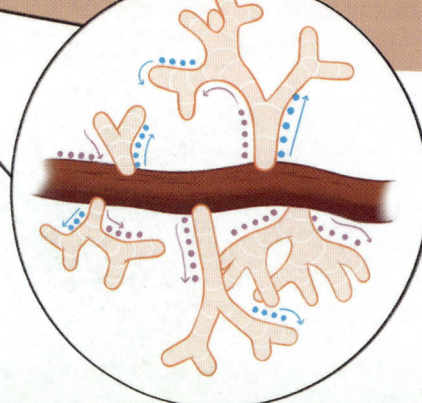

Map of fungal forest network

Hoof fungus

THE WOOD WIDE WEB

The network of fungi beneath a forest works a bit like the Internet, but for trees. Trees use it to share resources, such as water and nutrients. They can also use it to send chemicals to each other, to give a warning—and even to cause harm.

Network users

Within the wood wide web, trees can perform different roles. Some help their neighbors grow and thrive. Others use the web to steal from their neighbors, or to attempt to poison them.

Mother trees
These trees send sugars to nearby seedlings.

Dying trees
Nutrients can be shared before they die.

Trees under attack
Chemical signals can be sent to ask for help.

Hacker trees
Nutrients can be stolen from other trees.

Saboteurs
Toxic chemicals can be sent to other trees.

 **Sugars**

 **Nutrients**

Chemical signals

 **Toxic chemicals**

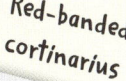
Red-banded cortinarius

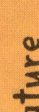

Nature

Common puffball

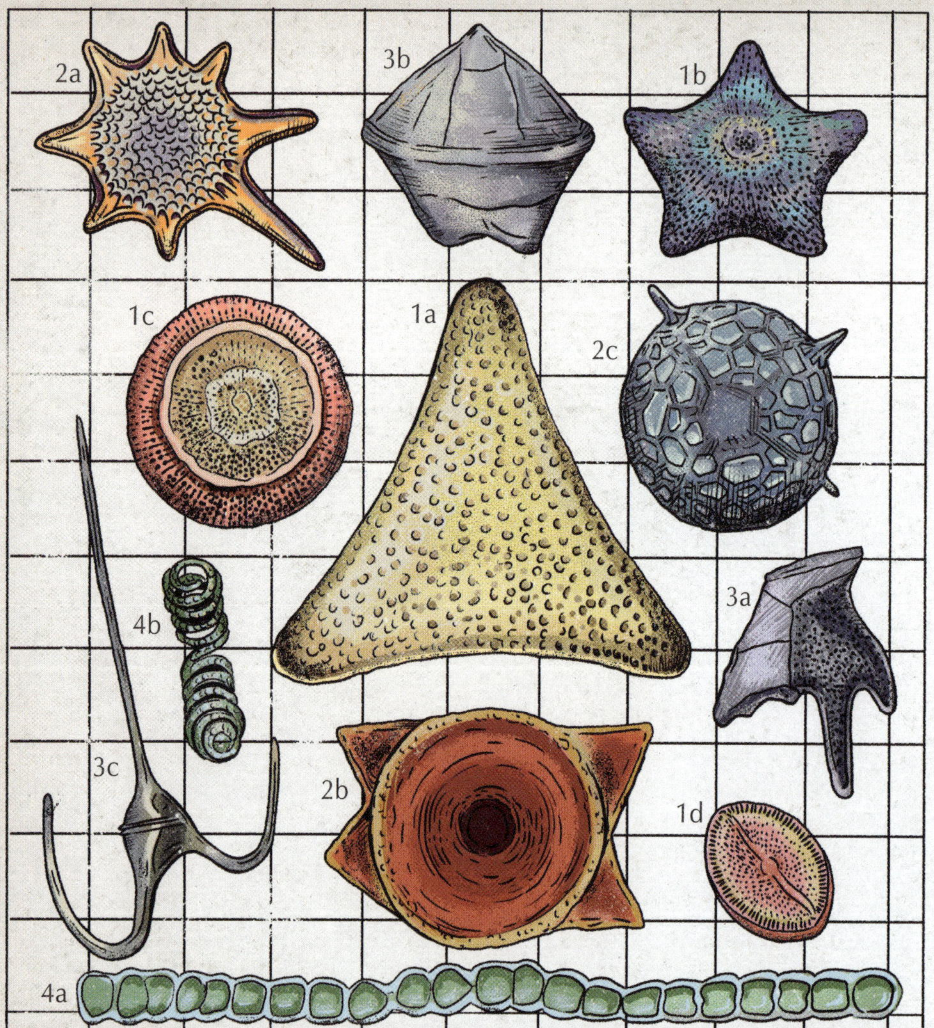

Salmonella
If eaten, this bacterium causes diarrhea, vomiting, and cramps.

Shigella
This bacterium causes a quick-spreading disease called dysentery.

Streptobacillus
If a rat carrying this bacterium bites you, you will get rat-bite fever.

Leptospira interrogans
This bacterium can cause kidney and liver failure.

Cholera
Water carrying this bacterium will make you very sick.

Escherichia coli
Some strains of this bacterium cause infections in the digestive tract.

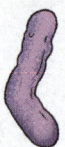

Bifidobacterium longum
This "good" bacterium helps keep your intestinal tract healthy.

Bacillus subtilis
This bacterium helps us break down food and fight off diseases.

MICROSCOPIC PLANKTON

Diatoms
These phytoplankton are related to larger brown algae. They produce a lot of oxygen.

1a) Triceratium favus
1b) Triceratium formosum
1c) Coscinodiscus sp.
1d) Navicula sp.

Dinoflagellate
Each dinoflagellate has just one cell in its body.

3a) Dinophysis tripos
3b) Protoperidinium leonis
3c) Tripos macroceros

Radiolarian
Delicate, spiky shells surround the bodies of these minute zooplankton.

2a) Heliodiscus
2b) Spongastericus quadricornis
2c) Spumellaria sp.

Cyanobacteria
These tiny, chainlike bacteria carry out photosynthesis, making energy from the sun's light.

4a) Cylindrospermum
4b) Arthrospira platensis

< Microscopic plankton
Plankton are tiny life forms that live in water. Some are plants, called phytoplankton, and others animals—zooplankton. The zooplankton eat the phytoplankton, and both are eaten by larger animals such as fish and whales.

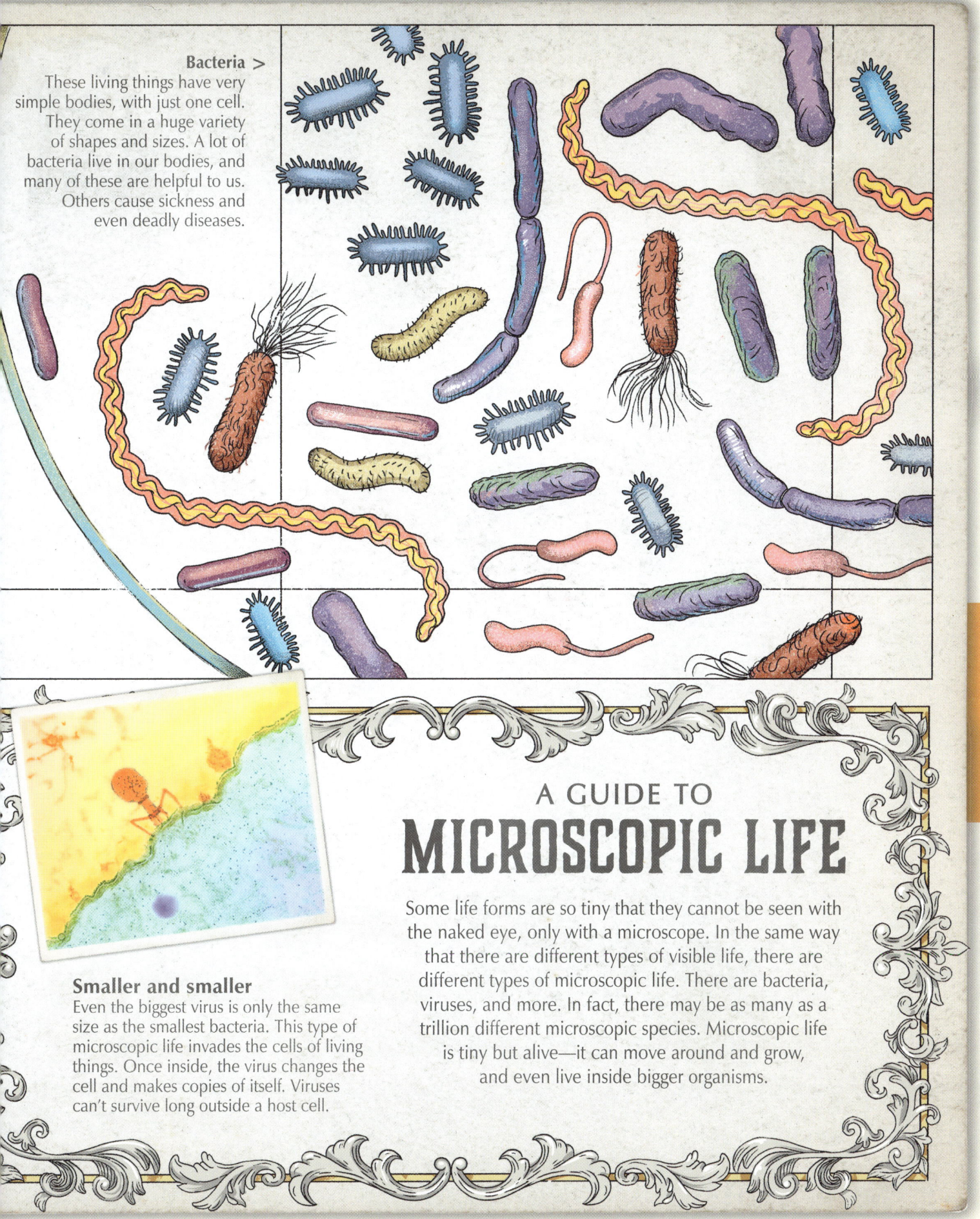

Bacteria >
These living things have very simple bodies, with just one cell. They come in a huge variety of shapes and sizes. A lot of bacteria live in our bodies, and many of these are helpful to us. Others cause sickness and even deadly diseases.

A GUIDE TO
MICROSCOPIC LIFE

Some life forms are so tiny that they cannot be seen with the naked eye, only with a microscope. In the same way that there are different types of visible life, there are different types of microscopic life. There are bacteria, viruses, and more. In fact, there may be as many as a trillion different microscopic species. Microscopic life is tiny but alive—it can move around and grow, and even live inside bigger organisms.

Smaller and smaller
Even the biggest virus is only the same size as the smallest bacteria. This type of microscopic life invades the cells of living things. Once inside, the virus changes the cell and makes copies of itself. Viruses can't survive long outside a host cell.

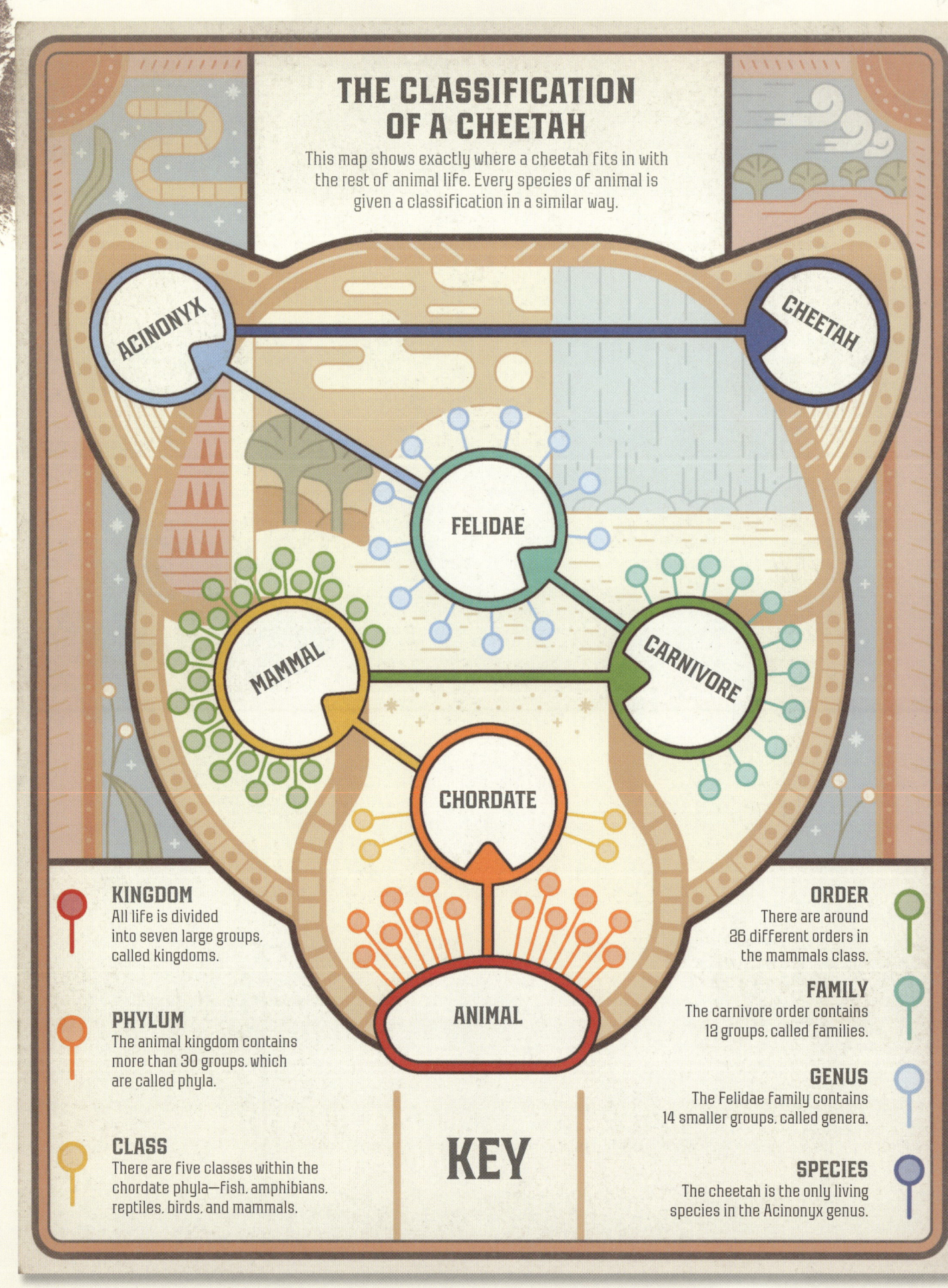

THE CLASSIFICATION OF A CHEETAH

This map shows exactly where a cheetah fits in with the rest of animal life. Every species of animal is given a classification in a similar way.

ACINONYX

CHEETAH

FELIDAE

MAMMAL

CARNIVORE

CHORDATE

ANIMAL

KINGDOM
All life is divided into seven large groups, called kingdoms.

PHYLUM
The animal kingdom contains more than 30 groups, which are called phyla.

CLASS
There are five classes within the chordate phyla—fish, amphibians, reptiles, birds, and mammals.

ORDER
There are around 26 different orders in the mammals class.

FAMILY
The carnivore order contains 12 groups, called families.

GENUS
The Felidae family contains 14 smaller groups, called genera.

SPECIES
The cheetah is the only living species in the Acinonyx genus.

KEY

ANIMAL GROUPS

There are a humongous range of animals on Earth, with different shapes, sizes, and habits. To keep track of what's what, scientists organize them all into groups, based on shared features. This system of organization is known as classification. The first grouping looks at whether an animal has an internal skeleton. After that the groups get increasingly more specific, with divisions based on whether an animal has scales, if it lays eggs, and so on.

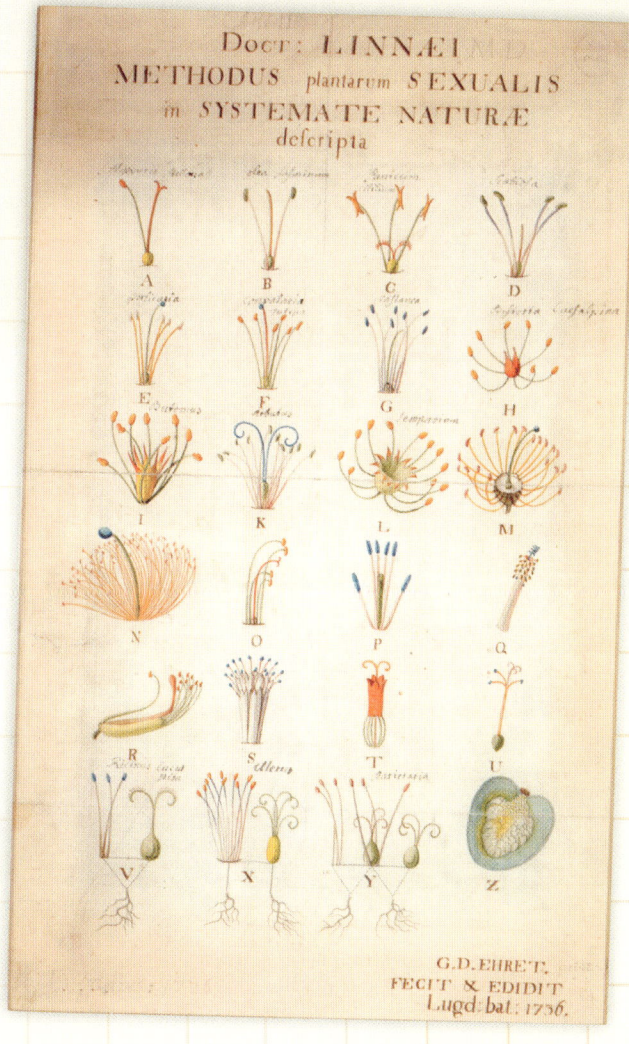

^
THE FIRST CLASSIFICATION

Scientists began trying to classify animals and plants in the 18th century. Two-part scientific names were suggested by a Swedish naturalist, Carl Linnaeus, in 1758.

WHAT'S IN A NAME?

The scientific names of animals are usually made up of two parts. The first part is the name of its genus—one of the groups the animal belongs to. The second part is its unique species name.

Common name

Lion

Scientific name

Panthera   leo

Genus   Species

CHEETAH The cheetah is a specific species, but it belongs to a number of other groups.

ACINONYX This is a genus within the Felidae family, which contains cheetahlike cats.

FELIDAE Also known as cats, this is a family of mammals.

CARNIVORE This order of mammals has sharp canine teeth used for ripping into meat.

MAMMAL Animals in this class usually have fur, and feed their babies milk.

CHORDATE This phylum contains animals with internal skeletons, called vertebrates.

ANIMAL This is one of the seven kingdoms of life. The others include plants and fungi.

INVERTEBRATES

When we think of animals, we often think of the cute, fluffy kinds we may have as pets. But those fluffy animals make up only a tiny part of the animal kingdom. In fact, the biggest group of animals, called the invertebrates, are not furry at all—they are smooth, slimy, or hard to the touch. They come in many different shapes and sizes. Insects, spiders, worms, crabs, and squid are all part of the invertebrate group, alongside all kinds of other animals.

INVERTEBRATE > GROUPS

There are 35 major groups of animals (phyla), and 34 of them contain invertebrates. The largest of the invertebrate groups is the arthropods, which includes insects, arachnids, crustaceans, and myriapods.

What are invertebrates?

Invertebrates all share some basic features. They have no internal skeleton, which is where they get their name from—"invertebrate" means "no backbone." They are also cold-blooded, and their young hatch from eggs.

Snail

No skeleton inside the body

Cold-blooded

Lays eggs

97 percent of all animals are invertebrates!

The Antarctic midge

Where can you find them?

Species of invertebrates live almost everywhere. They fly through the sky, walk on land, burrow underground, and swim through water. Some even live in freezing-cold, icy regions, such as in Antarctica.

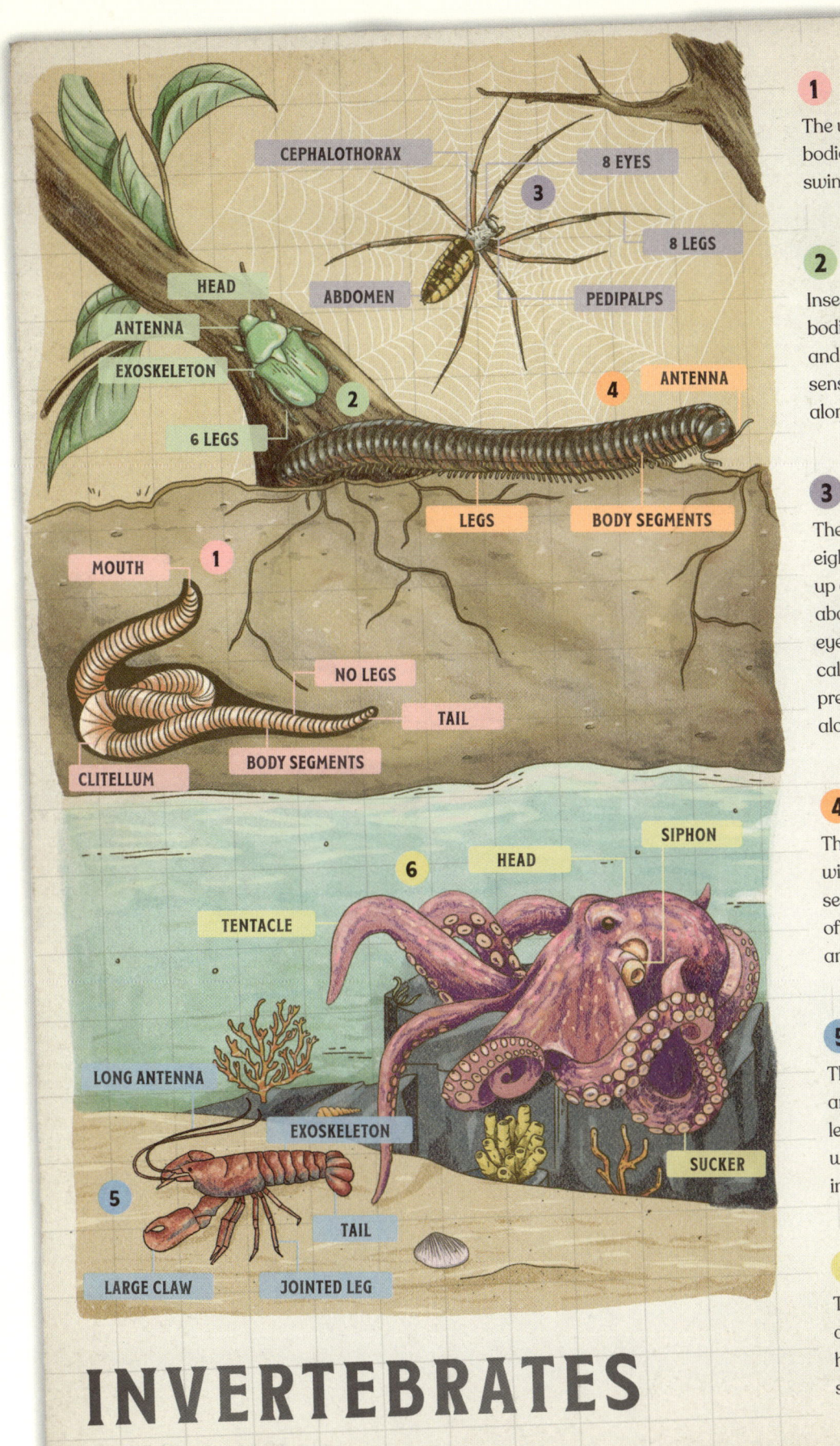

INVERTEBRATES

1 WORMS

The worm group all have long, thin bodies with no legs. Some worms swim, others burrow in the ground.

2 INSECTS

Insects have six legs, three-part bodies (head, thorax, and abdomen), and antennae, which help them sense things. Beetles are insects, along with ants, bees, and moths.

3 ARACHNIDS

The members of this group have eight legs, and their bodies are made up of two parts (cephalothorax and abdomen). Arachnids have many eyes, and specialized mouthparts called pedipalps for grabbing their prey. Spiders belong to this group, along with scorpions and ticks.

4 MYRIAPODS

The myriapods have bodies with many segments, and each segment has at least one pair of legs attached. Millipedes and centipedes are myriapods.

5 CRUSTACEANS

This group has a protective, armorlike exoskeleton and jointed legs. Almost all crustaceans live in water. Crabs and lobsters belong in this group.

6 MOLLUSKS

The mollusks all have soft bodies, and some of them, such as snails, have a thick outer shell. Octopuses, squid, and oysters are all mollusks.

Nature

A chart showing examples of groups from within the invertebrates

INSECTS

Insects are a type of invertebrate—they don't have a skeleton inside their body. Instead, they have a hard outer layer, called an exoskeleton. As adults, all insects have bodies divided into three sections, with three pairs of legs, and two pairs of wings—though the second pair can be very small. You probably noticed a number of different types of insects, but our world contains millions of them, including beetles, bugs, flies, moths, and dragonflies.

Three parts

All adult insects have bodies divided into three parts: a head, thorax, and abdomen. On the head is a pair of feelers called antennae. The legs and wings are connected to the thorax, and the abdomen contains many of the insect's vital organs.

Antenna

Head

Thorax

Abdomen

Wing

Leg

TYPES OF INSECTS

Beetles have a set of hard front wings, which cover and protect the set of flying wings beneath.

Wing case

Bugs have a sharp mouthpart, which they use to pierce animal or plant flesh, then suck up food.

Dragonflies have big eyes, see-through wings, and a long body, which usually has shimmering colors.

Moths have large wings, and antennae that are usually feathery. Most moths are nocturnal.

Many bees have yellow and black stripes, but they can be other colors, too.

1. Egg

2. Caterpillar

4. Butterfly

3. Chrysalis

Butterfly life cycle

Metamorphosis

Some insects, such as butterflies, ants, and flies, go through big changes as they age. This process is called metamorphosis. It happens in four stages: the insect begins life as an egg, hatches into a larva, forms a hard case called a pupa, then emerges from the pupa in its adult form.

< BUTTERFLY STAGES

A butterfly lays its eggs on a plant or tree. The larva, called a caterpillar, munches on the leaves when it hatches. It builds a pupa, called a chrysalis, around itself, then emerges as a butterfly.

Nature

POLLINATORS

What is pollination?

For plants to produce seeds, pollen from one flower must be transferred to another of the same type. Many plants use insects to carry their pollen, in exchange for a reward of sugary nectar. Insects that carry pollen are called pollinators. Honeybees are important pollinators—they visit many different flowers on their hunt for nectar.

The bee visits a flower to find sweet nectar.

Pollen from the flower sticks to the bee's body.

The pollen gets transferred to the next flower, pollinating it.

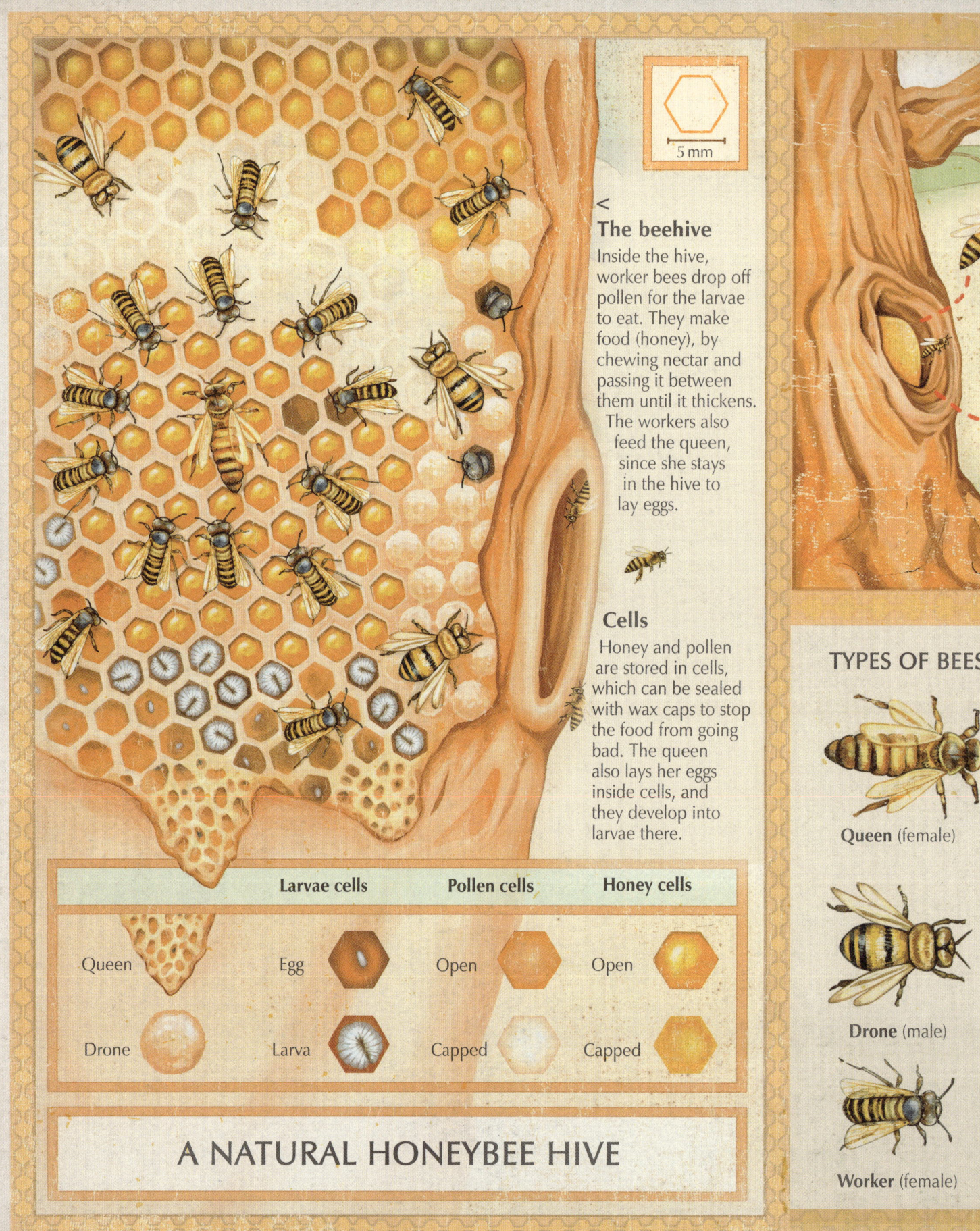

5 mm

<

The beehive

Inside the hive, worker bees drop off pollen for the larvae to eat. They make food (honey), by chewing nectar and passing it between them until it thickens. The workers also feed the queen, since she stays in the hive to lay eggs.

Cells

Honey and pollen are stored in cells, which can be sealed with wax caps to stop the food from going bad. The queen also lays her eggs inside cells, and they develop into larvae there.

	Larvae cells		Pollen cells		Honey cells	
Queen	Egg		Open		Open	
Drone	Larva		Capped		Capped	

A NATURAL HONEYBEE HIVE

TYPES OF BEES

Queen (female)

Drone (male)

Worker (female)

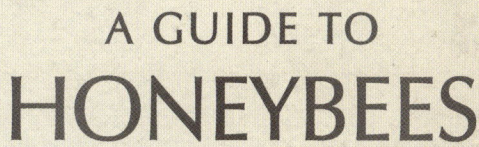

A HONEYBEE FLIGHT PATH

Apple tree

Common comfrey

Red clover

Goat willow

Dandelion

∧
Pollination

Plants need pollinators, such as bees, to help them make seeds. As a bee flies out from its hive, it visits a series of flowers, and is brushed with pollen by the anthers (male parts) of each one. When the bee flies on, it carries the pollen with it. At the next stop, the pollen sticks to the female part of the flower, called the stigma, and a seed can begin to form.

< ## Types of honeybees

Each beehive has just one queen. She lays all of the colony's eggs—up to 2,000 a day. Drones are male bees that mate with queens, usually from other hives, so they can produce eggs. Workers gather food and defend the hive. They have a stinger, unlike drones.

A GUIDE TO
HONEYBEES

Among the millions of species of insects, there are around 20,000 species of bees, and among the bees are honeybees. These busy creatures play a vital role in helping new plants grow, by carrying pollen from flower to flower on their hairy upper bodies. They visit flowers to collect nectar and pollen, which they carry back to their bustling hive.

Honeycomb

Worker bees build honeycomb using wax. They produce tiny slivers of wax from their bodies, then chew it to make it soft before adding it to the structure.

FISH

Fish spend their lives in water, and their bodies are perfectly adapted to it. They can breathe beneath the surface, and their streamlined, smooth bodies easily push through the water. Different fish also have unique features. Tiny, carefully camouflaged sea horses and colossal, razor-toothed sharks are both examples of fish. All of them live in water, and all are cold-blooded.

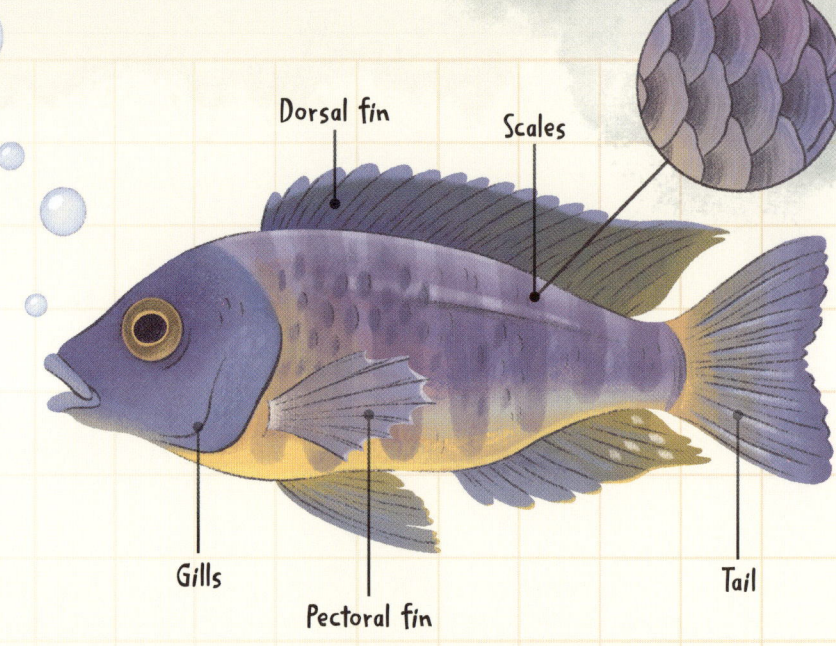

Dorsal fin

Scales

Gills

Pectoral fin

Tail

Parts of a fish

Many fish have fins on the top, bottom, and sides of their bodies to keep them balanced, and tails that flip sideways to push them forward through the water. The fish's body is covered in tiny overlapping scales, and it breathes through organs called gills.

TYPES OF FISH

There are thousands of different types of fish. All of them are organized into three main categories, based on their skeletons.

Hagfish

Koi

Motoro stingray

JAWLESS

These fish have muscly mouths, with no jaw bones. They were the first fish ever to exist, hundreds of millions of years ago.

BONY

As their name suggests, these fish have bones, in the form of internal skeletons. Their bones are hard, unlike the cartilaginous fish.

CARTILAGINOUS

These fish have skeletons too, but they are made of cartilage, not bone. Cartilage is hard and strong, but more flexible than bone.

FISH EGGS

Some fish give birth to live young, while others lay eggs. Fish eggs come in a range of forms, and here are a few examples.

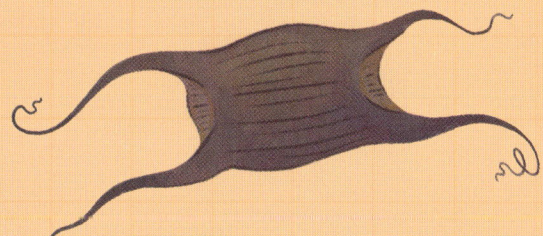

Egg cases

Some sharks and rays lay eggs in small leathery pouches, which are also called mermaid purses. The baby fish hatches inside the pouch then wriggles out.

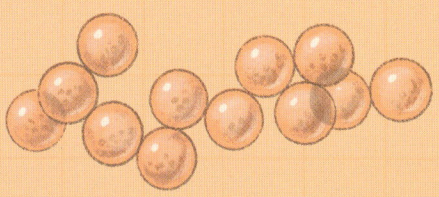

Sandy eggs

Grunions drag themselves out of the ocean and onto the shore to lay their eggs in sand. The eggs are eventually washed into the ocean, where they hatch.

Watery eggs

Catfish lay their eggs in nooks and crannies underwater. Some types of catfish will guard the eggs until they hatch.

∧

SHARKS

Sharks are also fish—cartilaginous fish, to be exact. Most of them are apex predators—expert hunters who are not hunted by other animals. Sharks have rows of incredibly sharp teeth, which allow them to slice into their prey.

SALT WATER AND FRESH WATER

Water is divided into the categories of salt and fresh. Salt water contains dissolved minerals, which make it taste salty. Most fish species live in either one type of water or the other. Some, such as salmon, travel from salt to fresh water to breed.

 ∨

EUROPEAN EELS

Eels are fish with long, snakelike bodies. They start their lives as eggs, then slowly grow through several stages before becoming adults. European eels do not go through their life cycle in a straightforward way. They make a journey that leads them around the edges of the Atlantic Ocean. Along the way, they transform into stages so different they were once thought to be separate species.

Not-so-European eels >

European eels reach their adult form in Europe, but they swim all the way to the Sargasso Sea—which is closer to the coast of North America—to lay their eggs. Once the eggs hatch, the young eels develop through a number of life stages, each in a different habitat and location.

KEY

Freshwater range of wild European eels

Spawning site of wild European eels

Spawning

Adult eels lay their eggs in the Sargasso Sea.

Sargasso Sea

Egg

The eggs float around until they are ready to hatch.

Snipe eel

There are more than 800 different species of eels! Most of them hunt other fish.

Giant moray eel

JOURNEY AND LIFE CYLE OF EUROPEAN EELS

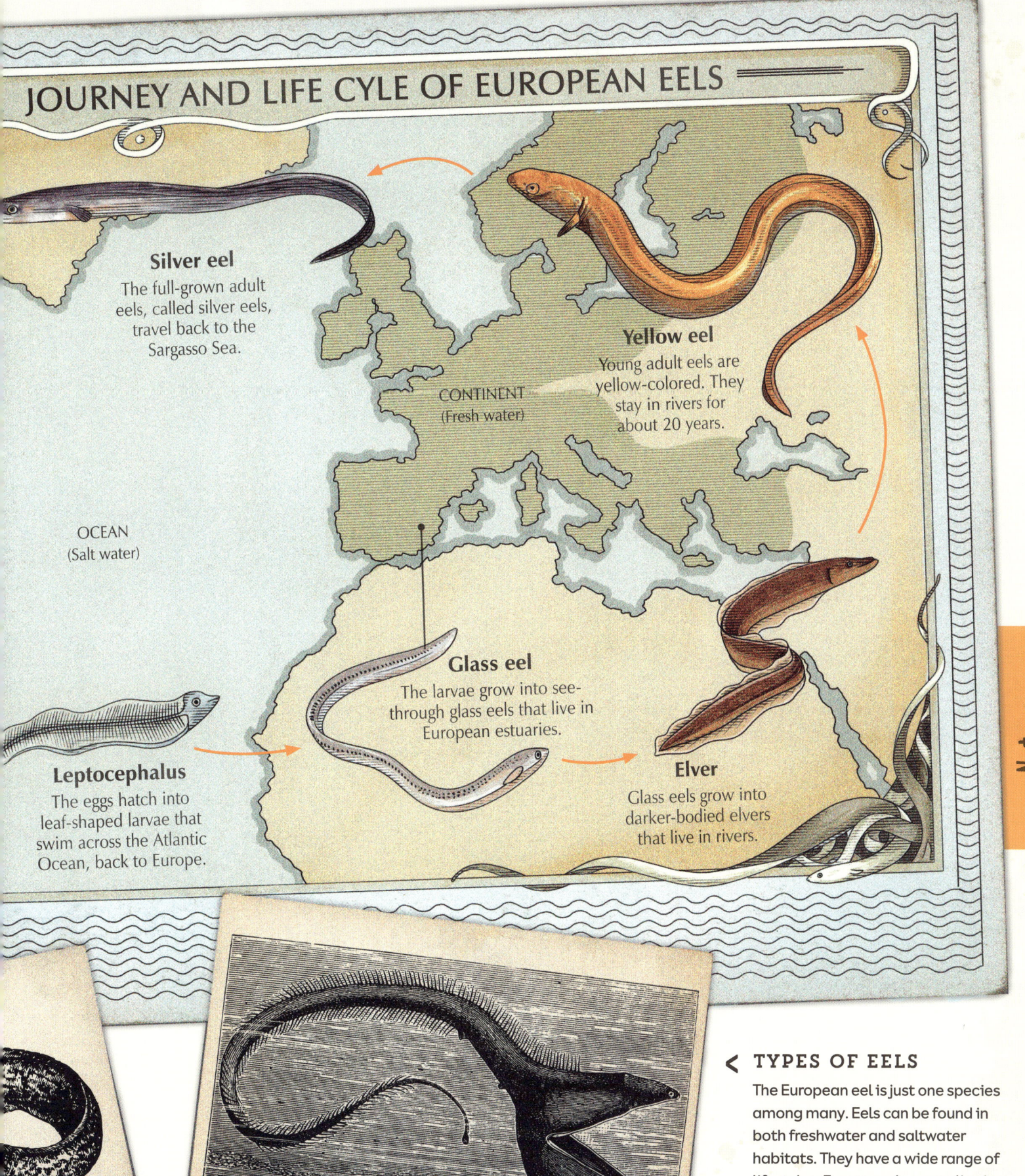

Silver eel
The full-grown adult eels, called silver eels, travel back to the Sargasso Sea.

Yellow eel
Young adult eels are yellow-colored. They stay in rivers for about 20 years.

CONTINENT
(Fresh water)

OCEAN
(Salt water)

Glass eel
The larvae grow into see-through glass eels that live in European estuaries.

Leptocephalus
The eggs hatch into leaf-shaped larvae that swim across the Atlantic Ocean, back to Europe.

Elver
Glass eels grow into darker-bodied elvers that live in rivers.

Pelican eel

< TYPES OF EELS

The European eel is just one species among many. Eels can be found in both freshwater and saltwater habitats. They have a wide range of lifestyles. For example, some live in the crevices of coral reefs, while others live deep down in the ocean, where there is no natural light.

TYPES OF AMPHIBIANS

Amphibians all have a few key things in common. They can breathe through their skin, which needs to be kept wet for this process to take place. They are cold-blooded, and most of them lay eggs. We divide amphibians into three groups, based on the shape of their bodies and how many legs they have.

Fire salamander

SALAMANDERS

These amphibians have lizardlike bodies, with four even-sized limbs.

Cane toad

FROGS AND TOADS

Amphibians in this category have long, strong back legs and shorter front legs.

CAECILIANS

Wormlike caecilians, such as this purple caecilian, have no limbs at all.

AMPHIBIANS

Frogs, toads, newts, and salamanders all belong to the same group of animals—the amphibians. Amphibians spend much of their lives in water, or at least close to water. This is because water is essential to their lifestyle—they must keep their skin wet to stay alive, and they lay their eggs in water. Once the eggs hatch, the newly hatched tadpoles go through a series of body changes before becoming adults, in a process called metamorphosis.

AN UNUSUAL FROG

Most frogs start as little tadpoles and grow into larger frogs, but the paradoxical frog is a little different. It has tadpoles measuring up to 8.6 in (22 cm) long, but an adult paradoxical frog is only 3 in (8 cm) long.

Front legs

Head

Trunk

Hind legs

PARTS OF A FROG

Frogs and toads are vertebrates—they have spines, like we do. Their internal organs are also very similar to ours. The four main sections of their body are head, front legs, trunk, and back legs.

LIFE CYCLE OF THE EUROPEAN COMMON FROG

1—FROG EGGS

A female frog lays lots of round, jelly-covered eggs, called frogspawn, in water.

 A FEW DAYS

2—TADPOLES

Tadpoles hatch from the eggs. The tadpoles live in water and have tails. They grow hind legs, then front legs.

 1-3 WEEKS

3—FROGLET

Over time, the tadpoles grow into froglets. They have four stubby legs and a shorter tail.

 12 WEEKS AFTER HATCHING

4—FROG

Finally, the froglets grow into adult frogs that can live in or out of the water.

 AROUND 14 WEEKS

REPTILES

Reptiles have existed for more than 300,000 million years, which is long before the first dinosaurs ever appeared. Almost all reptiles are meat eaters, with hunting skills matched to their environments. The one exception is tortoises, who eat plants—which is lucky, since they are much too slow-moving to be able to catch prey. Reptiles are found in almost every habitat on Earth.

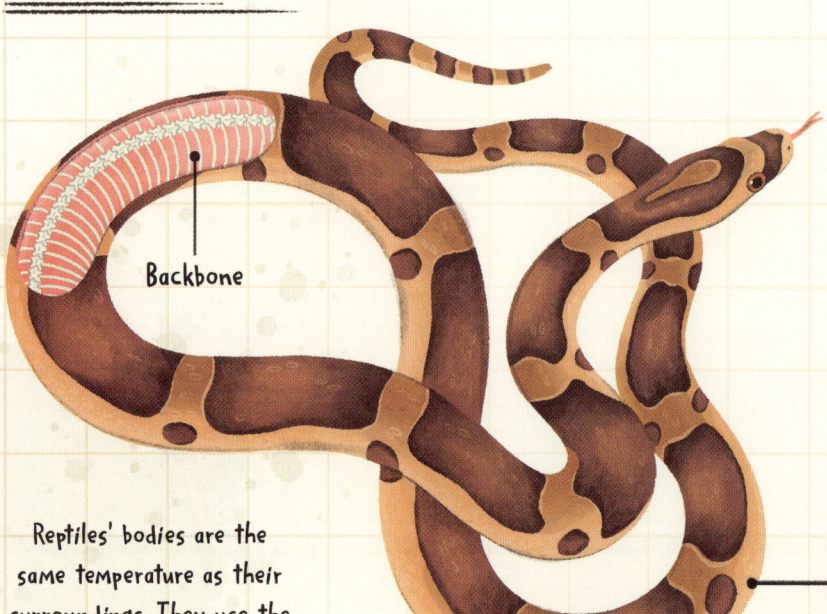

Backbone

Reptile features

All reptiles have a few things in common. They are vertebrates, with hard internal skeletons. They are cold-blooded and most of them lay eggs. Reptile skin is tough and waterproof, which allows them to live in extremely dry places.

Reptiles' bodies are the same temperature as their surroundings. They use the sun's heat to warm up.

Scales

An armor of hard scales protects the reptile's skin. The scales often overlap.

TYPES OF REPTILES

The different types of reptiles are divided into five groups, based on their body shapes and features. Some live on the land, others spend most of their lives in water.

Iguana

LIZARD

Most lizards have four legs and long tails, but some have no legs at all. This is the biggest reptile group, with more than 6,000 species.

TURTLES AND TORTOISES

These reptiles have hard protective shells on their backs. Tortoises live on land, and turtles in water.

Hawaiian green sea turtle

Baby viviparous lizard

< SHEDDING SKIN

Reptile skin does not stretch as the reptile grows. So, reptiles occasionally cast off their old skin, revealing a new one underneath. Some reptiles shed in sections, but snakes shed their whole skin in one long piece.

Eye spy

Reptile eyes look different depending on whether they are active in the day (diurnal) or night (nocturnal). A diurnal reptile's round eyes can take in a lot of daylight. A nocturnal reptile's slit-shaped eyes can close tightly to block out bright daylight.

Corn snakes hatching

Diurnal

Painted turtle

Nocturnal

Boa constrictor

^

YOUNG REPTILES

A few reptiles, such as the viviparous lizard, give birth to live young, but most of them lay eggs. Reptile eggs have leathery waterproof shells, to stop them from drying out. The young develop inside the egg, then break their way out.

SNAKES

Snakes have no limbs at all. They have jaws that allow them to swallow prey all at once. Some are venomous.

Nile crocodile

CROCODILES

Alligators and crocodiles have four legs, armored bodies, and sharp teeth. They are experts at hunting in shallow water.

TUATARA

This group is lizardlike. Only one species exists today, but there were more of them around 200 million years ago.

Blue viper snake

Tuatara

TURTLE RUN

Adult sea turtles are large and robust, but to become adults they must survive a daunting ordeal. They must run a gauntlet of challenges to even reach the ocean—only about one in a thousand leatherback hatchlings will survive the journey to adulthood.

2

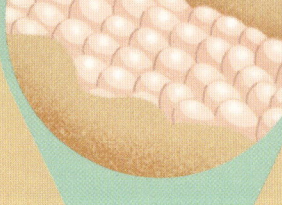

1

Returning home

Adult sea turtles return to the beach they hatched on to lay their own eggs. They can detect Earth's invisible magnetic field, and use it as a map to guide them back to their home beach, year after year.

THE MOTHER TURTLE LEAVES HER NEST AND HEADS BACK TO THE OCEAN.

1
BEACH BOUND
The female leatherback sea turtle crawls out of the ocean and up the beach to an area that won't be underwater during high tide. She uses her front flippers to dig a pit for herself, settles in, and uses her hind flippers to dig a hole for her eggs.

2
EGG LAYING
She lays 50 or more ping-pong-ball-shaped eggs into the egg hole. The soft-shelled eggs are protected by a thick layer of mucus. This means they do not break as they fall into the egg cavity.

3
BREAKING FREE
The eggs stay buried in the warm sand for 45 to 70 days. Then, the tiny turtle hatchlings break their way out of the eggs. They hide in the nest until all the eggs have hatched.

The journey of a leatherback turtle hatchling

Bright lights

Baby turtles head toward the brightest light they can see, which is naturally over the ocean. Electric lights, such as streetlights, can lead them astray, making them head inland instead of out to sea.

PREDATORS SWARM, EAGER TO MAKE A MEAL OF THE BABY TURTLES.

4
NIGHT RUN

The hatchlings wait until the sand cools—a sign that it is nighttime. Then, under cover of darkness, they crawl out and make their way down the beach toward the ocean.

5
FOLLOW THE LIGHT

The hatchlings use the slope of the beach and the glow of natural light over the ocean to help them find their way to the water.

6
JUST KEEP SWIMMING!

The hatchlings reach the water and begin to swim. Predators can spot them more easily in the shallows, where there is less water to get lost in, so they head toward deeper waters.

7
DINNER TIME

The hatchlings that survive the journey will be on their own, living in the open ocean with no support from their parents. They live on small sea creatures, such as mollusks and crustaceans, fish eggs, and seaweed.

BIRDS

Most birds have bodies that are perfectly adapted for flight, with light bones, feathers, and a smooth outline. Not all of them fly, though. Some groups, such as ostriches and penguins, are completely flightless but can run and swim. Birds can be expert hunters, and these you might see at dizzying heights on the lookout for small animals down below. Other birds stay closer to the ground, in search of seeds, fruit, or insects to eat.

Streamlined shape for flying

Wings

Beak

Feathers

Talons

Tail

Bird features

Birds are vertebrates, which means they have an internal skeleton made from bone. They are also the only animals to have feathers—light, soft structures made from keratin that keep the bird warm and allow it to fly.

TYPES OF FLIGHT

Green woodpecker

BOUNDING

To bound, a bird flaps its wings and then tucks them in, creating a bouncing flight pattern.

Hummingbird

HOVERING

To stay in the air in a fixed spot, a bird must hover, flapping its wings back and forth extremely quickly.

GLIDING

Some birds glide smoothly for long distances. They do not flap their wings until they want to rise higher into the air.

Kestrel

SOARING

To soar, a bird hitches a ride on a rising current of air. Birds can only soar in places where these air currents exist.

Eagle

Nests

Birds build nests to have a safe place to lay their eggs and raise their chicks. The nests are built from a wide range of materials, and their shape varies from species to species. The European robin builds a typical, cup-shaped nest, while the village weaver creates a more elaborate structure, with an extended entrance.

^
LIGHT AS A FEATHER

Bird bones are not solid. Instead, they are mostly hollow, with crisscrossing structures to support them. This makes the bones lightweight, allowing the bird to fly.

Village weaver nest

European robin nest

Nature

HATCHING

Breaking out

Many animals lay eggs, but only birds lay hard-shelled eggs, which hatch into baby birds. To get out, the chick must use its beak to break the eggshell. These pictures show what the hatching process looks like for a baby goose, or "gosling."

The gosling starts to move around inside the egg.

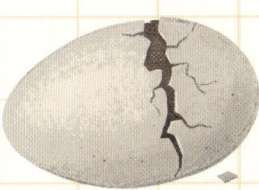

The gosling begins pecking at the egg, making a ring of holes.

The gosling's feathers dry out, it opens its eyes, and can walk around.

The gosling wiggles its way out of the egg, then rests.

109

FLYING HIGH

Some birds fly for extremely long periods of time, crossing continents, and not touching the ground at all for months at a stretch. These journeys can take birds to extreme heights above ground level, reaching even higher than airplanes fly. Here are just a handful of the world's most high-flying birds.

COMMON CRANE
33,000 ft (10,058 m)

30,000 ft
9,000 m
Mount Everest   Jet plane

25,000 ft
7,620 m

20,000 ft
6,000 m

15,000 ft
4,572 m

BALD EAGLE
10,000 ft (3,048 m)

PURPLE MARTIN
6,197 ft (1,889 m)

10,000 ft
3,000 m

5,000 ft
1,500 m

CANADA GOOSE
3,250 ft (900 m)

SEA LEVEL

A map showing the heights reached by some birds

RUPPELL'S GRIFFON VULTURE
37,000 ft (11,309 m)

BAR-HEADED GOOSE
23,000 ft (7,000 m)

FLIGHT LOG

Some Canada geese fly south for winter, traveling 1,500 miles (2,400 km) in a day.

If there is not enough food or water locally in the winter, bald eagles will fly south, or to the coast.

Purple martins fly from North to South America and back, every single year.

Common cranes make long migratory flights at high altitude. They fly in V- or Y-shaped groups.

The Ruppell's griffon vulture is the world's highest-flying bird. It soars through the skies, looking for food down below.

Bar-headed geese fly from their summer breeding grounds in central Asia to wintering grounds in southern Asia.

ROLLER-COASTER FLIGHT

Bar-headed geese change altitude as they fly. They follow the shape of the landscape as they move over it, shifting up and down, using drafts of wind to save their energy. Their annual migration takes them right over the Himalayan mountains, reaching extreme heights with very little oxygen for them to breathe.

Nature

MAMMALS

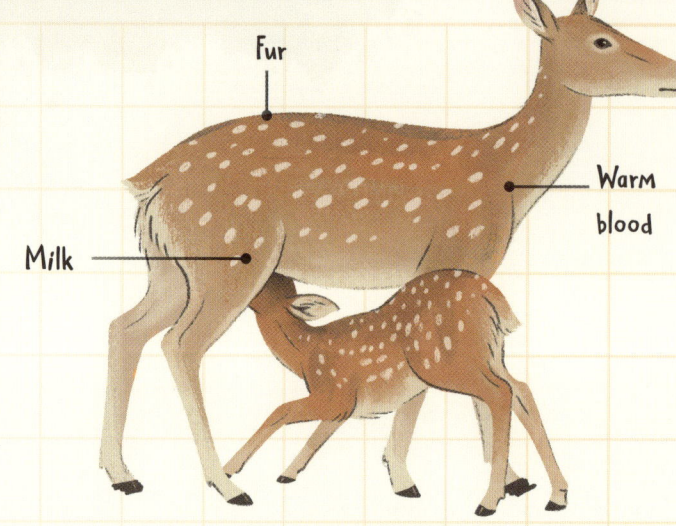

Fur

Warm blood

Milk

This is the animal group that includes you. In addition to humans, the furry animals we tend to keep as pets, such as cats and dogs, are mammals. Less furry mammals include whales, dolphins, and seals in the ocean, as well as bats and elephants on land. Altogether, there are more than 5,000 different types of mammals! Most of them give birth to live young, rather than laying eggs like birds and reptiles do.

Mammal features

All mammals have a few key features in common. They are warm-blooded, produce milk for their babies, and have hair on their bodies. Even whales have hair, although it's pretty sparse compared to a furry mammal such as a deer or bear!

TYPES OF MAMMALS

Mammals are organized into three main groups, based on how they produce their babies. The babies generally look like tiny, less-formed versions of their parents.

Platypus

Kangaroo

Elephant

EGG-LAYING MONOTREMES

Only two types of mammals lay eggs—the platypuses and echidnas, which both come from Oceania.

POUCHED

These animals, called marsupials, give birth very early. They take care of their babies in a pouch.

PLACENTAL

These mammals have babies that grow inside the mother, where they are attached to an organ called a placenta.

ALL AROUND THE WORLD

Mammals live all over the world in a huge range of environments. Most of them live above ground, but not all—some live underground or in water. Some mammals live in scorching desert temperatures, others in icy lands.

HIBERNATION

Some mammals use a clever technique to help them survive the winter, when food is scarce. They eat as much as they can in the fall, then curl up and go into a deep, sleeplike state, called hibernation. They sleep away the whole winter, then wake up again in spring.

v

MOVING MAMMALS

Mammal bodies are adapted to move in a huge range of different ways. Here are a few examples of incredible mammal movement.

RUNNING

Cheetahs have a very flexible spine, which lets them spring over a huge distance with each bound.

HOPPING

Rabbits have strong back legs, and can leap a long way into the air with just one push.

CLIMBING

Mountain goats are incredibly nimble. They can pick their way along narrow ledges in the mountains without falling.

FLYING

Bat hands have developed into full wings, with webs of skin between the fingers. They are expert fliers.

SWINGING

Gibbons have long, stretchy arms that they use to swing from tree to tree. This way of moving is called brachiation.

SWIMMING

Whales have smooth, streamlined bodies that allow them to move easily through the water.

DOMESTICATED ANIMALS

The word "domesticated" means made domestic, or taken into the home. We use it to describe animals that were once wild, but are now tame and kept by humans as food, or even as our pets. Over thousands of years, human involvement has changed animal species, sometimes creating an animal that looks and behaves very differently from their wild ancestor. Cows, sheep, goats, pigs, dogs, and cats are all examples of animals that have been domesticated.

Domesticated plants

People have changed plants over time, too. Plants with a desired feature, such as big leaves, were chosen, and their seeds were harvested and grown as food. This works because plant features are passed on from parent to baby. Cabbage, broccoli, kohlrabi, and kale all descend from one plant.

Broccoli

Large flower buds and stems

Cauliflower

Large flower buds

Kohlrabi

Large stems

Large leaves

Brassica oleracea

Kale

A GUIDE TO DOGS AND WOLVES

TAIL

Wolves have longer tails than dogs, which helps with balance and movement.

Domesticated dogs were once wild wolves, but their bodies have changed significantly over time. Wolf bodies were perfectly adapted for a wild life, hunting for their dinner. Dogs are pets, and don't need to hunt—but it does benefit them to look cute for their owners!

DOG

WOLF

HEAD AND SNOUT

Dogs have developed a muscle called the LAOM muscle, which allows them to change their expression and make "puppy dog" eyes. Wolves have a fixed stare.

Wolves have a longer snout than dogs, which probably allows for more smell receptors for hunting.

LEGS AND PAWS

Dogs typically have shorter legs than wolves, and can't run as fast.

Wolves have bigger paws in relation to their bodies than dogs, which helps stop them from sinking in snow during wild winters.

A map of a dog and a wolf's body

ANIMAL MIGRATIONS

A migration is a long journey—and some migrations are indeed very long journeys. Animals migrate to find food, to breed and produce young, or to find a warmer, easier place to spend the winter. Not all animals migrate, but those who do follow the same route every single year. Some migration routes are circular, while others are more back-and-forth.

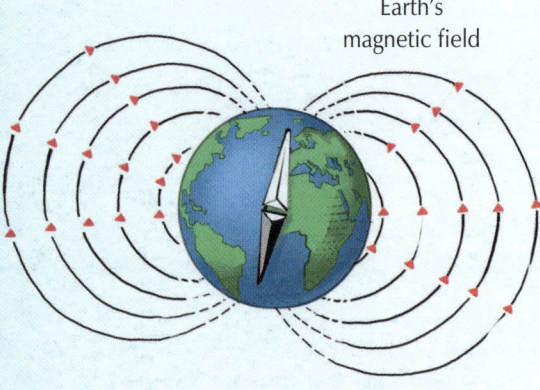

Earth's magnetic field

BUILT-IN NAVIGATION

Some birds and whales are able to sense the magnetic field that surrounds Earth. This information helps them find their way on their long migrations, using a kind of built-in compass inside their heads.

ANIMAL SPECIES KEY

GRAY WHALE

The gray whale makes the longest migration of all mammals. It travels up to 14,000 miles (22,530 km) between its summer feeding grounds in the Arctic and winter breeding grounds in Mexico.

MONARCH BUTTERFLY

Butterflies only have short lives, so they make their 3,000 miles (4,828 km) migration in shifts—it takes several generations to complete the whole journey.

ARCTIC TERN

The Arctic tern makes the longest migration of all animals, flying 18,641 miles (30,000 km) all the way from the Arctic to the Antarctic twice a year.

WHITE-BEARDED WILDEBEEST

These wildebeest follow a 1,000 mile (1,610 km)-long triangular route around the grasslands, in pursuit of water and fresh grass.

FEEDING

Food is always a good reason to make a journey. Gray whales swim north to feed on tiny amphipod crustaceans, which burrow in the mud of the seafloor. They can fill up on more than 2,200 lb (1,000 kg) of these shellfish a day.

Amphipod crustaceans

CLIMATE

Some animals migrate in order to spend the winter in a milder climate. Monarch butterflies fly south to escape freezing winter temperatures.

A sight to remember

Migrating animals use landmarks, such as the coastlines of countries they fly over, to help them find their way on their long journeys.

BREEDING

Another reason to travel is to reach breeding grounds. Arctic terns breed in the Arctic, in groups called colonies. The birds must all fly to their breeding grounds at the same time.

ANIMAL COMMUNICATION

Scientists believe that a humpback whale's song can travel up to 10,000 miles (16,093 km) through the ocean.

We talk to each other all the time. Communicating lets us share information and make friends, which makes our lives better and easier. Animals communicate with each other for the same reasons. Some of their communication is done with sound, like ours is. Certain sounds have meanings, which are understood by other animals of the same species, and sometimes even by animals of other species. Animals can also communicate in other ways, for example by using smell, color, or movements.

< COLOR CODING

Some animals can communicate by changing the color of their bodies. For example, the Humboldt squid sends flashes of red across its body when it is angry.

Body language

Many animals use their bodies to communicate. They might make a gesture, or a movement with meaning. Dogs move their tails in a wide range of different ways. Each movement tells other dogs (and us) how the dog is feeling: there is a different wag for excited, happy, anxious, and so on.

SMELL >

Animal noses can pick up messages too. Many animals use smells to mark their territories. Ants use smelly chemicals called pheromones to tell each other if there is danger, and where to find food.

The call of a blue whale can travel through 1,000 miles (1,609 km) of water.

118

LONG-DISTANCE COMMUNICATION

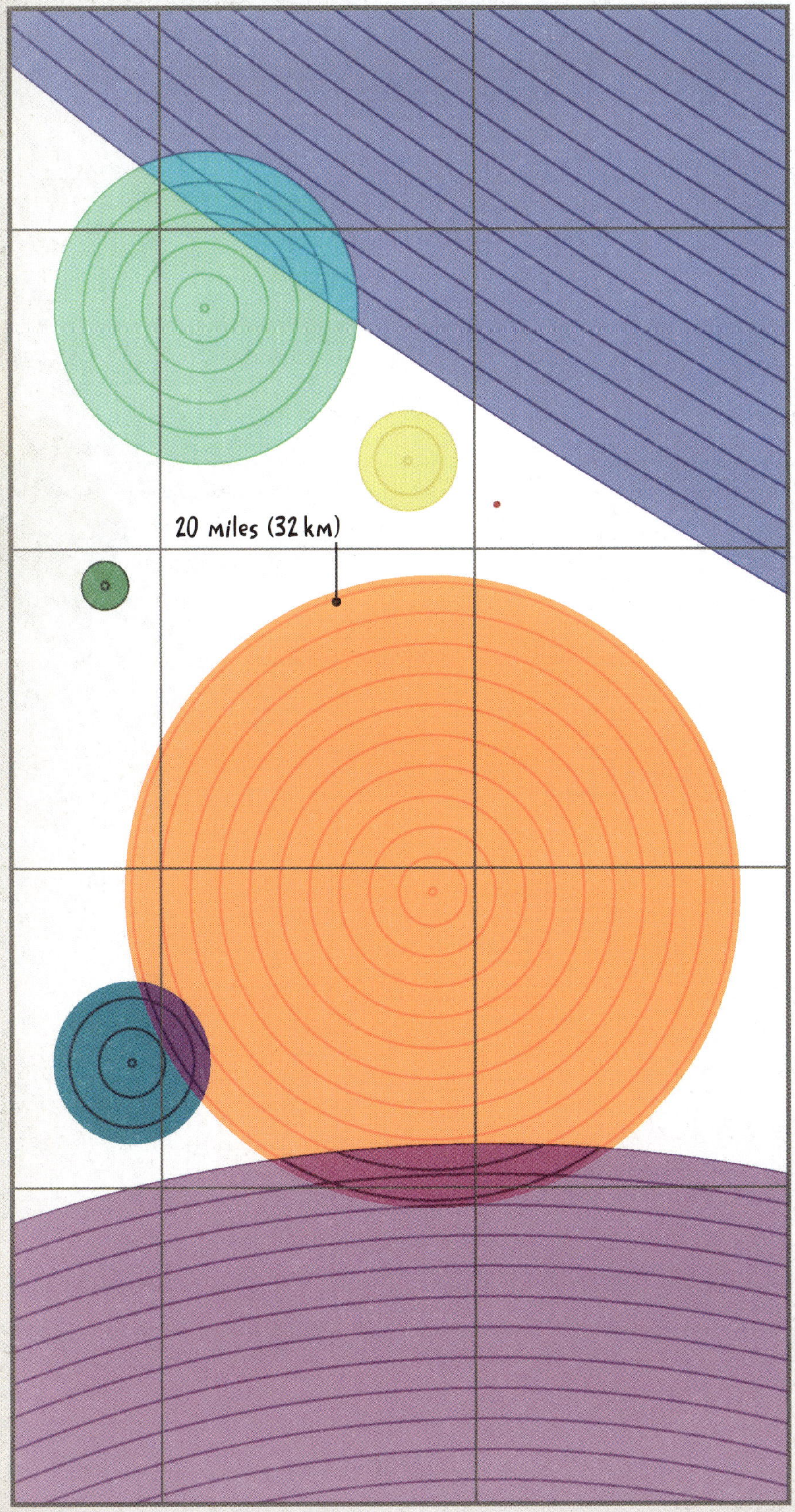

20 miles (32 km)

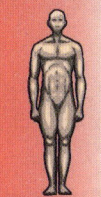

HUMAN

Whispers might not go far, but shouts can be heard up to 591 ft (180 m) away.

CICADA

Male cicadas make chirping sounds that can travel up to 1.5 miles (2.4 km).

HOWLER MONKEY

These monkeys' calls can travel 3 miles (4.8 km) across the rainforest.

LION

The loudest of the big cats, a male lion's roar can be heard 5 miles (8 km) away.

WOLF

Wolves howl to tell each other where they are, from up to 10 miles (16 km) away.

ELEPHANT

The vibrations made by an elephant's feet tell distant elephants where they are.

BLUE WHALE

Blue whales talk to each other with whistles, moans, grunts, and groans.

HUMPBACK WHALE

These whales sing long songs that can spread between them like pop songs.

Nature

PARTS OF A PLANT

FLOWER

The flower is where seeds form. The seeds can then grow into new plants.

LEAF

The leaves use sunlight to make energy, in a process called photosynthesis.

STEM

The stem carries water and nutrients around the plant.

All plants have leaves, stems, and roots, and many of them have flowers, too. Each part of the plant has its own job to do.

ROOTS

The roots take in water and nutrients from the soil.

KEY

— **WATER**—Like animals, plants need water to survive

— **NUTRIENTS**—Plants need to take in minerals to keep them healthy.

— **SUGAR**—Plants make their own sugary food inside their leaves.

A SEED'S JOURNEY

For a seed to grow, it needs soil, water, and light. But first, it needs a place to grow, in a spot with everything it needs, away from its parent plant. Seeds can be spread, or dispersed, in different ways.

KEY

••• Dispersal

● Silver birch seed

● Dandelion clock

● Viola seed

● Strawberry seed

● Lesser burdock seed

Water
Moving water can carry seeds away downstream.

TYPES OF PLANTS

Plants are divided into types based on how they look and how they reproduce. Roughly 400,000 species have been discovered, and most of them are flowering plants.

Moss

Conifer

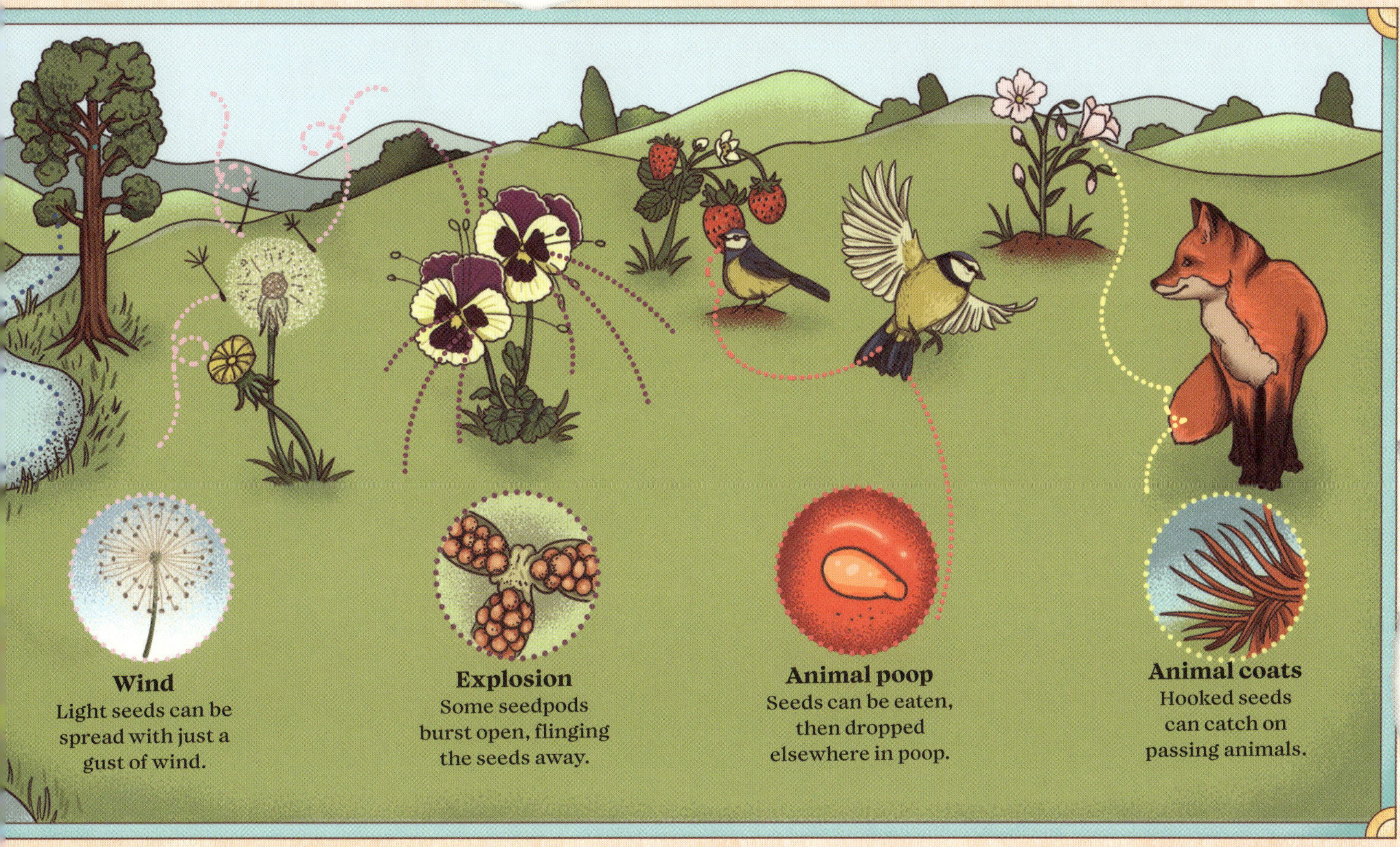

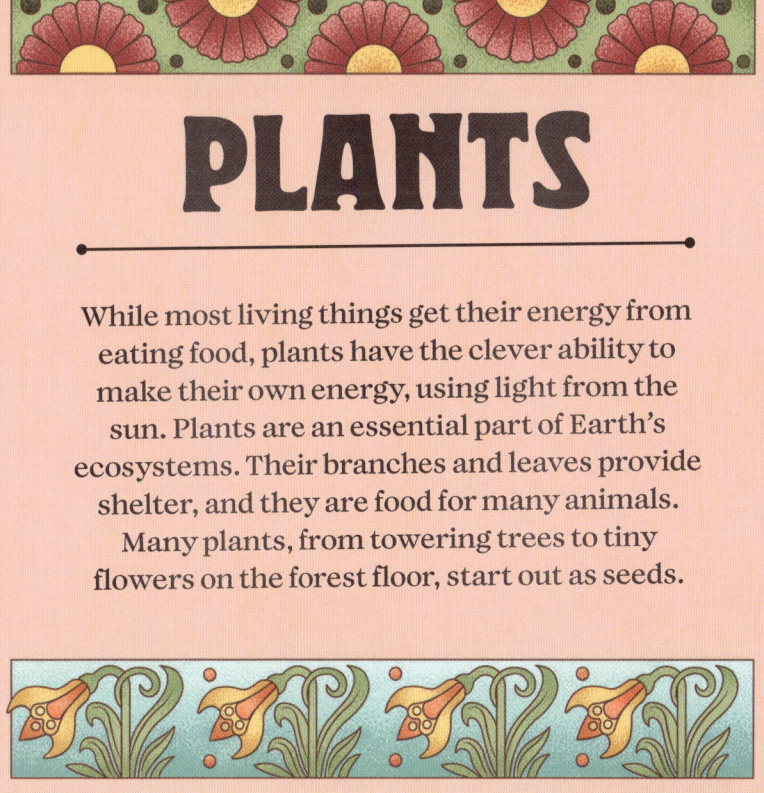

Wind
Light seeds can be spread with just a gust of wind.

Explosion
Some seedpods burst open, flinging the seeds away.

Animal poop
Seeds can be eaten, then dropped elsewhere in poop.

Animal coats
Hooked seeds can catch on passing animals.

Flowering plant

Fern

PLANTS

While most living things get their energy from eating food, plants have the clever ability to make their own energy, using light from the sun. Plants are an essential part of Earth's ecosystems. Their branches and leaves provide shelter, and they are food for many animals. Many plants, from towering trees to tiny flowers on the forest floor, start out as seeds.

TYPES OF TREES

BROAD-LEAVED

These trees have wide, smooth, flat leaves. They have flowers, and usually grow in places that are temperate—not too cold! Broad-leaved tree leaves come in a wide range of different shapes.

Oak

Flat, wide leaf

Thin, needlelike leaves

Pine

CONIFER

Conifers have thin, pointed leaves, known as needles. They have cones instead of flowers, and can grow in very cold places as well as mild ones. Conifer needles can be different lengths and colors, but they are always needle-shaped.

TREES

The only real difference between a tree and any other plant is that a tree has a big woody stem, called a trunk. The trunk gets wider and wider as the tree grows—some of the largest trees are over a thousand years old, and have trunks so wide that it would take dozens of people to circle them. Trees are essential for our survival on Earth—they absorb carbon dioxide, which can be harmful to us, and release huge amounts of the oxygen we breathe.

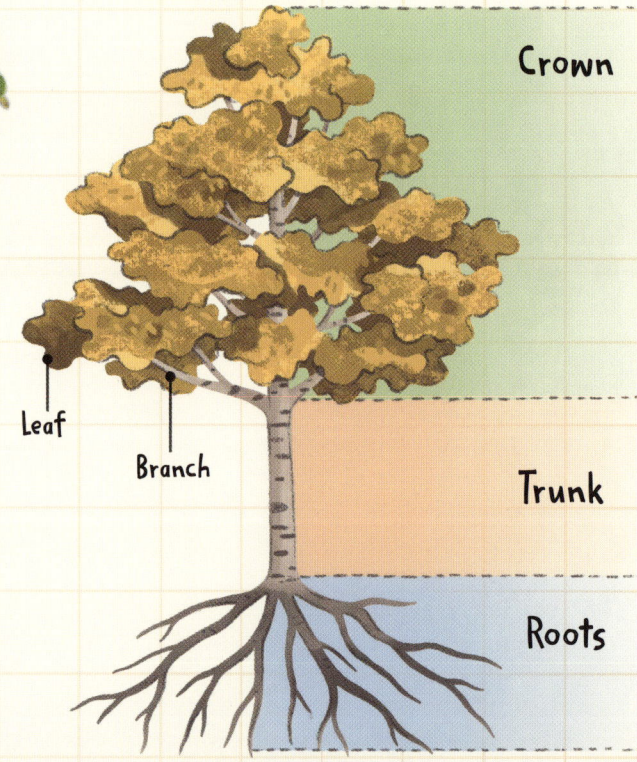

Crown

Leaf

Branch

Trunk

Roots

Parts of a tree

Each part of a tree has its own name. The roots branch out underground, absorbing water and nutrients for the tree and keeping it stable. The trunk supports the crown, which is all the leaves and branches.

Fruit and nuts

Many trees hide their seeds inside fruit, or nuts. Animals pick and eat these delicious offerings, taking them away from the parent tree. This helps the seeds inside find their way to a new patch of soil, where they can begin growing.

Pine cones have seeds hidden under each of their scales.

A peach has a seed hidden inside its pit.

DECIDUOUS OR EVERGREEN?

Cypress

Evergreen trees keep their leaves all year, without dropping them.

Birch

Deciduous trees have leaves that turn brown, gold, or red and fall off in the fall, then grow again in spring.

PHOTOSYNTHESIS

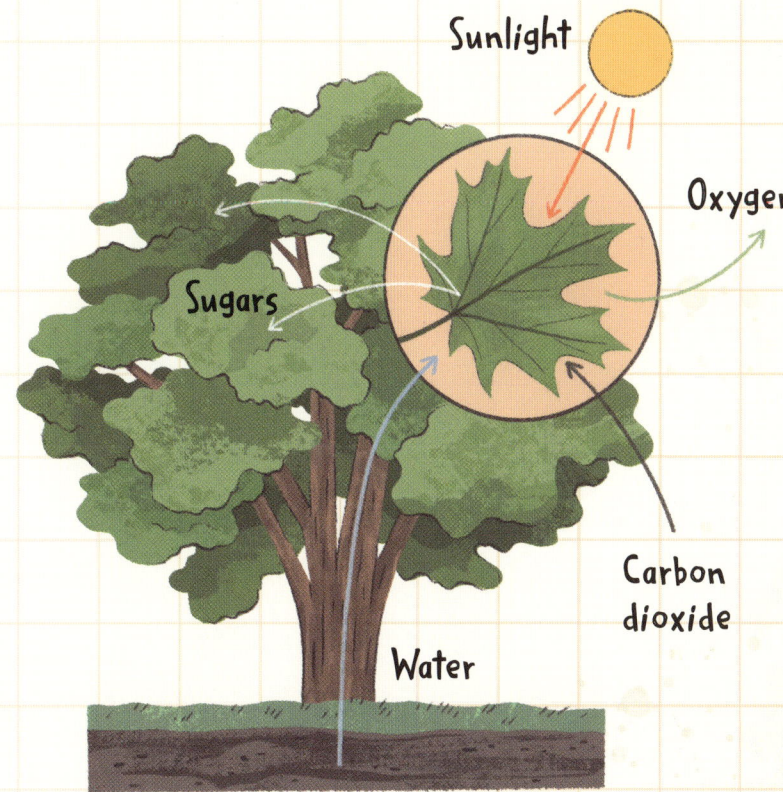

Sunlight

Oxygen

Sugars

Carbon dioxide

Water

Nature

Making food

Plants use light to make food, in a process called photosynthesis. Their leaves absorb carbon dioxide from the air and light energy from the sun, and turn them into sugars, which fuel the plant. Oxygen gas is released as a waste product of this process.

FIELDS FOR FARMING

Huge swathes of the Amazon Rainforest have been cleared away to make space for farming. In Brazil, land that was once rainforest is now cattle ranches, while in Bolivia it is now soybean farms.

CO₂

THE AMAZON'S LOCATION

KEY

SEA OR OCEAN	AREAS OF RAINFOREST
LAND	AREAS OF DEFORESTATION

CATTLE RANCHING

PALM-OIL FARMING

LOGGING

SOYBEAN FARMING

WHY IS DEFORESTATION BAD?

Trees absorb carbon dioxide (a gas that harms our planet) and release the oxygen we breathe. They also provide food and shelter for a huge range of plants and animals. The animals shown here are just a few examples of species that are threatened due to deforestation.

DEFORESTATION

EARTH WAS ONCE CARPETED IN THICK FOREST, BUT TODAY ONLY A FRACTION OF IT REMAINS. IT HAS BEEN DEFORESTED—CLEARED AWAY SO HUMANS CAN USE THE WOOD AND FARM THE LAND WHERE TREES ONCE GREW.

ORANGUTAN, INDONESIA

CANADIAN CARIBOU, ONTARIO, CANADA

FOREST OWLET, CENTRAL INDIA

A map showing the different causes of deforestation

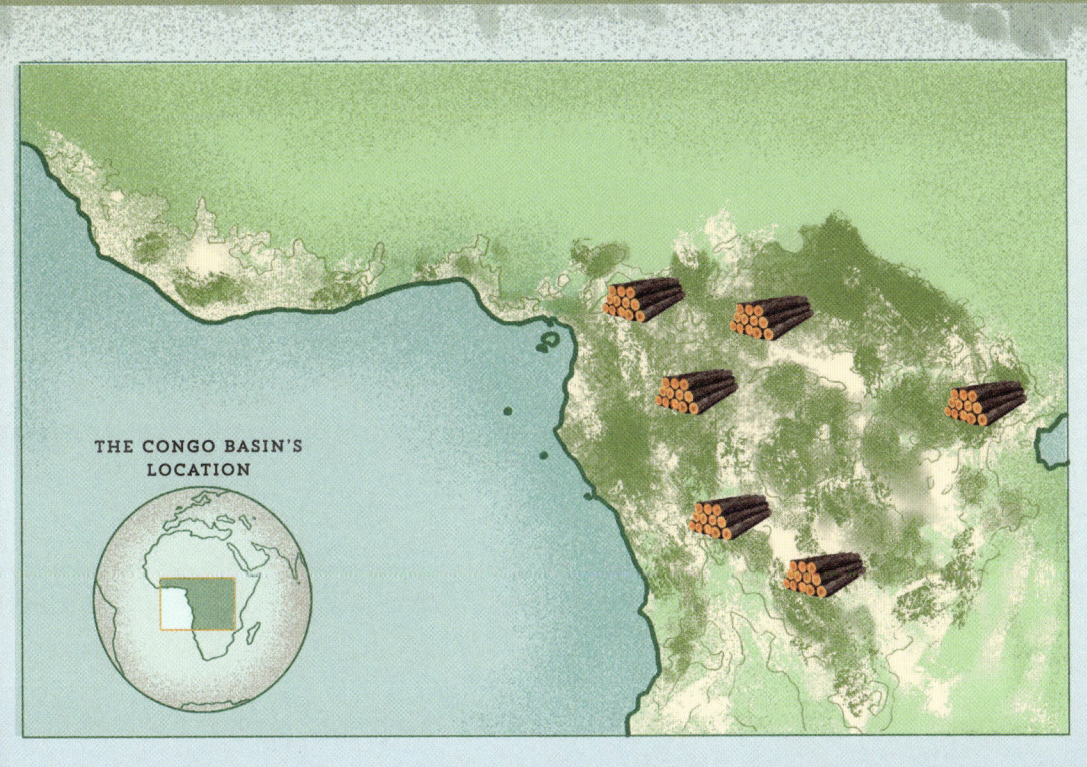

LOGGING

Much of the rainforest in the Congo Basin has been cleared, and the wood used to make furniture and paper. Cutting down trees in order to use the wood is called logging. Once a forest has been logged, it takes hundreds of years for the ecosystem to recover.

THE CONGO BASIN'S LOCATION

SPIX'S MACAW, NORTHERN BRAZIL (NOW EXTINCT IN THE WILD)

PALM-OIL PLANTATIONS

On the island of Sumatra, in Indonesia, huge areas of rainforests have been cleared to make space for palm-oil plantations. Very few of the animals that live in the rainforests are able to live among palm-oil trees.

SUMATRA'S LOCATION

MOUNTAIN GORILLA, UGANDA

PYGMY ELEPHANTS, BORNEO

CONSERVATION

Today, people are attempting to save the forests we have left. One way to do this is to recycle as much as possible, so that fewer trees need to be cut down to make new things.

MAINE PRAIRIE

Different grasses have been reintroduced to prairies in Maine, US. They are food for a variety of plant-eating animals, who are food for predators higher up in the prairie food chain.

SCOTTISH PEAT BOG

Healthy peat bogs absorb large amounts of carbon dioxide. Rewilding them can help reduce the effects of global warming.

BEAVERS

The Forest of Dean, in England, is now once more home to beavers.

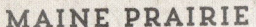

SPHAGNUM MOSS

HESPEROSTIPA COMATA

GRAY WOLF

Wolves were introduced back into Yellowstone National Park, US.

GIANT TORTOISES

were reintroduced to the Galápagos Islands, Ecuador.

AMERICAN BISON

These large animals have been reintroduced to the Montana prairie, US.

RETURN OF THE WILD

OVER HUNDREDS OF THOUSANDS OF YEARS, HUMAN ACTIVITY, SUCH AS HUNTING AND BUILDING, HAS LED TO MANY PLANTS AND ANIMALS DISAPPEARING FROM THEIR ANCIENT HOMES. NOW, SOME PEOPLE ARE TRYING TO REWILD AREAS OF LAND—BY BRINGING BACK THE ANIMALS AND PLANTS THAT ONCE THRIVED THERE.

NORWAY SPRUCE

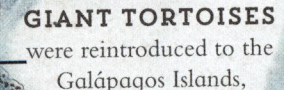

GIANT RIVER OTTER

The El Impenetrable National Park, Argentina, has had otters reintroduced.

CARPATHIAN FOREST

Forests of Norway spruce trees are being planted in the Carpathian Mountains, Romania, to create wildlife links between old-growth forests.

BROWN BEARS
These bears were reintroduced into the Pyrenees, France.

EURASIAN LYNX
The Swiss Alps, Switzerland, had lynxes reintroduced.

SHARAAN NATURE RESERVE
More than 120,000 native trees have been planted in this wilderness area in Saudi Arabia. Later, birds and animals will be reintroduced alongside them.

MORINGA PEREGRINA   ACACIA

BAMBOO-LEAF OAK

MOUNTAIN CHERRY

CHINQUAPIN OAK

MOUNT TSUKUBA FOREST
This forest in Japan contained mostly conifers. Adding more species has transformed it into a diverse mixed woodland.

BLUE WILDEBEEST
These animals were reintroduced into the Serengeti, Tanzania.

TAKAHĒ
These birds were reintroduced to Rotoroa Island, New Zealand.

PAINTED WOLVES
The Gorongosa National Park, Mozambique, has had these animals reintroduced.

GIANT PANDAS
Pandas were reintroduced into the Giant Panda National Park in China.

PLATYPUS
These animals were reintroduced to Sydney Royal National Park, Australia.

A map of rewilding projects around the world

The human effect
Humans have had a huge effect on the world around us. We destroy habitats so we can use the land for farming or building, and pollute the air with our cars and factories. This has a huge impact on wildlife, and has caused many species of plants and animals to become extinct.

Keystone species
Gray Wolf

Herbivore
Elk

Plant
Cottonwood

Keystone species
A keystone species is a type of plant or animal the rest of the ecosystem depends on. If we support a keystone species, we are supporting the plants and animals that depend on it, too.

Nature

DINOSAURS

Some of the biggest and most powerful animals to ever roam the Earth were dinosaurs—though many dinosaurs were not very big at all. This large group of reptiles roamed the Earth for almost 170 million years. Some were carnivores, which meant they hunted and ate other animals, while others, called herbivores, munched on leaves. Dinosaurs are now extinct, but modern birds are their living descendants.

When did dinosaurs live?

The dinosaurs lived during the Mesozoic era, between 252 and 66 million years ago. The Mesozoic can be further divided into three periods—the Triassic, Jurassic, and Cretaceous.

Many of the most well-known dinosaurs are from the Cretaceous period.

TRIASSIC PERIOD (252–201 MILLION YEARS AGO)

The first dinosaurs that appeared were small. It is likely that carnivores evolved first, followed by herbivores.

Nyasasaurus

Stegosaurus

JURASSIC PERIOD (201–145 MILLION YEARS AGO)

During the Jurassic, dinosaurs began to grow bigger. They evolved into new forms, with a range of lifestyles.

CRETACEOUS PERIOD (145–66 MILLION YEARS AGO)

In this period, dinosaurs became the most powerful animals on the planet, and some of them reached colossal sizes.

Tyrannosaurus rex

TYPES OF DINOSAURS

Dinosaurs are split into groups, based on the features they had in common. Those groups then fit into two main divisions (saurischians and ornithischians), based on the shape of the dinosaurs' hips bones.

Tyrannosaurus rex tooth

THEROPODS

The theropods walked on their two hind legs. They are the only dinosaur group that includes carnivores.

SAURISCHIANS

These dinosaurs had hips similar in shape to those of modern lizards. They usually had long necks, and large claws on their thumbs.

SAUROPODOMORPHS

This group walked on four sturdy, pillarlike legs, and had long necks and tails. Some of them reached enormous sizes.

THYREOPHORANS

This group had armored bodies, including thick plates of skin on their backs and spikes or clubs on their tails.

ORNITHISCHIANS

These dinosaurs had hips similar in shape to those of modern birds. They had a strong extra bone on their lower jaws, which helped to support a beak.

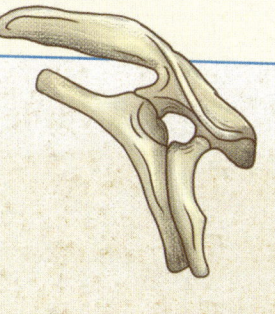

ORNITHOPODS

The word "ornithopod" means "bird feet." Ornithopods had sharp beaks. Some walked on two legs, others on four.

MARGINOCEPHALIANS

These dinosaurs had a wide range of unusual features, including head frills, spikes, horns, and domed skulls.

1 Allosaurus   **2** Diplodocus   **3** Ankylosaurus   **4** Iguanodon   **5** Triceratops

THE END OF THE DINOSAURS >

Around 66 million years ago, an asteroid hit Earth. It caused catastrophic changes to our planet, which the dinosaurs could not survive. Dinosaurs became extinct, along with many of the animals that lived alongside them.

CHAPTER 5

HISTORY

Today, there are about 8 billion humans on Earth. We permanently inhabit every continent except Antarctica, and have invented all kinds of technology, from computers to space rockets. But life wasn't always this way. People first appeared a few hundred thousand years ago. We were hunter-gatherers, moving from place to place, finding what food we could and using simple tools. Then, we began to settle down and started to farm. We grew villages into towns, towns into cities, and so on. People lived differently in different parts of the world, and developed new ideas that made their lives easier. Humanity's past is rich and complex! We call it our history.

EARLY HUMANS

The earliest human ancestors were apes that looked very different from us. Little by little we changed, becoming what we are today—a species called *Homo sapiens.*

Homo sapiens first appeared around 200,000 years ago. We were hunter-gatherers, who used simple tools and moved around in search of food. Since then, humans have come up with a huge range of new ideas, which have completely changed how we live.

< Our ancestors

Different species of humanlike creatures existed on Earth before modern humans did. Over time, they evolved, growing bigger brains and became able to walk on two legs rather than four.

Ardipithecus is thought to be an early human ancestor.

TOOL MAKING
A type of stone, called flint, is carefully struck against a rock to make sharp cutting and scraping tools.
1

CLOTHES MAKING
Furs are sewn together to make tunics, using a bone needle and thread made with plant fibers.
2

JEWELRY MAKING
Beads made of bone and amber are threaded together to make jewelry, such as necklaces and bracelets.
3

HUNTING
This group of hunters are off to bring home meat for the camp. They are armed with spears and bows and arrows.
4

GATHERING
Not all foods must be hunted. Some can simply be picked or collected, including nuts, fruit, and mushrooms.
5

ART
Paints made from colorful minerals are blown through hollow bones around hands, to create hand shapes on rock.
6

Prehistory time > line

The Stone Age, which can be split into three periods, was the time when humans used stone tools. The ages of metal-making followed.

3.5 million–11,500 years ago

Ivory (tusk) figurine

OLD STONE AGE (PALEOLITHIC)
This period covers more than three million years, during which humans carved simple stone tools and objects.

MIDDLE STONE AGE (MESOLITHIC)
We gradually learned how to make hunting tools for more specific tasks, such as harpoons for spearing fish.

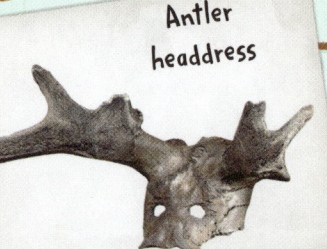

Antler headdress

c.11,500–6,500 years ago

STONE AGE SETTLEMENT

Here is a simple Stone Age settlement inhabited by hunter-gatherers, from around 200,000 years ago.

SHELTER

7 Huts are made from animal skins, stretched over flexible wooden poles. The skins overlap to keep the inside dry.

DOMESTICATED WOLVES

8 Wolves stay near the camp, because it is warm by the fire, and they may be able to beg for scraps of food from people.

PLAYING

9 Children play, chasing each other around the camp while the adults go about their daily tasks.

STORYTELLING

10 Writing hasn't been invented yet, so stories are passed down by word of mouth rather than in books.

COOKING

11 Meat and fish from the hunt, and gathered foods, are cooked over the fire.

Stone circle

c.6,500–4,000 years ago

NEW STONE AGE (NEOLITHIC)

Eventually, people began to farm for food instead of hunting. Our tools, however, were still made of stone.

BRONZE AGE

Finally, we discovered metal. Bronze was the first metal we used. It is easy to shape, but not that strong.

c.4,500–3,000 years ago

Bronze bracelet

c.3,000–2500 years ago

Iron dagger

IRON AGE

The discovery of how to make iron began this age. This metal could be made into stronger, sharper tools.

THE FIRST CIVILIZATIONS

A civilization is a society that has become highly developed. It has an organized leadership, with laws and a religion, and buildings designed for beauty not just function. Humans have existed for hundreds of thousands of years, but we only became civilized around 5,000 years ago, after we stopped living as hunter-gatherers and began to farm. Once we stopped moving, our settlements grew larger and civilizations began to develop.

Mesopotamia

The Mesopotamian civilization developed between the Tigris and Euphrates rivers in the Middle East. The world's first ever cities were built here, in about 7,500 BCE. They grew to contain complex, elaborate structures.

Ishtar Gate, Babylon

This grand gateway was the main entrance to the Mesopotamian city of Babylon.

Indus Valley Civilization

This civilization grew around the Indus River, in southern Asia, starting about 3,300 BCE. There were two large, carefully organized cities, and more than 100 additional towns and villages.

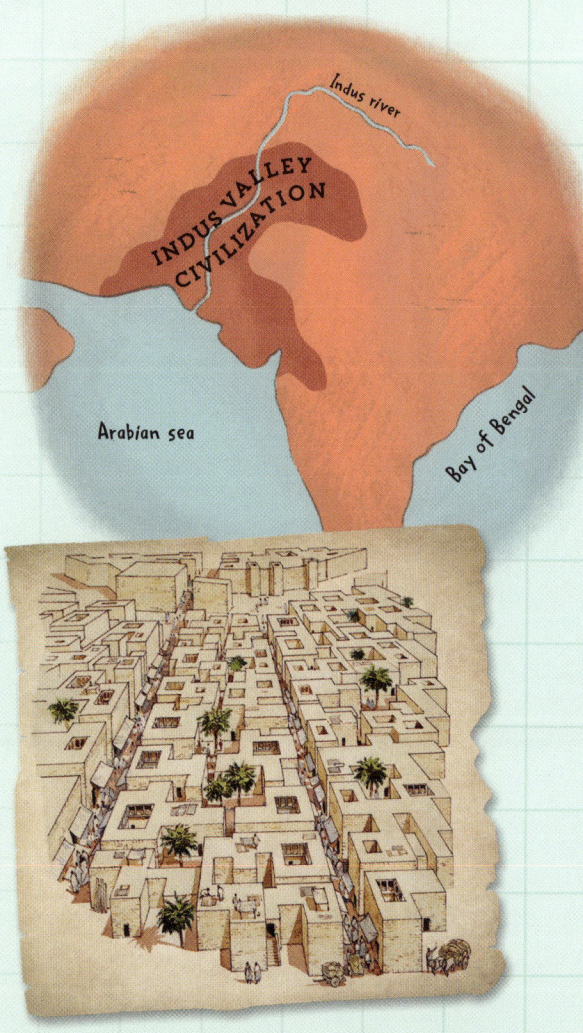

Mohenjo-Daro was the biggest city of the Indus Valley civilization. The city had a sophisticated water-supply and drainage system.

House in Mohenjo-Daro

FIRST WRITING SYSTEMS

As people began to settle down, record keeping became more important for activities such as trade—so people knew who owed what to who. Different writing systems appeared around the world.

CUNEIFORM WRITING

Mesopotamian writing used marks made by pressing a wedge-shaped tool into soft clay. It was used to record trades.

INDUS SCRIPT

The Indus civilization designed a script that appears on seals, which were pressed into clay to label batches of traded goods.

HIEROGLYPHICS

Ancient Egyptian writing used a series of picturelike symbols, each of which had a particular meaning. These characters are called hieroglyphics.

CHINESE

Writing began in China between 2,000–1,000 BCE. There were several different systems until just one was decided on, in around 200 BCE.

From hunting to farming

Gathering food by farming rather than hunting meant that people no longer had to move around. They settled down, and the settlements steadily grew. Many civilizations developed along rivers, because the land there was good for growing food.

TRADES

The early civilizations interacted with each other, which included trading. The Indus Valley people traded cotton, beads, copper, and bronze with people from Mesopotamia.

∨

Copper

Stone seals were used to record trades.

The seal was pressed in clay to leave an impression.

Cotton

History

135

ANCIENT EGYPT

In about 3100 BCE, a kingdom grew up around the Nile River in Egypt. It would become a powerful nation, controlled by rulers called pharaohs. The people of ancient Egypt worshipped many gods, including some pharaohs, who were believed to be gods in human form. To celebrate these deities they built elaborate temples, which housed towering statues. To honor some of their pharaohs after death they built colossal tombs—the pyramids, some of which are more than 328 ft (100 m) high.

The Giza pyramid complex includes three large pyramids for different pharaohs.

The pyramids

These great monuments starting being built around 2,630 BCE. Teams of workers hauled enormous blocks of stone up slopes and into place. It was backbreaking work, and slow—it took up to 30 years to build a single pyramid.

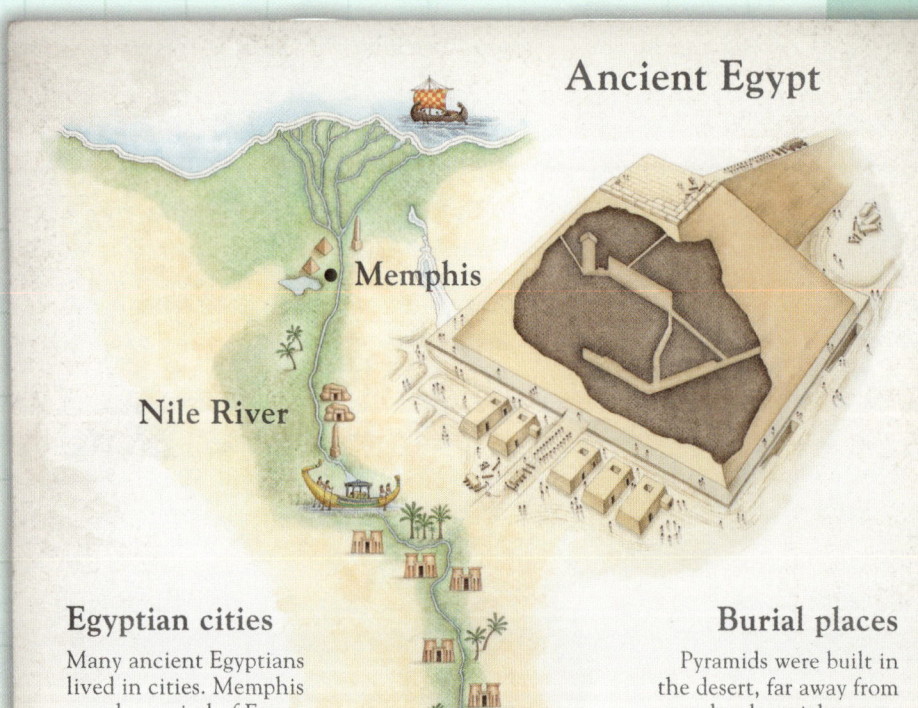

Ancient Egypt

Memphis

Nile River

Egyptian cities

Many ancient Egyptians lived in cities. Memphis was the capital of Egypt from around 3150 to 2686 BCE. It had around 30,000 inhabitants, and was one of the largest cities in the world.

Burial places

Pyramids were built in the desert, far away from people who might try to steal from them. If someone got in, they would need to find their way down tiny passages to the treasure-filled burial chamber deep inside.

‹

ALONG THE RIVER

Ancient Egypt grew around the Nile River. This river floods every year, which made the soil around it moist. This allowed crops to grow well, which meant there was plenty of food available to feed the growing civilization.

TUTANKHAMEN

A GOLDEN MASK

Who was Tutankhamen?

In about 1332 BCE, a boy around eight or nine years old was crowned pharaoh of all Egypt. His name was Tutankhamen, and he ruled until his death at the age of about 18. Tutankhamen's tomb was discovered in 1922, not inside a pyramid but cut into rock. He had been buried alongside hundreds of valuable objects, which were so well-preserved that they looked almost new.

<

BURIAL MASK

Like other pharaohs, Tutankhamen's body was mummified (preserved). His face and head were then covered with this elaborate mask, which is made from gold and semiprecious stones.

The boy king's body was placed inside a series of three coffins, including this one.

<

TOMB TREASURES

Among Tutankhamen's piles of belongings were gold jewelry, statues of himself, a board game, and richly decorated pieces of furniture. This photo shows the inside of part of the tomb—including a bed with a curly tail, painted to look like a cow. The boy king believed these objects would travel with him into the afterlife.

History

A JOURNEY THROUGH
THE EGYPTIAN AFTERLIFE

THE ANCIENT EGYPTIANS BELIEVED IN LIFE AFTER DEATH. THAT COULD BE A HAPPY ETERNITY IN A BEAUTIFUL LAND CALLED AARU, OR MISERABLE, ENDLESS DARKNESS. TO REACH AARU, A PERSON WOULD NEED TO BATTLE TERRIFYING GUARDIANS ON A DANGEROUS JOURNEY. HERE IS THE JOURNEY THAT THE BOY KING, TUTANKHAMEN, WOULD HAVE TAKEN.

OSIRIS	ANUBIS	RA

THE GODS

The pharaoh would meet a number of gods on his last journey. The sun god Ra took him on his boat to begin the voyage, Anubis watched over the weighing of his heart, and Osiris was waiting at the end, in his role as lord of the afterlife.

THE BURIAL CHAMBER

A wall was built over the entrance of Tutankhamen's burial chamber inside the tomb, to protect it from grave robbers. This is where the pharaoh believed his journey would begin.

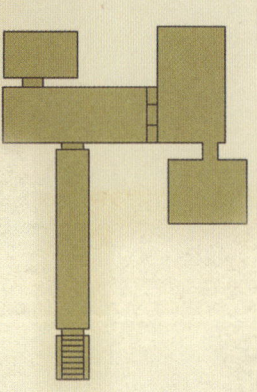

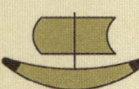
BOAT
The pharaoh began his journey into the afterlife onboard a boat.

SUNDIAL
The journey took 12 hours in total, and began at sunset.

JUDGE
The pharaoh had to deny wrongdoing in front of 42 gods before he could continue.

HEADS
A jackal and a ram's head tormented those who passed between them.

GATE
The pharaoh had to pass through 12 gates, each of which had challenges behind them.

GUARDIAN
Each gate had a terrifying guardian that the pharaoh would have to battle.

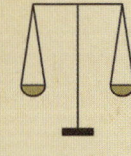
WEIGHING
The pharaoh's heart was weighed—if it was heavier than a feather, it was fed to a demon and the pharaoh could not pass.

AARU
The land beyond the last gate contained fields of reeds. This was the afterlife.

A map of the Egyptian afterlife

KIDNAPPING OF PERSEPHONE

Hades, god of the underworld, caught sight of beautiful Persephone and fell in love with her. He kidnapped her, and took her with him into the underworld. Persephone became the queen of the underworld, but was allowed to visit the living world once a year, in spring.

THE WAR OF THE TITANS

In a ten-year war, a new generation of Greek gods defeated and imprisoned the older gods, called the Titans. These new gods made their home on top of the tallest mountain in Greece—Mount Olympus. They became known as the Olympian gods.

ORACLE OF DELPHI

Pythia was the high priestess of the Temple of Apollo at Delphi. She was the temple's oracle, which meant she delivered prophecies (predictions about the future) from the Greek god Apollo. Many people visited to seek her advice.

ATHENA AND POSEIDON FIGHT FOR ATHENS

Athena and Poseidon both wanted to rule over Athens, and they decided to compete for the honor. Poseidon used his trident to produce a stream. Athena gave the people the very first olive tree, and won the contest.

ARTEMIS AND APOLLO

Artemis and Apollo were twins. Their father was Zeus, and their mother a titan named Leto. Leto fled from the home of the gods to hide from Hera, Zeus's wife, who was angry with her. She found a safe place on the Isle of Delos, where she was able to give birth to her children.

THESEUS AND THE MINOTAUR

Every year, the Athenians had to send seven girls and seven boys to be fed to a terrifying beast called the Minotaur, who lived in a labyrinth in Crete. Eventually Theseus, prince of Athens, went with them and killed the Minotaur.

MOUNT OLYMPUS

PHRYGIA

TROY

THE UNDERWORLD

AEGEAN SEA

DELPHI

ATHENS

DELOS

ICARIA

IONIAN SEA

SEA OF CRETE

CRETE

THE TROJAN WAR

The Trojan War began when the prince of Troy, Paris, kidnapped Helen, wife of the Spartan king, Menelaus. The war ended ten years later, when the Spartans gifted a wooden horse to the city of Troy. Once night fell, Spartan soldiers hidden inside the horse burst out and took Troy.

MIDAS AND HIS GOLDEN TOUCH

Midas was the king of Phrygia. He wished that everything he touched would turn to gold—and it did, including everything he wanted to eat and drink—and his beloved daughter. Eventually the curse was lifted and all returned to normal.

ICARUS

Daedalus, a great inventor, crafted wings for himself and his son, Icarus, to escape a prison. The father warned his son not to fly close to the sun, since the wax holding the wings together would melt. But Icarus did not listen. He flew too high, his wings fell apart, and he fell to his death near an island—Icaria.

GREEK MYTHS

Between around 1,200 BCE and 600 CE, the area that is now Greece was home to several Greek-speaking peoples we call the ancient Greeks. They lived in separate city-states. The states traded with each other and fought, but they all worshipped the same gods. The myths they wrote about these gods, and of heroic and tragic Greeks, survive today.

THE OLYMPIAN GODS

ZEUS
King of the gods and god of the sky

POSEIDON
God of the sea, horses, and storms

HERA
Queen of the gods and goddess of marriage

ATHENA
Goddess of wisdom and war

ARES
God of war and bravery

DEMETER
Goddess of harvests and fertility

APHRODITE
Goddess of fertility, love, and beauty

ARTEMIS
Goddess of hunting, wild animals, and childbirth

APOLLO
God of the sun, music, and dance

HEPHAESTUS
God of fire, volcanoes, and blacksmiths

HERMES
Messenger of the gods and god of journeys

HESTIA
Goddess of the home and hearth

History

A vast empire

The Roman Empire began in Rome, in Italy, in about 31 BCE. It then spread out around the Mediterranean and beyond. It was at its largest in 117 CE, under the emperor Trajan. After this, the empire gradually shrank again. Rome and the western half of the empire were conquered in 476 CE.

THE APPIAN WAY

^
ROMAN ROADS

The Romans built straight, paved roads, which connected their empire together and allowed goods and soldiers to move around easily. The Appian Way connected Rome and Brindisi.

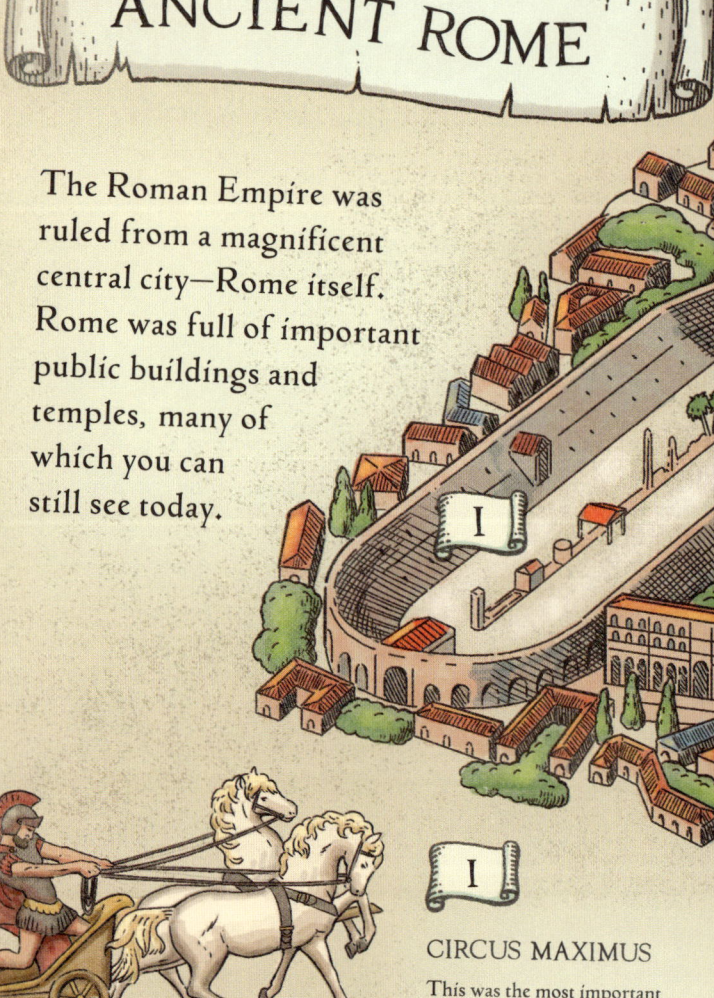

ANCIENT ROME

The Roman Empire was ruled from a magnificent central city—Rome itself. Rome was full of important public buildings and temples, many of which you can still see today.

I

CHARIOTEER

I

CIRCUS MAXIMUS

This was the most important racetrack in the Roman Empire. It hosted chariot races, during which teams of horses pulled their chariots and charioteers around the track at top speed.

II

EMPEROR AUGUSTUS

PALATINE HILL

This hill is thought to be the very spot where Rome was founded. It was home to several grand and sprawling palaces, which were built by a series of emperors, including the first emperor, Augustus.

III

THE GOD JUPITER

CAPITOLINE HILL

On this hill stand Rome's most important temples. The largest of them was dedicated to Jupiter, Roman god of the sky and king of all their gods.

ROMAN NUMERAL KEY

I	1
II	2
III	3
IV	4
V	5
VI	6
VII	7

IV

FORUM

This part of the city was a bit like a town square. It was a place where the people of Rome could gather and discuss government, law, and business.

CITIZEN VOTING

V

AQUA CLAUDIA

Eleven colossal aqueducts brought fresh water into Rome. The Aqua Claudia was one of them, built by Emperor Caligula.

EMPEROR CALIGULA

VI

THE TEMPLE OF CLAUDIUS

This temple was built to worship the Emperor Claudius, who, like many emperors, was declared a god after he died.

PRIESTESS OF THE TEMPLE

VII

COLOSSEUM

This building was a circus, or stadium, where men and beasts were made to fight each other to entertain huge crowds. Circuses were popular all over Rome.

GLADIATOR

IMPERIAL CHINA

China has been united as one country for thousands of years. Until the 20th century it was an empire—a country ruled over by all-powerful rulers called emperors. Many incredible inventions were first thought of in imperial China, including gunpowder, silk, paper, printing, the compass, porcelain, and mechanical clocks. The Chinese writing system was invented around 1,200 BCE, and uses more than 50,000 different symbols.

Ruling dynasties

From 221 BCE until 1911, China was ruled by a series of royal families, called dynasties. The leader of a dynasty was the emperor. Some dynasties ruled for hundreds of years, others were much briefer. At times, China was divided between multiple dynasties, which fought for control.

Qin Shi Huang was the first emperor of China.

Qin Shi Huang's burial site was filled with clay figures.

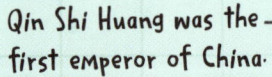

Silk moth cocoon

THE GREAT WALL OF CHINA

A series of colossal walls were built in the north of China to protect the country against invaders. At its longest, the wall was about 13,171 miles (21,197 km) long. Much of it still stands today.

THE SILK ROAD

Silk is a cloth, made from silk moth cocoons. China kept the knowledge of how to make silk secret, which made it extremely valuable. Silk was traded from China to countries in the west along a trade route that became known as the Silk Road.

Army of clay

When Qin Shi Huang died, an entire army of life-size terra-cotta clay warriors was buried with him. It is thought that they were meant to protect him in the afterlife. There were more than 7,000 soldiers, of varying ranks, all fully equipped for battle.

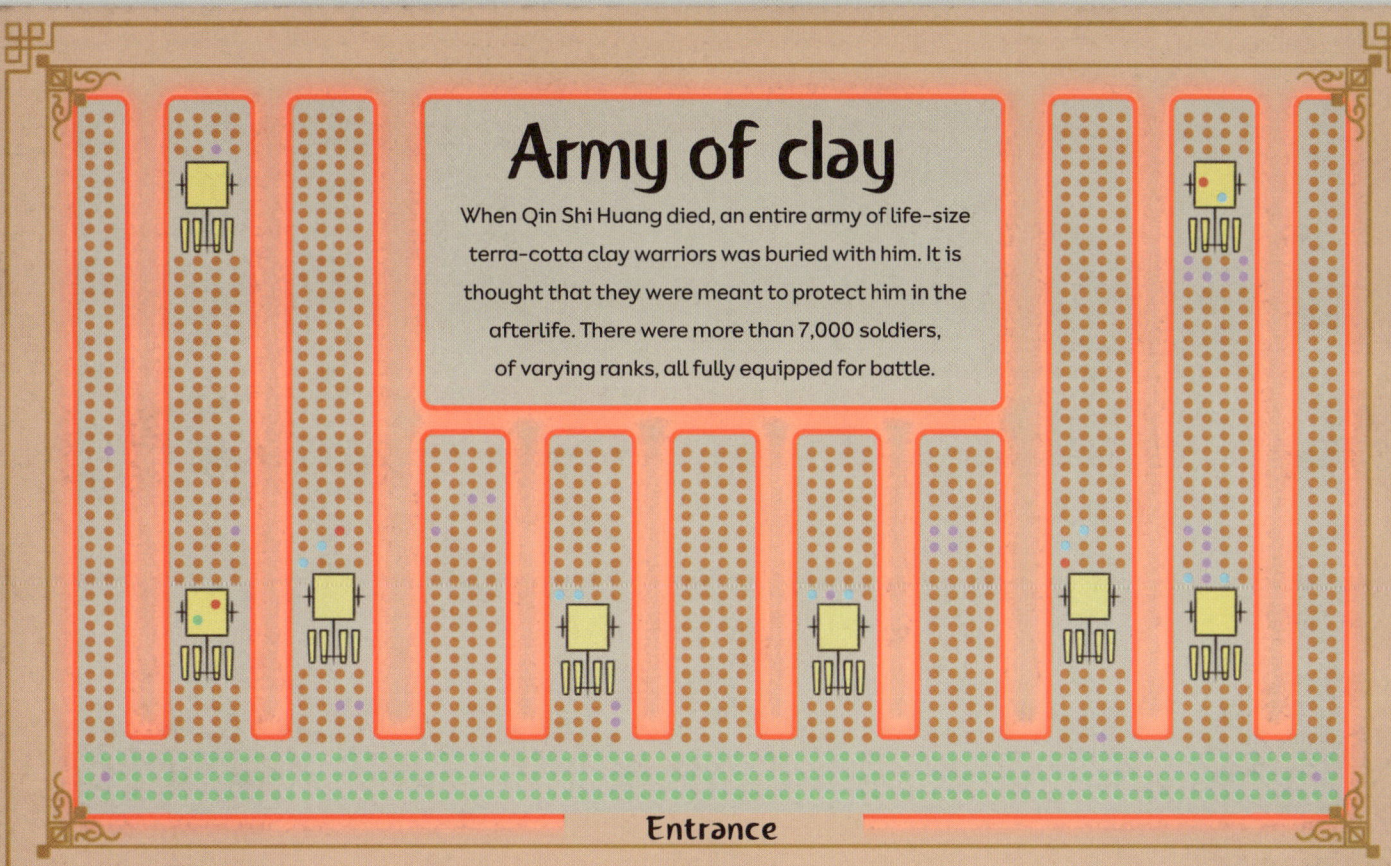

Entrance

General
Generals are the highest-ranking of all the warriors.

Officer
Officers are in charge of other warriors, and report to the generals.

Charioteer
The charioteers drive chariots. They wear protective helmets.

Archer
Rows of archers line up at the front of the army. They kneel or stand.

Chariot horse
Four clay horses pulled each chariot. The wood chariots rotted away.

WEAPONS

The terra-cotta army carried weapons made of real bronze. Different weapons were held by different types of warriors.

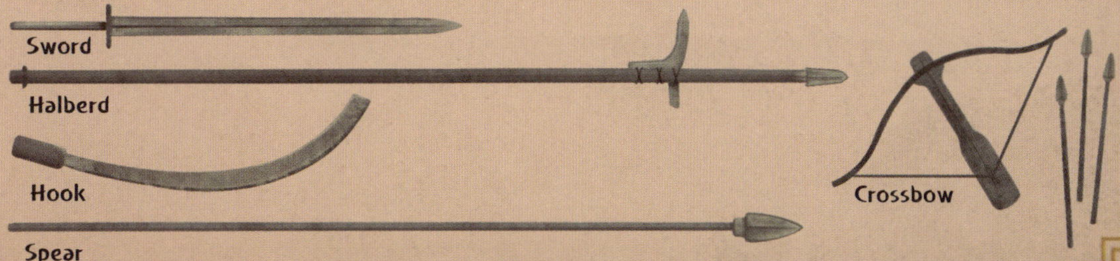

Sword

Halberd

Hook

Spear

Crossbow

MEDIEVAL CASTLES

During the medieval period (around 500–1,500 CE), Europe was ruled by a series of kings and their lords. They lived in stone castles, while most ordinary people lived in mud huts and worked on the land. There were often wars between different countries, and even within them, so castles were designed for defense, as well as for living in.

^ HILLTOP POSITION

Some castles were built high up on hillsides or hilltops. This gave them an excellent view of the surrounding land, and made them harder to attack, because an attacking army would have to travel uphill.

EVERYDAY LIFE

Outside the castle, most people were farmers. They grew crops and raised animals, and paid a proportion of them as tax to their lord. Life in the fields was hard, and usually short.

v

THE FEUDAL SYSTEM

Medieval society was very strict, and everyone had their place. The king or queen was all powerful, with everyone else arranged below them. At the very bottom of the system were the servants and peasants (farmers).

King — Queen

Lord — Bishop

Lady —

Knight — — Priest

Bishop — — Nun

Craftspeople — — Bailiffs

Servants   Peasants

A map of
Bodiam Castle

STONE WALLS

The castle walls helped keep out attacking armies. They were tall and also extremely thick.

TURRETS

These small towers were taller than the walls around them, which made them useful as lookouts.

ARROW SLIT

Narrow windows allowed defenders to fire arrows out, while being a tiny target for attackers.

BATTLEMENTS

These square openings at the top of the wall allowed defenders to shoot down at attackers below.

COAT OF ARMS

The pattern on each of these carved shields is linked to a particular noble family.

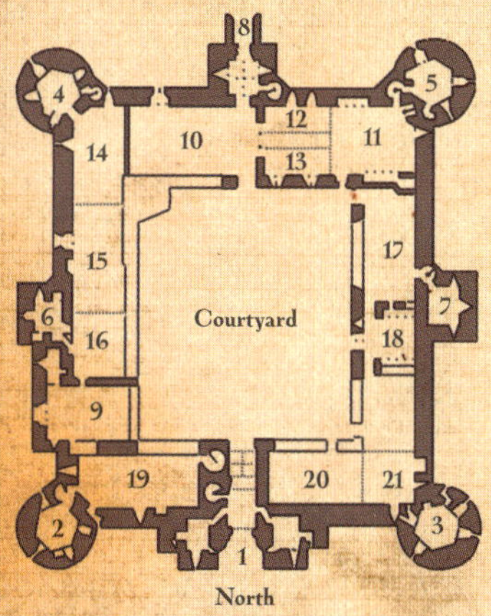

PLAN OF BODIAM CASTLE, 1391

Military, household, and religious rooms at Bodiam were all arranged around a central courtyard, which bustled with comings and goings.

Courtyard

North

1. GATEHOUSE
2. NORTHEAST TOWER
3. NORTHWEST TOWER
4. SOUTHEAST TOWER
5. SOUTHWEST TOWER
6. EAST TOWER
7. WEST TOWER
8. POSTERN TOWER
9. CHAPEL
10. GREAT HALL
11. KITCHEN
12. PANTRY
13. BUTTERY
14. ANTEROOM
15. HALL
16. CHAMBER
17. RETAINERS' HALL
18. RETAINERS' KITCHEN
19. HOUSEHOLD APARTMENTS
20. SERVICES
21. STABLES

A **Moat** *A water-filled moat made the castle that much harder for invaders to get to.*

B **Barbican** *This fortified gateway was positioned in front of the main gate, as an additional level of defense.*

C **Octagon** *This island in the moat may have had a guard posted on it.*

D **Gatehouse** *This was the main entrance to the castle. Holes allowed missiles to be dropped on any attackers.*

E **Postern tower** *This was the second entrance into the castle. It may have had a drawbridge.*

F **Drawbridge** *This wooden structure could be raised up, to cut off access to the castle.*

FACTORY LIFE

FROM VILLAGES...

For most of history, people lived in small clusters of dwellings. Most of them earned a living by working as farmers on shared land, or on land rented from lords. Only a handful of people had professions or ran businesses.

BEFORE 1750

...TO CITIES

After the Industrial Revolution, many people moved to live in cities. Factories needed plenty of people to work in them, which meant people were living and working closer together than ever before.

AFTER 1750

In around 1750, Britain went through a huge shift, known as the "Industrial Revolution," which later spread around the world. Steam-powered engines had been invented, which led to another world-changing invention—factories.

New technology

A series of inventions made making things quicker and easier than before, which meant products could be made in large amounts. People could only make one thread at a time before the spinning jenny came along—with which they could make eight.

① FARMING
Animals were raised for milk and meat. Crops such as turnips, carrots, and wheat were planted and harvested.

② FAMILY HOMES
People lived in small, simple houses. Most homes had only one story, and just one room.

③ COMMONS
Some land was held communally, which means it was owned by everyone, and everyone was allowed to use it.

④ SMALL BUSINESSES
Some people had specialized work. For example, blacksmiths made metal items and weavers made cloth.

⑤ GROCERY STORES
Since people could no longer grow their own food, they had to buy it. Grocery stores opened to sell food to workers.

⑥ PACKED HOUSING
Most people lived in single rooms or small apartments, packed together. They often shared space with other families.

⑦ BUSY STREETS
The city streets were busy, with people and horse-drawn vehicles pushing past each other to get around.

⑧ FACTORIES
The factories had rows of machines, which were powered by steam engines. Working in the factories was hard, dangerous, and dirty.

⑨ SMOG
The whole city was blanketed in a thick layer of smog—air polluted by smoke created by the factories.

∧
COAL POWER

Coal mining was important work! Steam-powered engines ran on coal—it was burned in order to turn water into steam, which powered engines. The invention of steam engines meant that trains could travel on tracks to transport people and goods more quickly.

THE BRITISH EMPIRE

The islands of Great Britain, equipped with a powerful navy, once ruled an empire stretching across much of the world. The empire's longest ruling monarch was Queen Victoria (1819–1901).

SIZE: 13.7 MILLION SQUARE MILES (35.5 MILLION SQUARE KM)

PEAK: 1919

26.4% OF THE EARTH'S LAND

WHY WERE EMPIRES BUILT?

Taking more land gave rulers access to workers, raw materials, goods, markets, and useful trading locations. Powerful countries used the resources from the places they conquered to make themselves even more powerful.

EMPIRES

When one country rules over many other nations, we say it has an empire. There have been empires throughout history—some rulers are always hungry for more. Beginning in the 1500s, European rulers became particularly power hungry, and expanded their empires worldwide. The countries they took are called "colonies."

Cotton plant

Diamonds

Gold

Fighting foreign power

Colonial rule was often cruel and unfair, and there were protests and uprisings against it. In India, Mahatma Gandhi led nonviolent protests against British rule, which eventually helped to gain Indian independence.

THE MONGOLIAN EMPIRE

This empire was started by Genghis Khan (1162–1227), in 1206. Skilled Mongol horseback warriors invaded and conquered their neighbors, until their empire covered a huge swathe of Asia.

Genghis Khan

17.8% OF THE EARTH'S LAND

SIZE:
9.3 MILLION SQ MILES (24 MILLION SQ KM)

PEAK: 1279

THE RUSSIAN EMPIRE

By the late 19th century, Russia was the biggest country in the world. Rulers such as Catherine the Great (1729–1796) fought wars against Persia and other neighbours, in order to expand its borders.

SIZE:
8.8 MILLION SQ MILES (22.8 MILLION SQ KM)

PEAK: 1895

Catherine the Great

Peter the Great

16.9% OF THE EARTH'S LAND

< **THE END OF EMPIRES**

Eventually, the European empires came to an end. Many colonized countries overthrew their oppressors, winning their freedom. In 1957, Ghana became the first African country to gain independence from Britain. Kwame Nkrumah (pictured) was its first leader.

REVOLUTIONS

What would you do if your life were extremely difficult, and the leaders of your country didn't seem to want to help? You might be tempted to try to change things. You could voice your opinion, and hope those in power would listen and try to help their country's people. But if that didn't work, and the unfairness continued, or got worse, you might, eventually, be tempted to revolt.

Protests can start revolutions!

A month before the Russian Revolution began, people gathered outside the winter palace to protest against the tsar.

< What is a revolution?

A revolution is a sudden change in the way a country is run. It generally brings in a whole new political system. Revolutions can be accomplished using peaceful protests, such as marches—but some involve fighting.

FRENCH REVOLUTION

By 1789 in France, food had become almost too expensive for ordinary people to buy, while rich people lived in huge houses and ate very well. The people rose up, took control, and sent hundreds of nobles to death by guillotine, including the king and queen.

RUSSIAN REVOLUTION

Russia's workers lived in terrible conditions, with a lot of work and not enough food. In the early 20th century they revolted. The tsar (king) was forced to step down, and Vladimir Lenin took power.

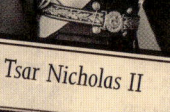

Tsar Nicholas II

Vladimir Lenin

King Louis XVI and Queen Marie Antoinette

FIGHT FOR AMERICAN INDEPENDENCE

Parts of North America were controlled by Britain starting in the 1600s. By the mid 1700s, Americans had had enough—they wanted freedom. But Britain wasn't willing to give up its colony without a fight. So, in 1775, the American Revolution began.

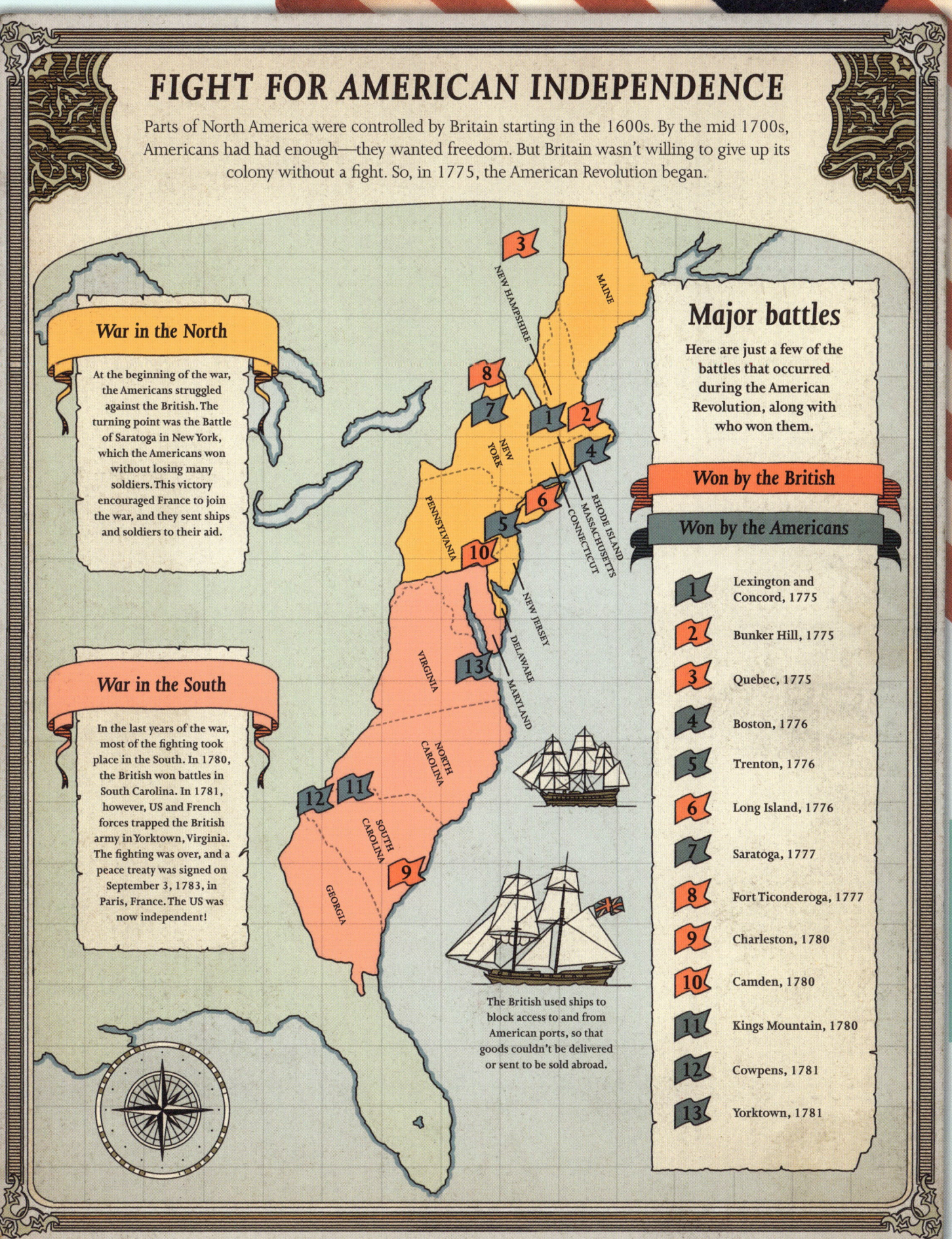

War in the North

At the beginning of the war, the Americans struggled against the British. The turning point was the Battle of Saratoga in New York, which the Americans won without losing many soldiers. This victory encouraged France to join the war, and they sent ships and soldiers to their aid.

War in the South

In the last years of the war, most of the fighting took place in the South. In 1780, the British won battles in South Carolina. In 1781, however, US and French forces trapped the British army in Yorktown, Virginia. The fighting was over, and a peace treaty was signed on September 3, 1783, in Paris, France. The US was now independent!

The British used ships to block access to and from American ports, so that goods couldn't be delivered or sent to be sold abroad.

Major battles

Here are just a few of the battles that occurred during the American Revolution, along with who won them.

Won by the British

Won by the Americans

1. Lexington and Concord, 1775
2. Bunker Hill, 1775
3. Quebec, 1775
4. Boston, 1776
5. Trenton, 1776
6. Long Island, 1776
7. Saratoga, 1777
8. Fort Ticonderoga, 1777
9. Charleston, 1780
10. Camden, 1780
11. Kings Mountain, 1780
12. Cowpens, 1781
13. Yorktown, 1781

History

WORLD WAR ONE (1914–1918)

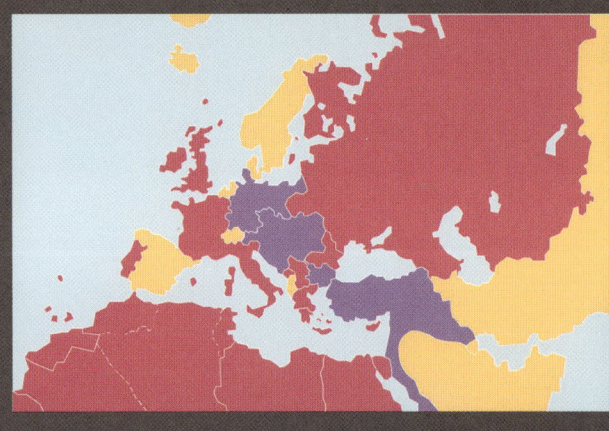

KEY ● Allied Powers ● Central Powers ● Neutral countries

World War I was triggered by the murder of the heir to the Austrian throne. Austria-Hungary blamed its rival, Serbia, and declared war on it. Each country's allies joined in, leading to a war between two sets of countries, or "powers," which included most of Europe.

1. Trenches
Soldiers spent their days in trenches—deep ditches dug down into the ground. It was filthy, and the trenches often flooded.

2. No-man's-land
Between the trenches belonging to each side was a space known as no-man's-land. Soldiers would climb out of the trenches to fight.

Tommy cooker
This small stove could be folded up. It was mostly used to make stews.

WORLD WAR

A. Women at war
With the men away fighting, women worked in offices, factories, farms, and stores—in roles that had once been taken by men.

B. Air raids
Britain was attacked from the sky by German airships known as zeppelins, which dropped bombs.

C. London Underground
People sheltered from the bombing in London's subway system. Many spent long nights trying to sleep on train platforms.

D. Rationing
Food was in short supply, so it was rationed—people were only allowed certain amounts of sugar, meat, butter, and milk.

E. Children and war
Children did what they could to help, for example by collecting books and blankets to send to soldiers at the front.

WORLD WAR II AT HOME

3. Tanks
World War I was the first war to use tanks. They had continuous tracks, which allowed them to move through trenches and barbed wire.

4. War at sea
Attacks from the sea were common during World War I. The largest warships were called battleships, and had large guns.

5. Cooking
It was difficult to cook in the wet trenches, so the soldiers ate mostly cold food, including bread, jam, and canned meat.

6. Weapons
The most-used weapons were rifles, grenades, machine guns, and explosive shells. Millions of weapons were made during the war.

Gas masks
These masks protected the wearer against poison-gas attacks.

Giant rats
Huge rats thrived in the trenches, making the soldiers' lives even more miserable.

ON THE BATTLEFIELD

WORLD WAR II

World War II started when Germany, led by Adolf Hitler, began invading other countries. Countries chose sides, and the Axis powers (Germany, Italy, and Japan) fought the Allies (France, Great Britain, the US, and the Soviet Union). Both sides used far more advanced military equipment than was used in World War I.

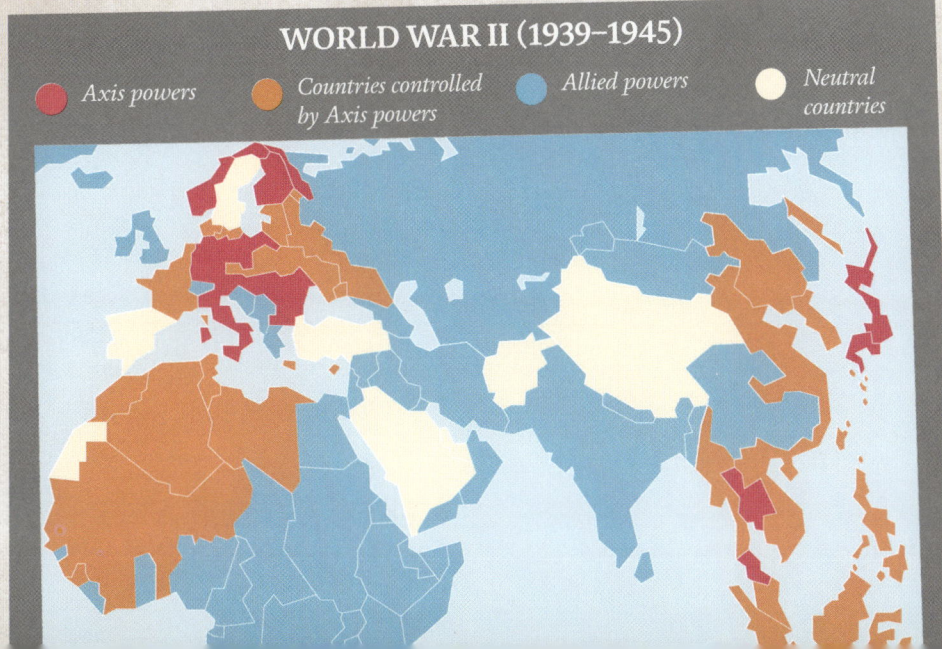

WORLD WAR II (1939–1945)

- Axis powers
- Countries controlled by Axis powers
- Allied powers
- Neutral countries

The US dropped two atomic bombs on Japanese cities, ending the war.

GLOSSARY

ADAPTED

How a living thing changes over time to better suit its environment

AFTERLIFE

Life or state of being that some people believe happens after death

AMPHIBIAN

Vertebrate that usually lives in water when young, before moving between land and water when fully grown

ANCESTOR

Person from whom someone is descended, such as a great-great-grandmother

ARCHITECT

Person who designs buildings

ATMOSPHERE

Layer of gases that surrounds a planet

ATOM

Smallest possible part of a chemical element. Atoms are made of protons, neutrons, and electrons

BIOME

Major landscape of the natural world, such as tropical rainforest, desert, or temperate grassland. Each biome has its own distinctive climate, vegetation, and animal life

BIRD

Egg-laying vertebrate that has feathers and is often able to fly

BLACK HOLE

Area of space with such a strong gravitational pull that it sucks in anything that comes too close, even light

CARBON DIOXIDE

Gas that forms a small part of the atmosphere. Some living things, such as plants, can use it to make food

CARNIVORE

Animal that eats other animals

CELL

Basic unit from which all living things are made

CELLULOSE

Tough substance that is found in the walls of plant cells

CITIZEN

Person who is a member of a particular state or country

CIVILIZATION

Culture and way of life of people living together in an organized and developed society

CLIMATE

Most common weather conditions in an area, over a period of time

CLIMATE CHANGE

Long-term changes in Earth's weather patterns

COMBUSTION

Chemical reaction in which a fuel, such as wood or coal, burns with oxygen from the air to release heat energy

CONSTELLATION

Group of stars in the sky that follow a pattern, and mostly represent animals, objects, or figures from mythology

DEFORESTATION

Clearing or cutting down of forests

DINOSAUR

Reptile that lived during the Mesozoic era, between 250 and 66 million years ago

ECOSYSTEM

Community of living plants and animals, and nonliving things such as air or water, which occupy the same habitat and interact with each other

ELECTRICITY

Type of energy caused by electrons inside atoms

ELEMENT

Basic building block of matter made from one type of atom

EPIDEMIOLOGY

Study of diseases

ENERGY

Property of an object that allows it to do something now or in the future. Different types of energy include kinetic (movement) energy and potential (stored) energy

EMPIRE

Group of countries or territories ruled by another country

EVOLUTION

Gradual change of a species, over many generations

EXOPLANET

Planet that orbits a star outside our solar system

FERTILIZER

Substance that is added to soil to help plants grow

FISH

Vertebrate that breathes through organs called gills and lives in water

FOOD WEB

Group of living things that are linked together by what they eat. For example, from a plant to a herbivore and then a carnivore

FOSSIL

Remains of a plant or animal, preserved inside a rock

FUNGI

Group of living things that includes mushrooms and toadstools

GALAXY

Large group of stars, dust, and gas, held together by the force of gravity. We live in a galaxy called the Milky Way

GOD

Supernatural being worshipped as having great powers, and who may sometimes influence human events

HABITAT

Place where a plant or animal normally lives

HERBIVORE

Animal that eats plants

INDUSTRY

Organization that produces (makes) something

INSECT

Creature with six legs and three body parts. Many also have wings

INVERTEBRATE

Animal that lacks a backbone

MAMMAL

One of a group of warm-blooded, often hairy vertebrates, whose females feed their young milk

MEDIEVAL PERIOD

Also known as the Middle Ages, the period in European history that lasted from about the 5th to the late 15th century CE

MIGRATION

Journey by an animal to a new habitat. Animals migrate to spend winter in warmer places, to feed, or breed

MOLECULE

Substance made from two or more atoms joined tightly together. The atoms in a molecule can be the same or different

MYTH

Ancient story that involves historical elements

OXYGEN

Gas that makes up 21 percent of the atmosphere

PANDEMIC

Disease that has spread across a whole country, or around the world

PARTICLE

Small part of a solid, liquid, or gas

PHARAOH

Ancient Egyptian ruler

PICOSECOND

Trillionth of a second

PLANT

Living thing from the group that includes trees, ferns, and mosses

POLLINATION

Transfer of pollen from the male part of a flower to the female plant of a flower. Pollination is essential for plants that make seeds

PROFESSION

Type of work that needs special training

PROTEIN

Substance made by all cells that is essential for life

PROTEST

Showing that you do not agree or approve of something

RECEPTOR

Cell or organ that can respond to stimuli such as heat and light

REPTILE

Animal group that includes turtles, crocodiles, and snakes. They have dry, scaly skin and typically lay eggs on land

REVOLUTION

Sudden and fundamental change in society brought about by an organized group of protesters

SETTLEMENT

Place where people have settled down and built homes

SOLAR SYSTEM

Sun and the planets and other objects that orbit it

SPACE

Place beyond Earth's atmosphere

STAR

Huge glowing sphere of gas that creates energy at its core

TECTONIC PLATES

Giant pieces of Earth's crust, which move around over millions of years

TRANSPIRATION

Loss of water vapor from a plant, due to evaporation

UNIVERSE

All space and everything in it

VERTEBRATE

Animal with a backbone

INDEX

ACKNOWLEDGEMENTS

The publisher would like to thank the following people for their generous assistance in the preparation of this book: Rituraj Singh for picture library assistance, Pankaj Sharma for DTP assistance, Helen Peters for compiling the index, and Polly Goodman for proofreading.

The publisher would like to thank the following for their kind permission to reproduce their photographs:

(Key: a-above; b-below/bottom; c-centre; f-far; l-left; r-right; t-top)

3 Dreamstime.com: Kaspri (cb); Youths (cla); Vladimir Yudin (cb/seal). 6-7 123RF.com: max776 (map). Dreamstime.com: Bbgreg. 8-9 Dorling Kindersley: © Kaley McKean. 9 Alamy Stock Photo: MMphotos (br). Dreamstime.com: Andreykuzmin (tl/background). NASA: SOFIA / Lim, De Buizer, & Radomski et al.; ESA / Herschel; NASA / JPL-Caltech (tl). 10 Alamy Stock Photo: MMphotos (cb/background). Dorling Kindersley: © Kaley McKean (tl, bl). NASA: (cb). 12-13 Dreamstime.com: Avictorero (background). 14 Alamy Stock Photo: CBW (tr); MMphotos (tr/background). Dorling Kindersley: © Kaley McKean (cl). Dreamstime.com: Artur Balitskii (bl); Bolotov (crb/background). 15 Alamy Stock Photo: MMphotos (background). 16-17 Alamy Stock Photo: MMphotos (background). Dorling Kindersley: © Kaley McKean (bc). 17 Dorling Kindersley: © Kaley McKean (r). 18-19 Dreamstime.com: Avictorero (background). 19 Alamy Stock Photo: MMphotos (br/background). Science Photo Library: Ron Miller (br). 20 123RF.com: leonello calvetti (ca). Alamy Stock Photo: MMphotos (tr/background). Dreamstime.com: Travelarium (bl). Getty Images / iStock: dima_zel (tr). NASA: JPL-Caltech (c). Science Photo Library: Mark Garlick (clb, cl). 21 Alamy Stock Photo: MMphotos (cla/background). Dorling Kindersley: Kaley McKean (illustrations). Dreamstime.com: Stockfotocz (cla). 22 Alamy Stock Photo: Dimitris K. (bc/background); Science History Images / Photo Researchers (bl); Pictorial Press Ltd (bc). Dorling Kindersley: Kaley McKean (cra). 24 Dorling Kindersley: Dave Shayler / Astro Info Service Ltd / Gary Ombler (br). 24-25 Dreamstime.com: Avictorero (background). 25 Alamy Stock Photo: MMphotos (cb/background, crb/background). NASA: JPL-Caltech / ASU / MSSS (cb); JPL (crb). 27 Dreamstime.com: Bbgreg (br). 28 Dorling Kindersley: © Kaley McKean (c). Dreamstime.com: Banluporn Namnorin (tr). Science Photo Library: ADAM HART-DAVIS (clb). 29 Alamy Stock Photo: MMphotos (backgrounds x4). Dreamstime.com: Banluporn Namnorin (clb). 31 Dorling Kindersley: Natural History Museum / Tim Parmenter (tl). 32-33 Alamy Stock Photo: MMphotos (background). 38 Alamy Stock Photo: MMphotos (bl/background). Dorling Kindersley: © Kaley McKean (cr). 40 Alamy Stock Photo: Classic Image (tr); Iconographic Archive (c). Dreamstime.com: Puntasit Choksawatdikorn (br); Serbysh (c/background, tr/background). Science Photo Library: Ziad M. El-zaatari (cb). 41 Alamy Stock Photo: MMphotos (tr/background). Dorling Kindersley: © Kaley McKean (tl). 42 Dorling Kindersley: © Kaley McKean (bl, cra). Dreamstime.com: Lou Oates (crb); Vadreams (br). 43 Alamy Stock Photo: MMphotos (background). 44-45 Alamy Stock Photo: MMphotos (background). 44 Dreamstime.com: Tiagoz (b). 45 Dorling Kindersley: © Kaley McKean (b). 46-47 123RF.com: atee83 / Attila Mittl (splats x3). 47 Science Museum Group: © Science Museum / Science & Society Picture Library (t). 50 Dorling Kindersley: © Kaley McKean (b). 51 Dreamstime.com: Piman Khrutmuang (bl). 52 Dreamstime.com: Bolotov (br). 53 Alamy Stock Photo: MMphotos (background). Dreamstime.com: Bolotov (bc/backgrounds x2); Liligraphie (tr/background). 54-55 Alamy Stock Photo: MMphotos (background). 54 Dorling Kindersley: Natural History Museum, London / Colin Keates (cra). 55 Dorling Kindersley: Oxford University Museum of Natural History / Gary Ombler (tc). 56 Alamy Stock Photo: MMphotos (bl/background). Science Photo Library: Science Stock Photography (br). Shutterstock.com: Daniel K. Driskill (bl). 57 Dorling Kindersley: © Kaley McKean (r). 58 Alamy Stock Photo: MMphotos (cr/background, bl/background). Dreamstime.com: Andreykuzmin (cl/background); Youths (cl); Bolotov (tc/background, crb/background); Karen Foley (bl); Darkbird77 (br/background); Oleg Seleznev (tr); Serbysh (tr/background). Getty Images / iStock: E+ / KenCanning (c); Pro-syanov (bc); javarman3 (cr). 59 Alamy Stock Photo: MMphotos (tr/background, cl/background). Dorling Kindersley: © Kaley McKean (b). Dreamstime.com: Andreykuzmin (tl/background); Kaspri (cr); Serbysh (cr/background); Anna Karaseva (tl); Rui Baião (c). Getty Images / iStock: Robert_Ford (cl); SteveAllenPhoto (cra). 60 Alamy Stock Photo: MMphotos (r/backgrounds x3). Dorling Kindersley: © Kaley McKean (clb). Dreamstime.com: Oksana Ermak (bl); Rangizzz (ca); Inga Nielsen (cra); Egon Zitter (crb). Getty Images / iStock: IanChrisGraham (cr). 61 Alamy Stock Photo: MMphotos (background). Dreamstime.com: Dewins (tr). 62-63 Alamy Stock Photo: MMphotos (background). 64 Alamy Stock Photo: MMphotos (tc/background). Dreamstime.com: Youths (bc). Getty Images / iStock: Rainer von Brandis (tc). 66 Alamy Stock Photo: Horizon Images / Motion (cra); MMphotos (cra/background, bl/background). 66-67 Dreamstime.com: Andreykuzmin (b/graph). 67 Alamy Stock Photo: Associated Press / Bullit Marquez (cla); MMphotos (cla/background). Dorling Kindersley: © Kaley McKean (tr). 68 Alamy Stock Photo: Heritage Image Partnership Ltd / Historica Graphica Collection (c); MMphotos (cl/background, crb/background); Stocktrek Images, Inc. / Walter Myers (crb). Depositphotos Inc: marzolino (tr). Dorling Kindersley: © Kaley McKean (b). 70 Alamy Stock Photo: MMphotos (br/background). 70-71 Dreamstime.com: Soulart2012 (background). 71 Dorling Kindersley: © Kaley McKean (b). 72 Alamy Stock Photo: MMphotos (l/backgrounds x4). Dorling Kindersley: © Kaley McKean (crb). Dreamstime.com: Mihai Andritoiu (l/seasons x4). 73 Alamy Stock Photo: MMphotos (backgrounds x4). Dorling Kindersley: © Kaley McKean (cra). Dreamstime.com: Ryan Deberardinis (bc). Getty Images / iStock: jerbarber (bl); mdesigner125 (crb). 74-75 Alamy Stock Photo: MMphotos (background). 74 Dorling Kindersley: © Kaley McKean (bl). 75 Alamy Stock Photo: Minden Pictures / Jim Brandenburg (bl); MMphotos (bl/backgrond). 76-77 Alamy Stock Photo: MMphotos (background). 76 Dreamstime.com: Piman Khrutmuang (bl/labels). Shutterstock.com: Wondermilkycolor (bl/tags). 77 Dreamstime.com: Piman Khrutmuang (bl/labels); Pixelrobot (tissue). Shutterstock.com: Wondermilkycolor (bl/tags). 78-79 Getty Images / iStock: taseffski (backgrounds x2). 79 Alamy Stock Photo: MMphotos (tr/background). Getty Images / iStock: E+ / 35007 (tr). 80 Alamy Stock Photo: MMphotos (r/backgrounds x5). Dorling Kindersley: © Kaley McKean (clb). Dreamstime.com: Onepony (cra); Sborisov (ca); Xi Zhang (cb); Saiko3p (br). Getty Images / iStock: Ahmed_Abdel_Hamid (crb). 81 Alamy Stock Photo: Chronicle (tr). Dorling Kindersley: © Kaley McKean (b). Dreamstime.com: Andreykuzmin (tc/background); Serbysh (tr/background); Rodrigolab (c); Prochasson Frederic (tc); Yurataranik (cla). 82 Alamy Stock Photo: MCLA Collection (clb). 82-83 Alamy Stock Photo: Penta Springs Limited / Artokoloro (background). Dreamstime.com: Tortoon (stains). 85 Alamy Stock Photo: Marina Josan (br); MMphotos (tl/background). Dreamstime.com: Bolotov (tc/background); Vladimir Yudin (tc/seal). 86-87 Alamy Stock Photo: MMphotos (background). 88-89 Alamy Stock Photo: MMphotos (background). 89 Alamy Stock Photo: MMphotos (clb/background). Science Photo Library: Biozentrum, University Of Basel (clb). 91 Alamy Stock Photo: The Natural History Museum, London (tr). Dorling Kindersley: © Kaley McKean (clb). Dreamstime.com: Pixworld (cb). 92 Alamy Stock Photo: era-images / Colin Harris (crb); MMphotos (crb/background). Dorling Kindersley: © Kaley McKean (b). 94 Dorling Kindersley: © Kaley McKean (bl). Dreamstime.com: Alfotokunst (cra); Cathy Keifer (crb); Dmass / Dave Massey (br). Getty Images / iStock: fabioski (c). Getty Images: mikroman6 (tr). 95 Alamy Stock Photo: MMphotos (cla/background). Dorling Kindersley: © Kaley McKean (br). Dreamstime.com: Bolotov (tr/background); Vladimir Yudin (tr/seal). 96-97 Alamy Stock Photo: MMphotos (background). 97 Alamy Stock Photo: Mateusz Atroszko (bc). 98 Alamy Stock Photo: MMphotos (cb/backgrounds x3). Dorling Kindersley: © Kaley McKean (tr). Dreamstime.com: Lukas Blazek (crb); Eamelrose (cb). Science Photo Library: Science Source / Tom Mchugh (clb). 99 Dorling Kindersley: © Kaley McKean (l). Dreamstime.com: Romannerud (br). Getty Images: Dmitry Miroshnikov (tr). 100 Dreamstime.com: Patrick Guenette (bl, br). 101 Getty Images: DigitalVision Vectors / ilbusca (bc). 102-103 Alamy Stock Photo: MMphotos (backgrounds x5). 102 Alamy Stock Photo: Karen Debler (cla); Krystyna Szulecka (cl); Minden Pictures / Michael & Patricia Fogden (bl); Florilegius (cra). Dorling Kindersley: Kaley McKean (crb). 104-105 Alamy Stock Photo: MMphotos (b/backgrounds x5). Dreamstime.com: Winai Tepsuttinun (tc). 104 Dorling Kindersley: Kaley McKean (c). Dreamstime.com: Shane Myers (br); Zina Seletskaya (cb). 105 Dorling Kindersley: Kaley McKean (cl). Dreamstime.com: Bobhilscher (br); Sandra Standbridge (tr); Danolsen (cra); David Havel (cb). Getty Images: Kuritafsheen (bl). 106 Alamy Stock Photo: MMphotos (cl/background); Nature Picture Library / Konrad Wothe (cl). 107 Alamy Stock Photo: MMphotos (tr/background); David Wilkins (tr). 108 Alamy Stock Photo: MMphotos (r/backgrounds x4); Nature Picture Library / Michel Poinsignon (tr). Dreamstime.com: Darrin Aldridge (ca); Feathercollector (bl); Dennis Jacobsen (crb); Birdiegal717 (bc). 108-109 Dorling Kindersley: Kaley McKean. 109 Alamy Stock Photo: Classic Collection (cra); Florilegius (ca). Getty Images / iStock: Nadtytok (tl). 112 Alamy Stock Photo: MMphotos (cb/backgrounds x3). Dreamstime.com: Josiah Garber (crb); SappheirosPhoto (cb). Getty Images: De Agostini Picture Library (clb). 113 Alamy Stock Photo: MMphotos (br/background, ca/background, crb/background); Pictures Now (tl/Polar beer). Dreamstime.com: Gary Gray (c); Serbysh (tl, cra/background, c/background, cb/background, bl/background); Wirestock (cra); Sdbower (cb). Shutterstock.com: Anne Coatesy (bl). 114-115 Alamy Stock Photo: MMphotos (background). 114 Dorling Kindersley: Kaley McKean (bl). 116-117 Alamy Stock Photo: MMphotos (background). 116 Alamy Stock Photo: Penta Springs Limited (br). Dorling Kindersley: Royal Geographical Society, London / Dave King (bl). 117 Alamy Stock Photo: MMphotos (tr/background). Dreamstime.com: Mariusz Prusaczyk (tr); Youths (tr/Stamp texture). 118 Alamy Stock Photo: MMphotos (backgrounds x2); WaterFrame (cl). Dorling Kindersley: Kaley McKean (cr). Dreamstime.com: Okemppainen (bc). 120 Dreamstime.com: Coffeechocolates (br). 120-121 Dreamstime.com: Claudiodivizia (Background). 121 Dreamstime.com: Coffeechocolates (br). 122 Alamy Stock Photo: MMphotos (l/backgrounds x2). Dreamstime.com: Jonathan Casey (cla); Elena Elisseeva (cb); Marek Mnich (ca). 122-123 Dorling Kindersley: Kaley McKean. 123 Alamy Stock Photo: MMphotos (bl/backgrounds x2). Dreamstime.com: Peter Hermes Furian (ca); Angelo Gilardelli (tc); Valerygreen (cl). Getty Images / iStock: Feellife (bl). 124-125 Alamy Stock Photo: MMphotos (background). 126-127 Alamy Stock Photo: MMphotos (background). 127 Dorling Kindersley: Kaley McKean (r). 128 Dorling Kindersley: Kaley McKean. Shutterstock.com: Ryan M. Bolton (br). 129 Dorling Kindersley: Kaley McKean (br). 130 Dreamstime.com: Kaspri (br); Vladimir Yudin (br/seal). 131 Alamy Stock Photo: Ivy Close Images (tc); MMphotos (backgrounds x2); PjrStudio (crb/bc). 132-133 Alamy Stock Photo: MMphotos (b/backgrounds x3). Dorling Kindersley: Kaley McKean. Dreamstime.com: Roywylam (t/paper texture). 132 Alamy Stock Photo: The Natural History Museum (cb). © The Trustees of the British Museum. All rights reserved: (br). 133 Alamy Stock Photo: PMN / Piemags (bc); Zev Radovan (br). Dreamstime.com: Raduang (cb). 134 Dorling Kindersley: Kaley McKean. Dreamstime.com: Andreykuzmin (br, cr). 135 Alamy Stock Photo: MMphotos (backgrounds x2). Depositphotos Inc: Chronicserotonin (cla). Dorling Kindersley: University Museum of Archaeology and Anthropology, Cambridge / Dave King (cb). Getty Images / iStock: DigitalVision Vectors / Nastasic (cra). Getty Images: Mint Images (clb). Harvard Yenching Library: Li Si, 280? -208 BC, Chinese [calligrapher] (bl). 136 Alamy Stock Photo: MMphotos (bl/background, tr/Postcard texture). Dreamstime.com: Kaspri (crb); Vladimir Yudin (crb/seal). Getty Images: Kitti Boonnitrod (tr). 137 Alamy Stock Photo: David Cole (bl); Dimitris K. (bl/background). Dorling Kindersley: Cairo Museum / Alistair Duncan (tl). Dreamstime.com: Bolotov (cr/background); Vladimir Yudin (cr/seal). 138-139 Alamy Stock Photo: MMphotos (background). 142 Alamy Stock Photo: MMphotos (clb/background). Dorling Kindersley: Kaley McKean (cla). Dreamstime.com: Chris Hill / Ca2hill (tc, cl/x2). Getty Images / iStock: Ari Sääski (clb). 144 Alamy Stock Photo: CPA Media Pte Ltd (crb); MMphotos (backgrounds x3); World History Archive (c); Julian Money-Kyrle (tr); Oleksiy Maksymenko Photography (bl). Dreamstime.com: Daboost (bc). 146 Alamy Stock Photo: Brian Jannsen (tr). Dorling Kindersley: Kaley McKean (bl). Dreamstime.com: Kaspri (br/Paper Texture); Rangizzz (tr/Paper Texture). Getty Images: Universal Images Group / Christophel Fine Art (br). 147 123RF.com: Sabphoto (Paper background). 148-149 Dreamstime.com: Bbgreg (Paper Texture). 149 Alamy Stock Photo: Chronicle (cra). Dreamstime.com: Geografika (cr). 150-151 Alamy Stock Photo: MMphotos (background). 150 Alamy Stock Photo: Pictorial Press Ltd (br). Dreamstime.com: Yuri Bershadsky (bl/Glass crystals); Macrowildlife (bl/Gold); Valentina Razumova (bl). 151 Getty Images: Bettmann (bl). 152 Alamy Stock Photo: Digital Image Library (br); MMphotos (tr/background); Heritage Image Partnership Ltd / © Fine Art Images (tr); GL Archive (bl); IanDagnall Computing (bl/Lenin); Dennis Hallinan (br/Queen Marie Antoinette). Dorling Kindersley: Kaley McKean (cla). Dreamstime.com: Photka (br/Newspaper Background); Prapass Wannapinij (bl/background); Korn Vitthayanukarun (br/Broken Glass Texture). Getty Images / iStock: spxChrome (br/Locket). 153 Getty Images / iStock: E+ / Belterz (tr). 154-155 Alamy Stock Photo: MMphotos (background). 155 Alamy Stock Photo: Science History Images / Photo Researchers (br)

Cover images: Front: 123RF.com: Duncan Noakes cb; Dreamstime.com: Mhprice / Michael Price cb/ (whale), Wesleyc1701 / Michal Janoek fcrb; Fotolia: Auris crb; Back: 123RF.com: max776 (map); Alamy Stock Photo: CBW bl, MMphotos (postcard x3); Dreamstime.com: Bbgreg (paper background x2), Bolotov (background x2), Feathercollector tl, Chris Hill / Ca2hill ca, cra; Getty Images: Kitti Boonnitrod tr